finding
our way

Edited by Linda Villarosa

Body & Soul:
The Black Women's Guide to
Physical Health and Emotional Well-Being

finding our way

The Teen Girls' Survival Guide

Allison Abner
and
Linda Villarosa

Illustrated by Arleen Frasca

 HarperPerennial
A Division of HarperCollinsPublishers

HarperCollins books may be purchased for educational, business, or sales promotional use. For information please write: Special Markets Department, HarperCollins Publishers, Inc., 10 East 53rd Street, New York, NY 10022.

Designed by Helene Wald Berinsky

Library of Congress Cataloging-in-Publication Data

Abner, Allison, 1959–
    Finding our way : the teen girls' survival guide / Allison Abner & Linda Villarosa.
      p. cm.
    Includes bibliographical references (p.).
    ISBN 0-06-095114-1
    1. Teenage girls—Life skills guides. I. Villarosa, Linda. II. Title
HQ798.A53 1995
646.7'00835'2—dc20   95-35964

96 97 98 99 00 ❖/RRD 10 9 8 7 6 5 4 3 2 1

CONTENTS

FOREWORD

Let's talk, ladies. It seems like these days a lot of young women don't have anyone to turn to. I was lucky to have a mother who, though she worked hard and even went to school while I was young, really believed in communication. If my brother or I had any problems, or we weren't doing our fair share around the house, Mom would sit us down and talk about it. Knowing that my mother would be there for me made me feel loved, and it made me know that there was always someone I could turn to when I had questions or doubts.

And like most people, during my teens I had my share of doubts: What would my future bring? Would I ace my biology test? How could I earn some money after school? Even with all my questions I kept on trying to be the best person I could. Growing up in East Orange, New Jersey, I didn't exactly live in the lap of luxury, but I always found something to do to discover my talents and have fun. I played on a championship basketball team, sang in church, acted in plays, rapped with an all-female group, and learned karate. I wasn't exactly sure where all this would take me, but I knew I liked myself when I was involved in things that challenged my body and my mind.

Through sports I learned to pull the two together, body and mind. Playing on a team taught me to push myself to new limits, not give up, and perform under pressure, all of which prepared me for my future. I also discovered through athletics how important it is to take the body I was given and use it to my advantage. Playing power forward in basketball I couldn't be skin and bones, so I used my height and solid build to compete. This experience taught me to love my healthy body, and, most important, to take care of it.

During my teens, I also found out that I felt good about myself when I went after a goal and reached it. Though my family supported me, it was up to me to envision my dreams and slowly, steadily try to get there. For example, I knew I loved rapping and acting. But it took years before I was actually rapping on an album or acting on the big screen. To get there I had to work to earn money as a cashier at a fast-food restaurant. In my spare time I wrote lyrics, practiced with a DJ, rapped in talent shows and at parties, and went to school.

Even with the rejection I sometimes faced, I gained strength and confidence knowing that I could reach my goals by believing in myself. I realized I didn't have to act phony or pretend to be somebody I wasn't to get ahead. People liked me and thought I was talented, because I was being me doing what I do best, and it showed. I felt proud when my hard work finally paid off, and I got a record contract and began acting professionally. I proved to myself that I could make it on my own, but I still have to stay focused on new goals to remain successful.

So when I say let's talk, I mean to each other. I know through rapping that communicating is one of the best ways for us to share our ideas and feelings, and to support each other for who we are and who we hope to become. *Finding Our Way* is a good place to start because we hear from different kinds of girls from all over the country speaking from their hearts about how they learned to believe in themselves or turn their lives around.

In fact, many of the problems I've faced as a young woman are covered in this book, like divorce, racism, violence, and losing a loved one, in the case of my brother. Though I was fortunate to be able to talk openly to my mother, I know a lot of girls aren't. So, not only does this book have a lot of good information and advice about how to take care of your body and deal with topics like your family, friends, stress, and sexuality, it can also be a way to break the ice with your parents or another trusting adult and your friends. It can help you start a conversation about something you normally would find too hard or embarrassing.

You can read examples of young women, Native American, Latino, African American, Asian, and white, who are reaching out to others. Cate Baker of ESTEEM, in Chapter 1, helps young women deal with eating disorders; Carolyn, in Chapter 13, talks about sharing her experience of rape with other teen girls on her reservation; and Linda Isakson of SEAC, in Chapter 8, gives step-by-step advice to other high school students on setting up environmental clubs. Their stories show that if you believe in yourself and your cause, you can take action that counts. Even if you never become a community leader, the important point is to begin discussing real issues so you can see that your feelings and ideas matter.

Like success, growing up doesn't happen overnight. You are guaranteed to face failures, rejections, and difficult times along the way. But if you're honest, express yourself, and hold onto your self-respect, you'll definitely be on the right track.

Peace out,
Queen Latifah

ACKNOWLEDGMENTS

We wish to thank the following people:

Nina Lederman, who knows a good hookup, which in this case became a great partnership.

Janet Goldstein for broadening the concept of this book and helping it take shape, and Betsy Thorpe for your insightful comments and attentive editing.

Peternelle van Arsdale and Kristen Auclair for taking on this project and seeing it through.

Our agents Barbara Lowenstein and Madeleine Morel for always looking out for us.

Antronette Y. Yancey, M.D., M.P.H., our medical adviser, for your expertise and care.

Elizabeth Puccini for your time and wonderful interviews and research. Your contribution is greatly appreciated and helped make this book so special.

Lisa Jacobs, Melissa Washington-Harris, Mark Gabor, and Martha Southgate for pitching in on writing and reporting.

Researchers Derrayle Barnes, Regina Cash, and Donna Holder for attentiveness to the facts, figures, names and addresses.

Jheryl Busby for helping deliver a wonderful addition to the book—the foreword—and to Queen Latifah for being an inspiration to so many young women.

Liza Brown and the young women at The Door who set us straight about what it's *really* like to be a teenager.

All of the doctors, scientists and other experts who offered us your time and invaluable information.

The incredible and brave young women who gave us your stories and a piece of yourselves so that others may learn from your experiences.

INTRODUCTION

Welcome to the rest of your life! Easy for us to say. We've been in your shoes and have made it through to the other side—into adulthood, that is—still alive and breathing.

It wasn't that long ago that we too were forging through adolescence, making plenty of mistakes, watching our bodies change, and plowing through mounds of school work. Both of us loved our parents and stayed tight with them throughout the teen years, but friends became the center of the social universe while boys acted like gravitational pulls, distracting our attention every time they entered our galaxies. To top it all off each of us was one of the only African American girls in our schools and neighborhoods. To say the least, our teenhoods were filled with confusion, loneliness, and excitement, in other words, all the normal feelings of adolescence.

It wasn't until we got older that we realized we weren't the only ones having a tough time through those years. Each of us honestly thought that nobody else was going through such difficulties on the inside, and having to act "normal" on the outside. Part of becoming an adult was learning how to face the painful and embarrassing moments of the teen years with compassion and a sense of humor. (We can both finally laugh now at some of the hideous clothes we used to wear that we thought we looked so hot in.)

Best of all, we're able to say we learned some of our most important life lessons during that time, like setting goals for ourselves for the long term, believing in our own intelligence—despite what anyone else has to say about it—and taking care of ourselves. These lessons came out of years of experience, trying to get to know ourselves and our worlds better. Out of every mistake or pain came new growth, out of new growth came strength.

We also noticed that the only way we were ever able to learn a lesson was if we listened to that little voice inside. We all have it. It's that same voice that gives you a "creepy" feeling about someone, sets off a creative light bulb in your head, or tells when you might be coming down with a cold. It's the voice that guides you to be your best, in body and in spirit.

The lesson that we learned (the hard way) and that all of you must learn is that being your best starts on the inside and radiates out, not the other way around. After all, looks can be deceiving. The real key to being your best, we now know, is staying healthy. That means being in excellent—or at least decent—physical shape no matter what size you are and feeling good emotionally and spiritually. Health is about balance in body and mind, the inner self and outer self.

That's why the book is broken down into two parts. The first half deals with the body: how it's changing, what it looks like, how to take care of it, what you put in it, how it works, and the choices you make with it. The second half is about life: how you feel about yourself, your family, your friends, your community, and some of the issues that you have to confront during your transition out of childhood and into adulthood.

One goal of the book is to help you think for yourself and make the right decisions. As young(er) women, both of us hated people telling us what to do, because we felt that if we had the right information, we could make our own decisions. The book is filled with stories of other young women who have confronted many of the same challenges you have, who speak very honestly about how their choices affected their lives. (Some of the first-person accounts are pseudonymous, at their authors' request.) It also has tips on dealing with real-life situations and phone numbers, books, and organizations to contact on any and every subject.

Another goal of this book is to inspire you to take action. Adolescence is a time of gaining independence, which means having to take responsibility for yourself and the world around you. The young women featured in the "What Are You Gonna Do About It" sections of each chapter have all felt fired up about a particular topic. Their dedication has motivated them to improve their communities. And each person has made a difference!

Finally, we hope this book will fill a void that's been missing from many young women's lives. When we first started putting this project together, we got the help of some very special teen women who set us straight about the essential ingredient the book would need in order to reach them. "We want to see ourselves in this book," they told us. They meant that they wanted a book that really spoke to them as African Americans, Latinas, Asians, Native Americans, whites, or any combo in between. They felt no books available dealt with the new multiracial, multicultural world we live in. Our sincere hope is that any young woman can pick up this book and see herself in it.

You may not realize it now, but the patterns you set for yourself today—what you eat, how you solve problems, what you do with your free time, how you choose the people you hang with—could have consequences for the rest of your life. Though this book won't cover each and every concern that pops up in your life during these sometimes turbulent times, it will give you a starting point from where you can begin to sort things out. Even when you have the right information, it still comes down to trusting yourself to do the right thing. And no matter what age you are, if you listen to that little voice inside it will always help you find your way.

Enjoy!

Allison Abner

Allison Abner

and

Linda Villarosa

Linda Villarosa

finding
our way

CHAPTER 1

GOOD BODIES

Body Image

It's hard to pass by a mirror without looking into it. Some young women like what they see, happy to know that the little-girl shape is changing into a womanly figure. Others don't like the young woman staring back whose hips have expanded or legs have filled out. These feelings—what a young woman thinks about her body—make up what is called body image. And most young women worry (even just a little bit) about something, whether it's one body part or the whole package, especially during the teens.

The Effects of Body Image

If you feel good about the way you look, that means you have a healthy body image. But the reality is that most of us are constantly worried that our bodies aren't perfect, even if we're normal. Many have what's called a distorted body image. So lots of young women freak out about their bodies, and experts now say that it's a *normal* part of being a teenager. It's pretty sad to think that too many young women actually hate their bodies so much that they end up feeling depressed, or worse, full of self-hatred and failure.

Though it may seem impossible to do, the ideal is to strive to love your body no matter what size or shape you are. Even if you can't totally accept every inch of your body, you may know someone who does. She's the one who seems to have it together: she has good grades, a lot of friends, and the best personality, even though she doesn't have a body like Cindy Crawford or Angela Bassett. She may not think she's the hottest girl in school, but she doesn't care either because she focuses more on her accomplishments than her appearance. What's best about her is that she oozes self-confidence, so she doesn't need to put other people down. Basically she loves herself just the way she is.

This can be you too, if you work at accepting yourself. If more of us did, we'd show those experts that it's normal to feel uptight about our changing bodies, but that we love them anyway. That's a healthy body image.

"Before I was too caught up in feeling fat and wanting to lose weight. Now I want people to like me for who I am, not what I look like."

AMY, 15, ONALASKA, WISCONSIN

I've always wanted to have a good body. Since about sixth grade I've watched my weight and sometimes tried to diet. In seventh grade some people would bring laxatives to school, and I started taking them all the time for a couple of months. Then my parents figured out that the laxatives were always missing from the bathroom at home. I got in some trouble, but really they just wanted to know why I was doing it. They tried to give me confidence by saying "You're so pretty, and you really shouldn't do that to your body. It's going to wreck it more than it will help it." I thought about it and realized they were right. I'd rather lose weight a healthy way, so I stopped.

Now I'm 5'8" and weigh 130, and I like my body. I've gotten really into athletics. I'm in poms (we do the half-time show during football games), and I'm also trying out for basketball and I'll go out for track or softball. I like to exercise at least once a day, running, lifting weights, and doing sit-ups. If I wasn't able to exercise a lot and gained a lot of weight it would really bother me. I've worked so hard to have this body and it has a lot to do with why I feel good about myself.

If I didn't have a fit body, I'm afraid I'd get made fun of by the other people at school. It happens all the time. At school people are so judgmental. If they make a comment about somebody, you try to do whatever you can to fit in, not too noticeable and not too invisible, not too preppy and not too grunge. You walk in school and if there's one thing wrong with you, you have a label.

Over the last couple years I think I've come to accept myself more than I used to. Before I was too caught up in feeling fat and wanting to lose weight. I always compared myself. Now I want people to like me for who I am, not what I look like. My family's support and the support I get from my boyfriend really helps. They tell me they like me how I am and I don't need to change.

Where Do Feelings About the Body Come From?

In our society, looks mean a lot. Open a magazine and there's a beautiful, bone-thin, generally white model with cool clothes and guys hanging all over her. Turn on the TV to music videos, and you'll see even more thin, beautiful young women. Those images make an impression on young women and affect self-esteem.

But think about this: how many of those media images match the real people you know? It usually takes hours and hours of work, make-up artists, starvation diets, and expensive clothes to achieve the fashion model look. Most friends, mothers, sisters, teachers, neighbors, counselors, and coaches don't look like the models on TV and in magazines. In fact, according to feminist author Susan Faludi, only 5 percent of all women have the ultra-thin, long-legged bodies that advertising agencies consider "ideal." Faludi notes that the average model is 5'7" and 115 pounds while the average real-life woman is 5'4" and 140 pounds and wears a size 14. Big difference!

After a while, seeing all those rail-thin, amazon beauties makes some young women feel insecure. They may end up either exercising their brains out, staying on a constant diet, or pouting in front of the mirror.

What Is Ideal?

Something else that affects our feelings about our bodies is our culture. African American, Latino, and Native American communities generally view the large bodies of our mothers, grandmothers, aunts, and sisters as a sign of power. For example, in Africa—past and present—a large body is a sign of prosperity and fertility, while a thin, frail body is a sign of poverty and hunger.

What's ideal? There is no ideal. Accepting your own unique body shape means feeling comfortable with yourself.

● ● ● ● ● ● ● ● ● ● ● ● **THE IDEAL BODY: RACE MATTERS** ● ● ● ● ● ● ● ● ● ● ● ●

When girls in a University of Arizona study were asked what the "ideal" woman was like the responses were quite different. White girls gave a description of the 5'7", 100-pound blond and blue-eyed Claudia Schiffer type. Black girls listed qualities such as a good personality, easy-going, ambitious and self-confident. And they described their physical ideal as having full hips, big thighs, and a little waist. Also, getting older didn't mean loss of beauty to the black girls as it did to the whites. While 90 percent of white respondents were unhappy with their body weight, 70 percent of African Americans were "just fine, thank you" with their bodies.

If you have a healthy body image and like the way you look, you're lucky. A lot of people don't and that can lead to other problems. When you put too much emphasis on your physical appearance it can cause you to feel obsessed, which means it's hard to think about anything else. These obsessions can lead to overeating or not eating enough, or make it impossible to accept your body the way it is.

Obesity

What Is It?

Here's the definition of obesity: a chronic condition in which the body stores too much body fat because calories aren't burned fast enough. Though not all doctors agree on one standard measurement, some of them believe that someone who is more than 20 percent above normal weight for her or his age and height is obese. However, that depends on build and muscle mass.

Though most people believe that people are big just because they eat all day, obesity is really caused by several different factors, including:

- overeating, usually foods high in fat;
- lack of exercise;
- medical disorders of certain glands, such as the thyroid;
- a lowered metabolism (the body's ability to burn calories), sometimes caused by going on and off of diets repeatedly;
- abuse and other emotional factors—some people get fat or thin to cope with painful issues in their lives.

Heredity also plays a large role in weight. According to a Harvard School of Public Health study, the offspring of two obese parents has an 89 percent chance of being obese as well. That's because the child inherits a large number of fat cells and/or slow metabolism from the parents. So it may take a lot less food to make that person fat than it does the person who has inherited very few fat cells and quicker metabolism, who can eat anything and everything and not put on an ounce. Still, remember this point: regardless of what you get from your parents, if you eat foods high in fat (pizza, burgers, fries, egg rolls) and don't do some kind of exercise several days a week, you will gain weight.

What's The Connection between Overeating and Obesity?

People become obese for a variety of reasons, including the combination of eating too much and not exercising. But that's not the only explanation. Surviving traumas like divorce, poverty, abuse or witnessing abuse may cause some young women to turn to food for comfort. Food provides a sense of being filled, rewarded or satisfied when there's no one else to turn to. Some women who come from families of drinking or drug addiction may imitate the behavior with food because it's the only example they have of how to cope with problems, and it seems less destructive than getting drunk or high.

It's not just eating too much that can lead to obesity. It may be hard to believe, but dieting, especially "yo-yo" dieting, can also cause weight gain. In fact, research shows that after each diet, 95 percent of dieters regain the weight and usually end up weighing 20 percent more than they did before the diet. This typical scenario explains how the cycle works:

1. After eating fatty foods and not exercising for a while, Tanya begins to gain weight.

2. Afraid of rejection from friends and family, she decides to go on a crash diet. Tanya stops eating breakfast and eats only salads for lunch and dinner.

3. Tanya gets on the scale and is excited to see that she's lost ten pounds. In the meantime, her body thinks she's starving and automatically slows her metabolism, the rate at which she burns calories.

4. At a party, Tanya falls off her diet and fills up on lots of high-fat food. "Screw it" she thinks to herself, and keeps eating. Like most people, Tanya can't keep up her low-calorie diet because her body cries out for more nourishment.

5. Tanya gains back all her weight. But worse than that, because dieting caused her metabolism to slow down, once she returns to her former way of eating she puts back on all of the weight she lost—and more.

A better way to lose weight: rather than go on highly restrictive diets that you can never really stick to, eat plenty of fruits and vegetables; cut down on heavy, fatty, fried foods; substitute chicken and fish for red meat (but don't eat it fried or with heavy, fatty sauces), and drink lots of water. (For more on weight loss, see Chapter 3.)

FAT PEOPLE GET A BAD RAP

FOUR MOST COMMON MYTHS

Myth: Fat people eat a ton of food and just need to diet.

Fact: Many fat people eat as much as or even less than people who weigh less than them.

Myth: Fat people are out of shape and need to exercise the weight off.

Fact: Though it's true that many large people are obese because they're inactive, a lot of others are in great physical condition. They exercise regularly and get good marks from their doctors after regular visits. However much they exercise, the amount of fat cells in their bodies will not change and they may always be large.

Myth: Fat people are sad and lonely because they don't have any friends or fun.

Fact: Because of the amount of ridicule that big people are subjected to by others, some may feel intimidated by certain social activities, like parties or the prom. But most fat people lead regular lives and have the same problems as everyone else.

Myth: All fat people need is to be told how fat they are in order for them to want to lose weight.

Fact: Telling a fat person that she's fat and needs to lose weight only hurts her feelings. If someone you know feels she's overweight and expresses an interest in losing some pounds, be supportive rather than harsh. But if she's happy just the way she is, it's up to you to accept her and get over your own prejudices about fat people.

What Are the Health Risks of Obesity?

Although every young woman should love her body rather than be obsessed with thinness, there are real consequences to being obese—weighing more than 20 percent over what is considered ideal. A number of serious health problems are connected to obesity, such as heart disease, cancer and diabetes. Obesity is also a big problem for young women of color. For example, in the African American, Latino, and Native American communities diabetes is a major risk factor for women, even teenagers, and high blood pressure is a serious problem for African American women. Also, being overweight can take a more subtle toll: in general, obese teens may feel slower and more lethargic than their thinner friends. Many feel too embarrassed to exercise—

because they're ashamed of letting others see their bodies in fitness clothing or insecure about being out of shape—although exercise should be a part of every young woman's daily routine.

Being fat can also wreak havoc on self-esteem. Because some people can be mean to large women, being fat can be isolating. Without friends and support overweight teens often feel alone or depressed. And this may make the problem worse, especially if the person turns to food for comfort.

FAT JOKES AREN'T FUNNY

Large women are most often the brunt of unfair stereotyping and abuse. Although it's not OK to make fun of people based on skin color or ethnic origin, it's still considered OK to make jokes about fat people, especially women. On his album "Talking Shit," comedian Martin Lawrence, for example, falls into hurtful stereotypes about big women, implying that all they do is eat. He says: "Women are always joking about their weight. People make excuses for weight. Ain't no excuses. It's my metabolism. No it's not. It's them Twizzlers in your g-d back pocket! Let the Reese's cups go. Get out of the Häagen-Dazs line . . . "

These kinds of hurtful comments lead to discrimination. A Harvard University study reported that large women are 20 percent less likely to marry than their thinner counterparts. They also make less money. Noted Deborah Gregory in "Heavy Judgment," an article that appeared in the August 1994 issue of *Essence*: "I have painfully discovered the extent of fat discrimination over the last ten years as I have vacillated between 140 and 235 pounds. I currently weigh around 200. What has come with the extra pounds is blatant professional and social discrimination, both to my face and behind my back—the kind that routinely dismisses my skills, talents and God-given physical beauty."

People who make fun of fat people often don't feel good about themselves. So they make fun of others to boost themselves. But people who really love themselves don't need to waste time tearing down other people. Everyone needs to deal with large people straight up the same way we want people to deal with us.

What to Do About Obesity?

First things first: Your goal is to be healthy. So if you're a large young woman who sticks to a low-fat eating plan that includes lots of fruits, vegetables, and water; who enjoys exercise; who's got lots of energy; who doesn't have serious health problems; and who loves every inch of her big self, then you probably don't need to lose weight. On the other hand, if your size is leading to health problems; if you feel tired and out of breath all the time; if you know you're eating too much of the wrong foods; if you don't exercise; or if you're using your weight as a shield against hurt and pain, then it may be time to take a hard look at your body and consider a weight-loss plan.

For help, Dr. John Foreyt, who works with obese teens and is the co-author of *Living Without Dieting*, offers these suggestions:

- Go to a doctor or health clinic. A medical professional can run tests to determine whether you're at risk for diabetes or high blood pressure, either of which should be addressed above all else.
- Get informed. Start by reading up on health and nutrition (how about Chapter 3 in this book?), and talk to your medical practitioner about exercise and a low-fat, low-salt nutrition plan.
- Devise a strategy that works for you. If you're one of those rare, highly motivated people who can exercise and eat right on your own, then try to do that. Since support is key, you may want to start a "healthy eating" group or a "walking women" group so you have some company.
- Find a program that works for you. Whether it's through your church, synagogue, community center, school, or local health clinic, find an exercise and nutrition program that's convenient and that suits your needs. If you need to be around people your own age, find a teen group, or if you need to be around all women, seek out a women's organization.
- If your weight is making you feel bad or you're gaining weight because of an emotional problem, find someone to talk to such as a parent, trusted friend, or school counselor. Talking about what's bothering you is also a first step toward healing.
- Seek support. This is key, especially if you're planning to lose weight. Experts have found that the more friends and support you have, the more likely you are to stick with a program. Besides that, studies show that having supportive relationships gives you a higher self-esteem and improves the quality of your life.
- The goal is to be healthy, not skinny. That means no dieting, only healthy eating and exercise.

"Trying to be large, myself, and beautiful seems to be hard for some people to accept. But no one else has the right to make me feel bad because of the way that God made me."

ROXY, 18, WHEATON, ILLINOIS

I'm a large woman, though I have no idea how much I weigh. I'm 5'6", and I look like I weigh 250. I think I'm very pretty. And strong: I work out three or four times a week, bike riding and lifting weights. I'm very social and outspoken, not afraid to be myself.

I've always been large, but it was third grade that I got made fun of for my weight. I learned really quickly to tune them out. I drew into myself, became a bookworm. I started to read the classics and developed hobbies. The people who rejected me at school made me more into myself.

High school was different. My brother's older so I had instant friends, unlike junior high where I didn't have any friends. I worked in the athletic department as a student trainer with the football players. They took care of me, so no one would make fun of me. I wasn't as alone in high school. As a trainer I would be at school until eight at night, on weekends for games.

I don't want to sound like I'm perfectly on top of my life, because I'm not. I have bad days. But overall I'm happy. Still, I have a lot of anger and it's not bottled up. When I get angry I get really nasty. That's one of the mechanisms that I've learned and a lot of anger I can direct in the right place because of people making fun of me. It's from people calling me things like "lard ass."

I started college when I was sixteen, and it really helped that the first course I took was on self-esteem and being large. Having a large authority figure express that I was OK and large helped me feel really good. Most of the women in the class were around forty years old and had decided to stop dieting and begin to love themselves. We'd exercise three times a week, then go over magazine and media images, and health issues. Our teacher gave us permission to love ourselves. Seeing these women in their forties just learning to love themselves was so hard. I don't want to be like that. I want to love myself now.

Trying to be large, myself, and beautiful seems to be hard for some people to accept. I've decided that those who are down on me don't add up to the number that support me. No one else has the right to make me feel bad because of the way that God made me. I've become very adamant about that.

Eating Disorders

Adolescence is a time of change and during this period, many young women are dissatisfied with their bodies. This dissatisfaction sometimes begins before puberty, as studies show that girls as young as nine years old are already beginning to diet. At an early age many start to believe that the ability to control weight is an achievement more satisfying than performing well in sports or in the classroom.

What Are Eating Disorders?

An eating disorder is a problematic and distorted concern about food and weight. People who have an obsession with eating (or not eating) use food to mask deeper problems that center mainly around how they feel about themselves, which is pretty awful most of the time.

Eating disorders fall into three categories: anorexia, bulimia, and overeating. People who suffer from anorexia have an intense desire to be thin and starve themselves into dangerously low body weight.

Common symptoms are:

• weight loss, often in a short period of time;
• intense fear of becoming fat, regardless of low weight;
• distorted view of the body, for example someone believing they're too fat, when in reality they may be dangerously thin;
• perfectionism;
• loss of menstruation (period);
• dizziness and fainting spells;
• restricting food intake (strict diets or fasting);
• fear of food, or being at an event where she might have to eat;
• strange behavior while eating, like counting bites, moving food around the plate without eating it, and preparing meals for others without eating;
• becoming withdrawn or isolated from friends;
• severe mood changes, including irritability and depression;
• obsession with exercising, or wanting to be in constant activity to "burn off calories."

Bulimics also want to be thin but go through cycles of first starving, then eating uncontrollably (bingeing), and finally "purging," that is vomiting or using laxatives to get rid of just-eaten food.

Common symptoms are:

• bingeing, or secretively eating unusually large amounts of food at one time;
• purging by throwing up or using laxatives or diuretics;
• fasting or starving for days at a time;
• obsession with food and weight and fear of being fat;
• disappearing to the bathroom after meals;
• frequent weight fluctuations, sometimes within ten to twenty pounds;
• swollen face, broken blood vessels under the eyes because of vomiting;

• complaints of sore throat, fatigue and muscle aches;
• tooth decay;
• mood changes, including depression, guilt, and self-hatred;
• strong self-criticism and need for approval from others.

Like bulimics, overeaters binge on large amounts of food beyond the point of feeling full, but don't purge afterwards. Some people have suffered from two kinds of eating disorders. For example, someone may start out overeating but then begin to purge afterwards, which are symptoms of bulimia. Or a bulimic may stop bingeing and purging but continue to starve, which is anorexic behavior.

Side effects of bulimia and anorexia can be very serious. Both cause malnutrition, which can affect mental performance, bone growth and normal development. Over the long term it leads to heart, kidney and liver failure. Constant vomiting can cause bad breath, rotting teeth, a torn esophagus (passageway from the throat to the stomach), and intestinal disorders. Many of these harmful consequences are permanent and life-threatening, especially if they go untreated.

CAN'T STOP MOVING: EXERCISING TOO MUCH

Are you hyper? Not just regular hyper, but the kind of hyper where you have to be moving all the time because you want to burn off calories, reach a new exercise goal, or you get depressed when you can't work out? Though exercise is one of the best health benefits we can give ourselves, some of us go too far. Like bulimia and anorexia, overexercising can be a type of eating disorder. Young women who exercise too much may be trying to deal with problems such as low self-esteem or depression.

Here are some signs that may point to an exercise disorder:

• exercising several hours a day, several days a week.
• exercising according to what was eaten earlier or will be eaten, for example: "I ate two donuts, so I'll run three miles," or "I can only work out for three hours, so I'll just eat a salad for dinner."
• believing that exercise is a must, not a pleasure: "It's a sin not to exercise. I don't have a choice."
• exercising despite an injury or illness.
• exercising to look thin, not to be healthy.
• feeling anxious, restless, irritable, or guilty when not able to exercise.
• focusing too much on challenge or setting new goals rather than being satisfied by what is achieved.

- taking time from school, homework or work to exercise.
- exercising to the point of exhaustion and injury, and continuing to exercise despite it.

If you or someone you know is suffering from compulsive exercising, there are some things to do to help:

- Cut back on your exercise routine. Try alternating strenuous and light workouts every other day. And take at least one or two days off.
- Don't exercise if there's any pain. Pain does not make gain. It just makes more pain.
- Change types of exercise. Switch bicycling with walking, etc.
- Get other hobbies besides exercise and working out. It'll make you more interesting.
- Sit with your feelings. If you feel anxious or depressed, do nothing but sit and try to figure out why, or what it is you really want. Distracting yourself with a workout won't make the feelings go away.

For more information on compulsive exercising, contact: Anorexia Nervosa and Related Eating Disorders, Inc. (ANRED), at P.O. Box 5102, Eugene, OR 97405; (503) 344-1144.

"I know my eating disorder is a coping mechanism, thinking that losing weight will solve all my problems."

JENNY, 18, WAPPINGERS FALLS, NEW YORK

My eating disorder started at the end of my sophomore year, when I was sixteen. I had always been really self-conscious about my body. I had been a dancer since childhood, but I was never one of those stick-thin, toothpick dancers. I actually have a normal body, but most kids in ballet don't. Even at the age of eight I was comparing myself to others, and I always felt like the fattest kid there.

Then when I went to boarding school I didn't exercise as much because they didn't have as many dance classes as I had been taking. It was a very different environment than I was used to, and I found myself thinking about food a lot. There were so many things we weren't allowed to do. Our lives were so regulated, and there was very little room for freedom. I would just think about lunch or dinner the whole time.

Plus, my sophomore year I had a really beautiful roommate. Everything she did was perfect without even trying hard. I would be up 'til three in the morning, she would be in bed at eleven, and we'd both have the same grades. And she was gorgeous, she knew how to dress. It seemed like everything was easier for her. She also had the perfect boyfriend. I just never really fit in at this school and she did.

Just before the eating disorder started, I was having a bad time. I was partnering with two guys in a dance recital, and they were going to have to lift me. I weighed 135 and was 5'5", and I felt fat, even though I wasn't. I had also just been totally dissed by this guy I had been in love with, my first love. I had also heard rumors that my brother was dealing drugs back home. And someone outside the family pointed out that my father drank a lot. I had never viewed it as a problem, but it got me really concerned.

The first time I vomited it was at night, like always because I stayed up later than other girls in my hall. I remember psychoanalyzing myself, thinking of my brother, my father, my boyfriend, dancing, my perfect roommate. Also, I had always been the perfect little daughter. Nothing I ever did was wrong, so I finally wanted to do something drastic and shocking, but not have people find out. It was this huge, ugly secret of mine, but I could still carry on the facade of being the perfect little daughter. In a weird way, I wanted to have something wrong with me, but still look perfect. That was empowering, to have my own secret.

My eating disorder was in full swing my junior year. Vomiting and eating was taking over more and more of my thoughts. It got to the point where I was lying during study time so I could sneak out and go to another building to throw up. I was thinking about it all the time. I was obsessed.

I finally went to the school psychologist, but he was such a joke. I realized I'd have to tell my parents if I wanted to get therapy. I spent all of Christmas break trying to get the nerve to tell them. I knew they'd be disappointed, because it would hurt them and worry them. When I told my mother her first reaction was, "You know better than that."

During the summer after junior year I went to a treatment center for intensive outpatient therapy, family, group, personal, plus medical. I got on Prozac and that with therapy helped get me over the hump. Towards the end of my senior year, I had a relapse where I threw up three times in three months, which isn't horrible considering I used to throw up three times a day. My therapist said I wasn't recovered yet, and it really bummed me out. So I started vomiting again. At this point, however, I've stopped.

I know my eating disorder is a coping mechanism, thinking that losing weight will solve all my problems. I just have to gain confidence and get my priorities straight. Right now I'm working out a way that doesn't involve getting it through guys or other people's opinions. Until I accept the way I am, I'll never be satisfied.

Who Gets Eating Disorders?

About 7 million women and 1 million men have eating disorders in America, and the majority of cases—86 percent—begin during the teen years. Women are more at risk than men because our value is more appearance-rated. And because adolescence is a time of self-discovery—and confusion and insecurity—teenage girls are especially prone. Those who regard super-skinny supermodels as the ideal women are at highest risk.

For a long time experts didn't focus on young women of color when researching eating disorders because many come from communities that accept voluptuous figures. Experts believed that because many young women of color look at skinny models and say "why don't they put some regular looking women in these ads" that they wouldn't fall victim to the media images that push thinness. But no one lives in a vacuum; these images have started to influence young women of color, too. Native American, Asian, Hispanic, and African American young women are showing up in treatment centers in growing numbers.

Young women of color who are most prone to eating disorders live in predominantly white neighborhoods or go to mostly white schools and are exposed to images of ultra-thin, mostly white models on a daily basis. So even those who are ambitious or successful in school, sports, dance, acting, or other activities may feel they have to conform to those standards of beauty in order to get ahead.

Women of all colors can also develop eating disorders as a means of coping with sexual, emotional, or physical abuse. Though not much research has been done in this area, a lot of girls and young women who have been traumatized try to stuff their feelings or starve them away. Unfortunately until the matter of both the eating disorder and the abuse is addressed, neither goes away.

What young women who suffer from eating disorders have in common is the belief that being thin will offer a greater sense of self-esteem and power. In other words, thinness has become associated with attractiveness and attractiveness with success and success with acceptance.

EATING DISORDERS AND RACE

• A 1993 *Essence* magazine survey of 2,000 women concluded that "African-American women are at risk for and suffer from eating disorders in at least the same proportions as their white counterparts."

• Among Chippewa women living on a Native American reservation in Michigan who participated in a University of Nebraska Study, 75 percent reported dieting to lose weight in potentially hazardous ways, including vomiting, using diet pills, and starvation.

FAMOUS WOMEN WHO HAVE
.... SUFFERED FROM EATING DISORDERS ....

Great Britain's Princess Diana
Grammy Award–winning singer Karen Carpenter, who died as a result of
anorexia
Supermodel Beverly Johnson
World champion gymnast Christy Henrich, who died as a result of
anorexia and bulimia
Academy Award–winning actor and exercise guru Jane Fonda
Television actress Tracey Gold
Tennis star Zina Garrison

What to Do about an Eating Disorder?

If you think you have an eating disorder, get help. Talk openly with someone
you love and trust. Or call an organization that specializes in the problem.
(Some organizations have toll-free numbers that you can call anonymously.)
It may be very difficult, but admitting the problem is an important first step.
See the list at the end of the chapter for resources.

Identifying whether a friend or family member has an eating disorder can
be difficult. Many times young women who have a problem with food hide
the behavior, become defensive or shut down and don't want to talk about it.
If you know someone who is on her way to developing an eating disorder or
is already there, here are a few ways to help her cope:

• Plan very carefully what you want to say, who is the best person to
say it, and when it should be said. The best time is during a calm,
private moment when you can speak without interruption.
• Start by letting her know that you care about her and are concerned.
Using confrontational phrases like "I know what you're doing" or
"You have a big problem" may turn her off. Instead tell her what
you've noticed, such as changes in her weight, eating habits, or signs
of depression. Let her know you're interested in her feelings, and
try not to get caught up talking about food, dieting, and her weight.
If the conversation starts getting too heated, let it go until a better
time.
• Don't come to the conversation with unrealistic expectations. You
are not a miracle worker and cannot get her to stop starving or purging. Only she can. But you can be a good listener and encourage her
to get help.

ESTEEM

Cate Baker was like most anorexics: a high achiever, very bright, with unrealistic expectations of perfection and low self-esteem. For two years she struggled with her body and was severely underweight. Finally, in recovery for anorexia in her senior year in Bangor, Maine, she decided to take action. She applied for a grant, and with the money wrote an eating disorders handbook and started a peer support group at Bangor High for others like her.

When she got to Duke University a year later, she and four fellow students got together to form ESTEEM, or Educational Support to Eliminate Eating Misconceptions. "Suffering from an eating disorder can be so isolating and shameful," says Cate, "and activism is a great way to build solidarity, optimism, and a sense of power."

The group meets weekly to provide support and also offer educational speakers, peer counseling, and outreach at local high schools in Durham, North Carolina. "I've had a lot of mentors and I get excited about teaching," Cate remarks energetically.

ESTEEM's vice president Armide Bien-Aime, from Evanston, Illinois, joined the group her freshman year at Duke. Though she has never been diagnosed with an eating disorder, Armide admits to being an exercise addict and would hate to miss working out a minimum of four hours a day. "I learned a lot about the media, the body's physiology, and decided to focus my energy on things outside of exercise," she recalls.

Being Haitian in a predominately white school has allowed her to reach out to other women of color. "A lot of groups target white women, but at Duke we have large Asian, Hispanic, and African American populations. So I like to discuss how we all feel about our bodies and food. What we found out is that we all have similar issues, like among Japanese students eating disorders are filtering more into their culture as they become assimilated, just like in the black community." Cate remarks on how far the group has come, with the help of members like Armide, saying "When I see our progress as a group, I'm convinced that there's nothing we need to be ashamed of and we don't need to feel alone."

For more information on ESTEEM, contact Duke Student Health Education, P.O. Box 3886, Durham, NC 27710; (919) 684-3620 ext. 343/325. You can also ask about Cate's booklet *The Perfection Trap: College-Age Women and Eating Disorders* ($2).

NIP AND TUCK: PLASTIC SURGERY FOR TEENS

Every year about 22,000 teens go to plastic surgeons to have one or more body parts worked on. Some young women (and men) have corrective or reconstructive surgery done, while others have surgery for cosmetic reasons. Reconstructive surgery involves repairing a birth defect, injury, or the effects of a disease. This would include repairing burns and scars, removing birth marks, fixing deformed ears, or repairing a broken nose from an accident. Cosmetic surgery is strictly to change a feature that the person doesn't like, such as getting a nose job, in hopes of enhancing self-image.

The most popular types of plastic surgery among young women are:

RHINOPLASTY (NOSE JOB): This surgery, which is done entirely inside the nose, requires the surgeon to scrape away bone and cartilage (sometimes breaking the nasal bone first). The bone is reshaped and held in place by a splint to set for a week. Usually there is significant bruising and swelling afterwards. Though the bruising disappears after several weeks, the swelling may take up to a year to go away completely. The cost of a nose job runs between $2,000 and $5,000, depending on where you live and what doctor you use.

Rhinoplasty is increasingly popular in the African American community for people who want to make their noses look less "African," meaning broad and flat. Though a surgeon can reconstruct a more slender nose, she cannot entirely change the shape and general structure.

LIPOSUCTION: Liposuction requires a small incision to be cut and a tube placed just under the skin. With a vacuum-like suction, fat deposits are sucked out. The incision will leave a small scar and healing from bruises takes several weeks. Though this operation sounds simple, it should be performed only by a surgeon who specializes in liposuction. Otherwise you could end up with rippled, uneven skin or nerve damage.

Most plastic surgeons will not perform this procedure on just anyone. Here's the catch, to get liposuction you have to be physically fit and within normal weight. But most people who want the surgery are overweight. So who gets it? Women who have "stubborn spots," or pockets of fat that don't go away after exercise and healthy eating. And even they have to pay from $2,000 to an unbelievable $10,000.

MAMMOPLASTY (BREAST JOB): The most common types of plastic surgery for the breasts are augmentation and reduction. Augmentation involves making an incision below the breast just large enough to slip in an implant. Since the recent controversy surrounding silicone implants, most doctors use saline (salt and water) implants as an alternative. Silicone implants not only have a tendency to leak, but some women have claimed that their silicone implants have led to autoimmune deficiency and cancer. Recovery takes several weeks, during which time bandages, sutures, and support bra are worn. Afterwards, two small scars will remain under the breasts. Augmentation involves general anesthesia and costs $2,000 to $4,200.

Breast reductions are usually done for women who suffer from back problems or other discomfort, bra-strap scars, or ridicule because of their large breast size. While the patient is under general anesthesia, the doctor cuts around the nipples and lower breast, and may have to reposition the nipple after removing excess tissue. Recovery can take several months and involves wearing bandages, sutures, and, later, a tight-fitting bra. Two small scars will remain near the bra-line under both breasts. The cost is $4,000 to $6,000.

BLEPHAROPLASTY (EYE JOB): The options for blepharoplasty include removing puffy bags under the eyes, lifting droopy lids, creating double folds for hooded eyes, or pulling up eyes that are slanted. The procedure involves making incisions on the upper or lower lids, and tightening the muscle or removing excess skin. Most patients get surgery in the doctor's office and leave with small bandages over the incisions. Recovery time is a few weeks, and the cost ranges from $2,000 to $5,000.

Teenagers rarely get eye jobs, although eye surgery has become popular within the Asian community. Many get it to create a more European look that exposes the lid. This can sometimes leave the patient with sad-looking eyes, however, instead of luscious lids.

Some people think plastic surgery is just like getting braces for crooked teeth: if you can fix it, why not? Others believe that the pressure for young women to look a certain way is so strong that we can't even feel good about ourselves unless we look "perfect." Often perfect means trading in distinguishing features for a standard look.

And all this despite the risk. Teens aren't even advised to get plastic surgery on certain body parts until they're at least sixteen, or when they stop developing. However there are some doctors who will perform surgery prematurely, to the detriment of their patients. Aside from the bruising, swelling, and pain that comes from surgery, each patient runs the risk of infection, excessive bleeding or clotting, scarring, or, at worst, a botched job. Some patients come out of the ordeal only to discover they're even more unhappy with their new feature than they were with the original.

If you're considering getting plastic surgery ask yourself a few questions first:

- Why do I want this procedure done?
- What do I expect plastic surgery to do for my life?
- Are there other issues I need to focus on besides looks that might make me feel better about myself?

- Am I trying to conform to a certain look, group of people, or culture? Is anyone else pressuring me to change my features?

These questions are especially important for people who want to change their features to look less "ethnic." A lot of people feel so ashamed of their wide nostrils or slanted eyes that they turn to plastic surgery to look beautiful. Sadly, instead of dealing with issues of racial identity, pride, and acceptance, they resort to drastic measures to fix themselves.

If you're considering plastic surgery for any reason other than reconstructive, seriously question what you want the surgery to address. Sometimes a visit to a therapist would be a better first step.

For more information write or call:

American Academy of Facial Plastic and Reconstructive Surgery, 1110 Vermont Ave. NW, Suite 220, Washington, DC 20005; (202) 842-4500. Ask for *The Teen Face* booklet (it's free), or try the Facial Plastic Surgery Information Service at (800) 332-FACE.

American Academy of Cosmetic Surgery, 401 N. Michigan Ave., Chicago IL 60611-4267; (312) 527-6713. Provides info on selecting a certified surgeon as well as pamphlets and info on procedures.

American Society of Plastic and Reconstructive Surgeons, 444 E. Algonquin Rd., Arlington Heights, IL 60005; (708) 228-9900. For answers to your questions, call its Plastic Surgery Information Service at (800) 635-0635.

How to Feel Good About Your Body

Accepting that the body is changing and will go through many stages before we reach full adulthood is easier said than done. But here are ten tips given by psychotherapist Julia Boyd, author of *In the Company of My Sisters: Black Women and Self-Esteem*, and Monica Dixon, M.S., a registered dietitian who holds body-image workshops:

- Stop comparing yourself to others. Magazine and television ads are designed to make you doubt your breath, underarm odor, or any other part of your body you may feel you have to "fix" with a product. Comparing yourself to models who comprise only a small percentage of the population will of course leave you with negative feelings about yourself. (Especially since their photographs are often enhanced to give them even thinner bodies and impossibly flawless features!) Honor your own body and remember that being unique is what makes us special.

- Don't buy into the myths. Being beautiful and thin will not make your problems disappear. Only dealing with your problems will. And thinness can never replace the hard work it takes to become successful. So be realistic and ask yourself "what will being thin really do for my life," "whose standards am I trying to live up to anyway," and "what other things aside from my body can I change to improve my life."

- Write down the names of the ten women you admire most. Recognizing that our role models come in an assortment of different sizes and shapes lets us know it's who these women *are* that matters most, not how they look.

- Focus on the positives. Make a list of everything positive about you, including your achievements. Put down in separate 3 x 5 cards what you do have going for you, "I have strong arms," "I aced my biology exam yesterday," "I am determined," or "I am a giving person." Carry these cards with you and peek at them throughout the day.

- Throw out the scale and get a telephone tree. First of all, don't get caught in the trap of weighing yourself every day. Whether you've gained or lost pounds isn't the point. It's how healthy you are and how you feel about yourself that matters. So, when you look in the mirror and it ruins your whole day, have two or three phone buddies you can talk to for at least ten minutes. It's important to have support, especially when you feel you're all alone.

- If you're into reading, go to the library or bookstore and get books on women who have dealt with life struggles, such as *I Know Why the Caged Bird Sings* by Maya Angelou or *I, Rigoberta* by Rigoberta Menchu, a Guatemalan woman who won the Nobel Peace Prize. Try to find similarities with these women in your life.

- Make a collage that focuses on your goals. Go through newspapers and magazines and find photographs, headlines, or artwork that speaks to who you are and where you want to go in life. Take the finished masterpiece and hang it on your wall. Some alternatives to the fashion mags are *National Geographic*, *Life Magazine*, *Ms.*, *A Magazine*, *YSB*, and *Women's Sports and Fitness*.

- Get informed. Find out what "healthy" is and share the information with your friends. Better yet, ask your teacher if you can get extra credit by giving a report to the class comparing fact and fantasy of what a healthy body is.

- Look in the mirror with an accepting and loving eye. At least once a day take the time to look at your body from head to toe and say to yourself, "I accept myself just the way I am." No matter how hard you may wish to, you'll never be able to cash in the body you were given for another one. So rather than comparing and setting impossible goals, concentrate on enhancing how you feel about yourself on the inside by accepting yourself on the outside.

- Get moving. Start out small, try a few stretches first, then put on some music and dance for a few songs. If you like to exercise then set a realistic goal every week. But try to do something. Moving our bodies helps us get to know ourselves better, gives us a sense of power. Movement and exercise can also help us get out of a funk and feel good about what our bodies *can* do. But be careful not to make exercise an obsession.

Where to Turn

Recommended Reading
For Body Image

The Beauty Myth: How Images of Beauty Are Used Against Women, Naomi Wolf, Doubleday, 1992.

BodyLove: Learning to Like Our Looks and Ourselves, Rita Freedman, HarperCollins, 1990.

Body Traps: How to Unlock the Cage of Body Obsessions, Judith Rodin, William Morrow, 1992.

Fat Is Not a Four-Letter Word, Charles R. Schroeder, Chronimed Publishing, 1992.

Shame and Body Image: Culture and the Compulsive Eater, Barbara McFarland and Tyeis Baker-Baumann, Health Communications, Inc., 1990.

SomeBody to Love: A Guide To Loving the Body You Have, Leslea Newman, Third Side Press, 1991.

For Eating Disorders

Focus on Eating Disorders, M. Sean O'Halloran, ABC-CLIO, 1993. A textbook and excellent resource for other books and videos on the subject.

Making Peace With Food: Freeing Yourself from the Diet-Weight Obsession, Susan Kano, HarperCollins, 1989.

Overcoming the Legacy of Overeating: How Your Mother Influenced Your Eating Patterns and How You Can Change Them, Nan K. Fuchs, Lowell House, 1990.

Overcoming Overeating, Jane Hirshmann and Carol M. Hunter, Addison-Wesley, 1988.

So You Think You're Fat?, Alvin, Virginia and Robert Silverstein, HarperCollins Children's Books, 1991. Intended for teenagers.

Straight Talk About Eating Disorders, Michael Maloney, M.D., Dell Publishing, 1993. Written for teens.

When Food's a Foe: How to Confront and Conquer Eating Disorders, Nancy Kolodny, Little, Brown and Co., 1992.

Support Groups and Organizations

American Anorexia Bulimia Association, 293 Central Park West, suite 1R, New York, NY 10024; (212) 501-8351. For East Coast referrals or information. To request an information packet send a self-addressed 9" x 12" envelope and include $3 for postage and handling.

Anorexia Nervosa and Related Eating Disorders, Inc., P.O. Box 5102, Eugene, OR 97405; (503) 344-1144. Provides free and low cost information about anorexia nervosa, bulimia, compulsive eating, and compulsive exercising. Leave your name and address for free packet of information on eating and exercise disorders.

Melpomene Institute for Women's Health Research, 1010 University Ave., St. Paul, MN 55104; (612) 642-1951. Helps girls and women link physical activity and health through research, publication, and education. Call for information packet called Large Woman: Enhancing Body Image, Fitness and Health.

National Association of Anorexia Nervosa and Associated Disorders, P.O. Box 7, Highland Park, IL 60035; hotline (708) 831-3438. Offers free services, including counseling, information and referrals, self-help groups.

National Association to Advance Fat Acceptance, P.O. Box 188620, Sacramento, CA 95818; (916) 558-6880 or (800) 442-1214. A nonprofit organization working to eliminate discrimination based on body size; also provides fat people with the tools for self-empowerment. This group has more than fifty local chapters throughout the country and distributes information and literature.

Overeaters Anonymous World Service Office, P.O. Box 44020, Rio Rancho, NM 87174-4020; (505) 891-2664. Overeaters Anonymous is a fellowship of individuals who are recovering from compulsive overeating. There are no dues or fees for members. Write for information about meetings offered in your area.

CHAPTER 2

GOOD OUTSIDES:
SKIN, HAIR, EYES, TEETH, NAILS

Bodies require regular maintenance. That's why it's crucial to take good care of the only skin, hair, eyes, nails, ears, and teeth we have. Doing so is just common sense: taking care of what you've got will prevent bigger health problems that can occur later in life. Plus, caring for your body is a sign of self-respect and pride.

What follows is some basic information and advice on personal body care.

Skin

It may seem weird to think of your skin as an organ, like the kidney or the heart, but that's what it is. The skin protects the inner parts from the environment, helps regulate body temperature and provides the sense of touch.

There are two layers to skin: the *epidermis*, which is the outer layer, and the *dermis*, a thicker inner layer containing blood vessels, nerve endings, hair and oil glands. The epidermis contains the brown pigment called *melanin*, which gives us our skin color. Darker skinned people have more melanin, while fair-skinned people have less. Going out into the sun stimulates the production of melanin and gives us darker skin—a sun tan—temporarily (read more about this on page 29).

Our skin shade is determined by nature and our parents. Aside from letting us know what hue a person is, skin color doesn't say much else about a person. Unfortunately too many people make judgments about each other based solely on skin color. And some actually believe that one skin tone is better than another and pick friends accordingly. This is racism, and it's not cool (read more about this in Chapter 8). Remember, skin shade is a matter of melanin and nothing more.

Skin Care

The skin needs special care, including daily cleansing, using a washcloth or loofah pad to remove the dead skin cells, oil, sweat, and grunge that accumulate during the day. This is especially important if you tend to have oily skin or perspire a lot from exercising or playing sports.

The more delicate skin of the face needs extra special care. It requires at least two washings a day with a mild fragrance-free cleanser, followed by a splash of cool water. Stay away from abrasive scrubs, like the apricot type, especially if you are light-, medium- or brown-skinned because it can cause blotching and scarring.

After you wash and pat dry, apply an oil-free moisturizer with sunscreen. Regardless of skin tone, everyone needs extra protection from the sun's harmful rays to keep from damaging the skin and to reduce the risk of skin cancer. The sunscreen should be at least SPF (sun protection factor) 15, and be sure to pick a moisturizer that says "non-comedogenic," which means nonclogging.

One of the best things you can do for your skin is to drink six to eight glasses of water a day. Water replenishes lost moisture, helps the body flush out toxins, and keeps the elasticity in your skin. (Smoking also decreases the skin's elasticity and can make it look grayish, not sexy!)

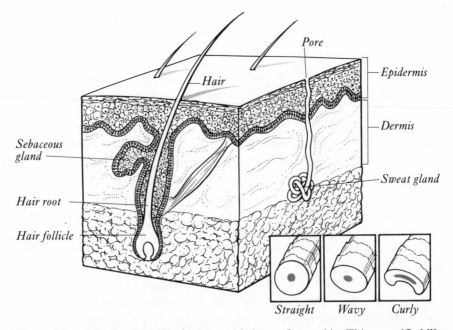

Pore

Hair

Epidermis

Dermis

Sebaceous gland

Sweat gland

Hair root

Hair follicle

Straight   *Wavy*   *Curly*

Your epidermis is showing! That's the outside layer of your skin. This magnified illustration also shows what's below the surface. Inset: A close-up view of three hair types.

Skin Problems

The following are common skin problems that most of us have suffered from at some point or another.

ACNE

Almost everyone has faced the mirror to find a small volcano about to erupt on their chins or foreheads. The urge to pick at it or cover it up is generally overwhelming—anything just to make it go away. But the pimples seem to multiply, and pretty soon it becomes too depressing to deal with.

Don't worry. As bad as it may seem, there are ways to help control acne. As menacing as it looks, acne is just the clogging of the pores with a natural lubricant called *sebum*. Blackheads are dried sebum pushed to the surface; whiteheads are a combo of sebum, oil, and bacteria trapped just under the surface; and the larger cysts—the big painful zits—are pus-inflamed follicles deep within the skin.

We get acne from:

- heredity, which means from parents (thanks Mom and Dad);
- oily skin;
- bacteria on the skin living in sebaceous (oil) glands, where sebum is produced;
- oil-producing hormones that plague us throughout puberty, and sometimes beyond (that's why acne is usually at its absolute worst during the teen years);
- being stressed out;
- hair- and skin-care products containing oil.

If you have clear skin and only an occasional small flare-up, give yourself weekly facials. Mild scrubs purchased at a health-food store or homemade treatments (steaming the face with a hot washcloth, cleansing gently, and then applying a drying mask for twenty minutes, followed with a cold rinse) can clean out and close up the pores and make the skin feel refreshed.

For acne that stays like a bad house guest, take action. You may be able to treat breakouts with drugstore products, such as a non-abrasive, oily skin cleanser and a gel or lotion containing benzyl peroxide (such as Clearasil) to dry the skin. These products may help, but you may also require advice from a dermatologist (skin doctor). She may prescribe the following:

- Oral or lotion antibiotics that kill the bacteria.
- Retin A, which is a vitamin A lotion that keeps off dead skin that can clog pores.

- Glycolic acids, made from fruit, which are generally prescribed to older patients (sixteen to eighteen years old) who have milder acne. These acids can also be purchased at a drugstore in lesser strengths called alphahydroxy acids (AHAs).

HOW TO BEAT A ZIT INVASION

Whether you go to the dermatologist or stick with over-the-counter products, here are some tips to help beat a zit invasion. Keep them in the forefront of your mind around your period when hormonal changes may increase breakouts:

- Keep your face or other affected areas (chest or back) clean. Wash when you wake up, after exercising or sports, when you come home from school, and before bed at night.
- Keep your hands off your face. Squeezing zits may make that one go away (or just make it bigger), but traumatizing the skin will actually cause more outbreaks and scarring. This is especially true for dark-skinned folks who scar more easily than those with fairer skin.
- Use oil-free products. This includes soap and lotions, as well as makeup foundation (which should be water-based) and haircare products.
- Try keeping your hair off your face. Dirt and oil from your hair can cause breakouts.
- Eat raw carrots and drink water. Carrots contain lots of vitamin A, a nutrient which promotes healthy skin, and water helps the body flush out dirt and toxins. Though diet is not the most important factor, try to avoid salty foods, like nuts, fast foods, and shellfish, which can make acne worse.
- Learn to deal with stress. Try exercising, meditating, and talking about your problems to keep negative, anxiety-producing feelings under control.

"The first thing people notice is your face, and I had all these things everywhere."

KELLY, 17, PORT WASHINGTON, MARYLAND

I started getting acne in my preteens, like twelve, and it wasn't anything bad because I had clear skin to begin with. Then one day it just broke out so bad, it looked like I had hives. I got the itches and my face broke out everywhere. It was a mystery.

I ended up going to the dermatologist and the allergist to find out what was going on. The hives stopped, but my face was still a wreck. I looked terrible. The doctor said it was a case of bad acne, but I don't know what caused it. I went to the dermatologist and got all this medication for my face: face wash, oral antibiotics, and lotion for the itching all two times a day. It took about three weeks and then it cleared up and looked good.

But after I sat out in the sun, I broke out again. It looks better now, but it's left scarring from the first time. I had black circles from where the bumps were, but they're starting to go away.

When this first started, I felt terrible. Everyone who saw me would say "What's wrong with your face." I took it offensively and said something smart back, like "It's not your problem, don't worry about it." If someone came off nasty, I would give a nasty response. If not I would try to explain just to get them out of my hair.

I hated my skin. I remember calling my mom on the phone and crying to death because I felt like I was ugly. The first thing people notice is your face, and I had all these things everywhere.

Even my sister made nasty remarks about my face. She was joking, but I didn't think it was funny because I was so sensitive about it. I said something back to her about being fat. It made me angry that my own sister would make comments knowing I was sensitive.

I suspect that my problem is stress. I go to a competitive college-prep school and I'm under enormous stress. Right now I'm trying to get my college applications filled out and keep my grades up with a tough workload. I'll be stressed out for a while, until I get into a good college. When my face breaks out more than usual, it's because school is stressful.

Now, even though I'm very self-conscious about how I look, I'm learning to live with the breakouts. I feel much better about my skin.

Other Common Skin Problems

HYPERPIGMENTATION/BLOTCHING

Just as the sun can stimulate the melanin in our skin, so can other factors. Acne, insect bites, hair gels, too much sun, medications, or any irritation can cause our skin to react and create skin discoloration and blotching.

If your skin has dark patches or spots, try to follow a few of these tips:

- Don't squeeze or pick at your face.
- Avoid abrasive scrubs or soaps.
- Always wear sunscreen with SPF 15, especially if you're being treated for acne because the skin is extra sensitive.
- Avoid hair gels or wearing your hair on your forehead, as many of these gels are harsh and can burn the skin.
- Ask your doctor if medication you may be taking is causing an allergic reaction in the sun.

A dermatologist can prescribe effective bleaching creams that will clear up the blotching in a few weeks. Be careful about purchasing drugstore fade creams. Experts have found that the active ingredient hydroquinone may cause cancer and is often not very effective. Instead, try an alphahydroxy acid lotion.

KELOIDS

Some of us tend to overheal when we get a cut. Instead of the skin returning to normal, the cut heals as a raised scar called a keloid. Though keloids are much more common in blacks, anyone who comes from a family that's prone to keloids will probably get them.

They can be from small scrapes, burns, acne, or surgery. Most keloids are small enough to live with, but others may need special care to remove the scarring. A dermatologist can inject the keloid with cortisone to try to shrink it. If that doesn't work, she may suggest plastic surgery on another visit. The scar is actually reopened and removed. Other surgery might involve sanding the skin.

If you have keloids, talk to your doctor about keeping some cortisone in your medicine cabinet for minor cuts. And definitely consult a dermatologist before getting any piercing or tattooing.

DRY SKIN

Persistent dry skin can be a drag, especially on the elbows and knees. Dark-skinned people are prone to "ashy" skin, or dry spots, that seem to need constant moisturizing. The best remedy for dry skin is using a loofah to slough off dead skin, then putting oil or moisturizer on the skin just after bathing, while the skin is still moist.

ECZEMA

Eczema is a word that actually describes a variety of skin problems, including red, itchy, blistering, or scaly skin conditions. There are several kinds of eczema, but the most common is atopic dermatitis (AD), caused by allergies or heredity. Three percent of Americans suffer from AD, according to the American Academy of Dermatology, and most get it any time between infancy and young adulthood. In adolescence AD usually appears on the elbows, back of the knees, ankles, wrists, face, neck, and upper chest, though it can affect all areas of the body.

Sometimes chemicals or irritants like lotions, detergents, alcohol, bleach, wool, tobacco smoke, and even change in temperature or stress can cause breakouts. A dermatologist can help you develop ways to manage AD, including dealing with emotional issues that can greatly aggravate an episode. She can also prescribe cortisone or tar creams to contain the affected areas and antihistamines to control the itching.

A WORD OF WARNING TO SUN GODDESSES

To put it simply, the sun is stronger than it used to be. As the ozone layer of the atmosphere has eroded, the rays of the sun have become much more powerful. That's why everyone—including people with dark skin—must wear sunscreen of at least sun protection factor (SPF) 15 to avoid damaging the skin and to reduce the risk of skin cancer.

The risk of skin cancer is real: one in one hundred Americans contract melanoma, a deadly form of cancer of the skin. To prevent it, doctors advise wearing hats, sunglasses, long-sleeved shirts, and staying out of the sun between 10 a.m. and 2 p.m. when the sun is strongest. And use sunscreen, of course.

Also keep a careful eye out for any unusual dark spots or moles. Dermatologists recommend using the ABCD warning signs:

A is for asymmetry, if one side of the mole doesn't look like a mirror image of the other.
B is for border, if there are ragged, notched, or blurred edges to the mole.
C is for color, if it is a mixture of black, brown, and tan shades.
D is for diameter, if the mole is any bigger than a pencil eraser.

Any one or all of these require a doctor's attention.

Extreme exposure to the sun before you're eighteen puts you at highest risk for skin cancer.

TATTOOING AND BODY PIERCING

Tattooing and piercing are both ancient body adornments brought to America from Asia, Africa, the Pacific Islands, and other parts of the world where tribal people originated the customs. Since the sixties these body adornments have been picking up in popularity. Now it's fairly common to see nose rings and ankle tattoos on top fashion models as well as regular people. But before you decide to get pierced or tattooed, consider these points:

- If you're prone to scarring or keloids, don't have tattoos or piercing done at all. You'll probably be disappointed with the overgrown scar tissue, and that could mean getting rid of the nose post or doing plastic surgery to remove the cupid heart.
- Think ahead. These procedures are permanent, so consider whether or not you want to have a purple dolphin on your shoulder or pierced eyebrow years down the road.
- Think about your livelihood. Some employers will not hire you if you

have visible tattoos or piercing in parts other than your ears. Holes sometimes don't close because you've pierced cartilage (soft bone, like that in the upper ear and nose). And although tattoos can be removed with laser surgery, it takes numerous visits and it is costly.

- Consider what parents, other relatives, and friends will say. Not that your decision should be based solely on the opinions of others, but are Mom and Dad going to have a huge hissy fit if you show up with a tattoo on your wrist?
- Have piercing done by a dermatologist. With a doctor you can be assured to have a safe and sterilized procedure. Otherwise you run the risk of infection.
- Never share needles. If you don't use a fresh, sterilized needle, you could contract an infection or a virus, including hepatitis or HIV. Don't be afraid to ask where the needle came from.

If you're planning to pierce, follow these specific guidelines:

- Use stainless steel posts with stainless steel backings. Other materials may irritate the skin.
- For the first few weeks after you've pierced, rotate the posts three times daily.
- Swab the pierced area and post with alcohol or hydrogen peroxide twice a day and after exercising.
- Don't wear doorknocker earrings or anything large and weighty, as it can cause the earlobe to tear. (A doctor can repair a torn earlobe with surgery, but why go through that?)

If a tattoo or piercing causes an infection that doesn't heal within a few days, go to the doctor. Waiting too long may mean having to surgically remove a post or repair a tattoo wound.

Hair

For many of us our hair makes just as much of a statement as our clothes do. Whether hair is straight and long enough to sit on, dreadlocked, permed and dyed, or shaved off altogether, it speaks to our taste and style, our individuality, and our culture.

Hair grows out of openings, or pores, in the epidermis called *follicles*. The shape of our follicles determines the amount of curl in our hair. Very curly hair comes out of a flat or oval follicle and slants backwards to create spirals; wavy hair comes from an oval follicle and grows out in a slanted direction; and straight hair comes from a rounded follicle and grows—you guessed it—straight.

Though the shape of our strands may differ, the structure of each of our individual hairs is the same. Each strand grows from the root and is kept nourished and lubricated by the sebaceous glands in our skin. The hair strand is made of *keratin*, the same kind of protein that our nails are made of.

Hair Care

What your hair requires is an individual matter depending on what styles you like to wear, whether you chemically treat your hair, what type of skin you have, and what special attention your hair and scalp might need. The first rule no matter what type of hair you have is to go easy. The second rule is to be patient. As with your entire body, the goal is to have hair that looks healthy and that means making the most of the type of hair you were born with.

Peggy Dillard Toone is a model who now owns Turning Heads Salon in New York City and styles for top fashion magazines like *Vogue*, *Elle*, and *Essence*. To shed more light on some hairy issues, Peggy answers the top ten most asked questions:

What's the deal with shampooing? How often should I do it?

Let's back up and start with before the shampoo. If you have curly hair, you might want to do a preshampoo condition with jojoba oil by massaging it into the scalp and leaving it on for at least an hour. Or you can wrap your head in a scarf overnight. It's a great way to lift dirt and oil from the hair.

Washing once or twice a week is enough, and every day isn't necessary. But if you sweat or exercise a lot, your scalp will secrete salts that dry and create flaking or dandruff, not to mention an odor. And if your hair is especially oily or you use lots of styling products you might need to wash more often. When you wash, massage the scalp gently.

What kind of shampoo should I use?

Be sure to use a pH balanced shampoo, preferably an herbal-based rather than detergent-based one because they're too harsh and drying.

Should I use a conditioner after every shampoo?

For all hair types I recommend using a homemade rinse from two tablespoons of apple cider vinegar and a half-gallon of water after shampooing. For dry hair, you can use an herbal conditioner, and definitely avoid balsams. They are too waxy and heavy for the hair.

What styling aids should I use and which should I avoid?

Avoid alcohol, balsam, petroleum, mineral oil, and harsh chemicals. Go for the herbal-based products made with natural oils. Jojoba oil is best because it's closest to our natural sebum. And try to stick with products that have been researched and on the market for awhile.

Should I comb my hair one hundred times a day?

Definitely not. That puts too much stress on the hair and only breaks it off. Combing and brushing is for distributing the oils from your scalp throughout your hair. It's best to massage your scalp first, then use a wide-tooth comb to detangle and style. Brushing is good for distributing oil, but never brush while your hair is wet.

How often should I get a haircut?

If you're trying to maintain a style, cut your hair every four to six weeks. If you're trying to grow your hair, cut it every fourteen weeks.

My hair is bone straight and I want to perm it. What should I do?

First do a strand test to see how, or even if, your hair will take the perm. But I wouldn't recommend a perm for really straight hair because it's such a harsh treatment and usually leaves your hair very dry. Plus it takes a long time to grow out. Consider setting it in a curly look every now and then using a spiral curl or hot stick.

My hair is really thin, but I want to color it. Is it possible?

Your best bet is to avoid permanent colors and go with a cellophane. They add weight and thickness, especially if you cut your hair in a layered look.

I love trying out new styles and experimenting with color, but I can't afford a salon. What can I do on the cheap?

You're best off with a semi-permanent hair color because it washes out after five shampoos. Then style your hair using a wet-set.

Can you name a couple of easy ways to set my hair?

Regardless of hair type, you can use a few texturizing styles. While your hair is still wet, use an herbal styling gel or lotion. Then you can either braid your hair, or separate it and put it in lots of twists, rollers, or coils. When your hair dries, comb it out using your fingers and take out the gel stiffness with a little oil.

. . . . **HAIR FACTS** . . . .

- Hair grows about a half-inch a month.
- Fifty to 150 hairs fall out every day.
- Scalp hairs grow for two to five years, then rest for two months before shedding.
- A healthy head of hair has 80,000 to 150,000 hairs.

. . . .

Is That Snow on Your Shoulders?

Few things are more embarrassing than wearing a dark shirt and having someone point out the cluster of small white flecks collecting on your shoulders. Or being on a date when the scalp itch just won't quit. If this has been you, you probably already know you have dandruff, flaky dead skin that has built up in your scalp. But what to do?

First, wash your hair *at least* once a week, or after two to three days because that's when dandruff generally shows up. Try a good dandruff shampoo with tar, salicylic acid, or selenium sulfide to help slough off the dead skin.

If you find that your dandruff hasn't gone away after a few washings, speak to a dermatologist so she can prescribe a stronger shampoo to combat the flaking.

To Curl or Not to Curl

A lot of us covet hair that's the exact opposite of what we were born with. Curly-haired people want straight hair. The straight-haired want curly. So stylists make a fortune trying to give us what we want but don't naturally have through perms, straighteners, colors, and other kinds of chemical treatments.

Chemically processing or coloring your hair usually strips it of its natural oils and can make it look dull. Sometimes the chemicals lead to hair loss. Follow this advice—especially if you're doing it yourself at home.

- Always follow directions. These products are laboratory tested and meant to be used according to directions. If you have questions, call the number on the product box.
- Don't relax hair that's already been chemically treated, such as dyed

or permed hair. If you have permed your straight hair, relaxing it to knock out the curl will leave you very disappointed.

• Never use professional kits at home. These are meant for salon use by professionals.

• Before you or your stylist perms, straightens, or colors your hair, do a strand test first. This is a quick dress rehearsal for your hair to see how it will react to the chemicals. If your stylist refuses, don't let her work on your hair. You don't know what you're getting and you may pay big bucks for something you hate.

• Use moisturizing shampoo and conditioner especially for chemically treated hair. You may want to follow it up with leave-in conditioner.

• Stay away from gels and mousses that contain alcohol, which leads to drying. Try to avoid daily styling with heat: hot curlers, blow dryers, curling irons.

• Think mild. For curly heads who want to relax, consider a texturizer, which is milder than a straightener. For straight heads who want curl, think about a body perm rather than a curl perm.

"What I really want is hair like Janet Jackson's."

ALICIA, 15, SIOUX CITY, IOWA

"People always say, 'I wish I could have your hair.' But I like Cindy Crawford's hair."

AMANDA, 16, SIOUX CITY, IOWA

ALICIA

I'm African American, and use straightener to relax my hair. I put it up in a barrette and curl my bangs under. What I really want is hair like Janet Jackson's. Her hair is curly, but I don't know if it's natural or not.

AMANDA

My hair is naturally straight and really thin and used to be really long. I just chopped six inches off the back and ten inches off the bangs. It still is down to way past my shoulders, but I don't really like it. I used to have a perm and I didn't like that either. But everybody I guess seems to like my hair. People always say, "I wish I could have your hair." But I like Cindy Crawford's hair.

ALICIA

At my school it's like if you have curly blond hair past the shoulder and winged up—that's the kind of hair that's real cool. In gym class people spend the whole time trying to fix their hair. They bring curling irons to school, blow dryers to school, I mean, just to fix their hair after gym class. They spend two hours on their hair, get up earlier just cause of their hair.

AMANDA

They're trying to impress other people. And they don't even need to. With the people I hang out with it doesn't really even matter. If you were bald they wouldn't care. As long as you are a cool person. My best friend is like this blond model, and I'm like far from it, and she just doesn't even care. My friends don't even care how your hair looks.

ALICIA

Guys aren't really into their own hair. But they look at girls' hair.

AMANDA

I don't agree with you on that. My ex-boyfriend, kind of, he doesn't care. He's like, your hair is your hair and it's not his problem.

ALICIA

You're right, I think they pay attention more to the body than the hair.

AMANDA

Girls who spend a lot of time on their hair are trying to impress guys. And the guys at my school, if they want me, they know that, hey, this is what you get.

ALICIA

That's true.

LET ME RUN MY FINGERS THROUGH YOUR DREADLOCKS

Long, beautiful dreadlocks are busting out all over. Locks, which originated in ancient times in the African country of Ghana, became popular because of Jamaican people like the late reggae king Bob Marley. As part of their religious practices, Rastafarians like Marley let their hair grow out uncombed until it matted into naturally formed sections. Jamaicans coined the term "dreadlocks" because the police "dreaded" any rebel seen wearing them. For African Americans, locks have become a statement of Afrocentricity; they proclaim "I'm proud of being black."

"Anyone can get locks," says Annu Prestonia, a "locksmith," who operates out of Khamit Kinks, a salon in Brooklyn where many New Yorkers go to get locked. "I've seen locks on blondes with straight hair, but the straighter the texture, the longer it takes the hair to lock." That's because locking requires the hair to twist upon itself, a time-consuming process which is started by one of three ways:

- Palm-rolling, in which each section is literally rolled between the palms of the hands until the hair catches on itself.
- Coil technique, which uses rubber-coated wires to wrap the hair around and is left in for six weeks, or until the hair begins to lock.
- Two-strand twist, that calls for two pieces of hair twisted together to form the individual locks; this style is left for three months until it locks. The two-strand twist is also good if you want to experiment with locking before taking the plunge.

Maintaining locks is easier than most dos because they require washing only about once or twice a week with a shampoo and conditioner. They are then palm-rolled wet, using an organic liquid oil to keep the hair moist. If your hair is very curly or very dry, you should oil your locks three times a week. But don't palm-roll dry hair or it can weaken the hair roots, which are the locks' support, and can break the lock off. Touch-ups are required once every four to six weeks, to clip the fuzz that peeks out through the locks, as well as a good hot oil treatment.

Although locks can be the ultimate fashion or Afrocentric statement, getting them started and maintained by a professional can be costly. Khamit Kinks charges from $90 to $175 to start and $75 for maintenance visits. If you live in an area where this style has caught on, you may be able to get an independent stylist to lock your locks for much cheaper. But be sure you know what you're locking yourself into—the only way to lose locks is cutting them off.

Nails

Getting Nailed: Five Common Nail Problems and What to Do

Finger- and toenails are nothing more than protein that grows from the nail center just below the cuticle called the *matrix*. Most of us take our nails for granted, biting them nervously or neglecting them until a hot date forces us to pamper them. Here are five common problems that can easily be treated to keep naturally nice-looking nails:

• Weak and brittle nails. This happens from lack of moisture in the nail and can be treated by soaking your nails in water for fifteen minutes. Afterwards, clean nails, apply polish—which helps keep moisture in—and rub moisturizer into your hands. Keep the polish on for six days, then remove it and let the nails breathe for one day before reapplying polish. To maintain nice nails, wear gloves when working with detergents or cleaners.

- Hard or cracking cuticles. Cuticles need to be softened and massaged back to keep from getting bad hangnails and cracked skin. Try soaking hands, and then, with a moist washcloth, work the cuticle back by rubbing it. Never use a hard instrument or scissors to push or trim them back. Keep your cuticles soft by applying moisturizer often.

- Fungal infections. Fungus is in our carpets, shoes, backyards, even our salads (mushrooms are a fungus, don't forget). Most of it is harmless, but when it infects our nails it can cause cracking, crumbling, thickening, and yellowing. The good news is that fungus is so common that it's easy to treat. If you see fungus taking over your nails, go to the dermatologist and she'll give you an anti-fungal cream or pill to take.

- Nail treatment blues. Nail treatments such as acrylic wraps are fine every so often, but not every month. Your nails need breathing room for at least a month until the next time. And FYI: many people are allergic to the acrylic and have to find another nail treatment that their nails can tolerate.

- Bruised or bleeding nails. If you're an athlete, artist or someone who likes to work with your hands, you probably bang your nails up a lot. Aside from not using your nail as a screwdriver, there are a couple of things you can do. If it's a minor bruise, you can try massaging the nail and icing it to take some of the sting and swelling out. But if it's bleeding from an injury, it's best to go to the doctor to let her drain the bruise. Either way, you'll probably have a purple nail for a good six months until the new one grows in.

NAIL FACTS

- Nails grow about one-eighth of an inch a month.
- Nails grow faster in hot weather than cold.

Eyes

According to studies, people who wear glasses are perceived as honest, sensitive, and intelligent.

"People tell me that I look prettier with my glasses on—and smarter."

MADIA, 14, ALBANY, GEORGIA

When I was in first grade I started having trouble reading the blackboard from the back of the room, and by third grade when I was nine it got pretty bad. I had to keep asking my friend behind me what it said on the board. I even had headaches from straining my eyes. Finally my mom took me to an eye doctor and he said I needed glasses. I got my first pair of glasses at that clinic, and the next pair I got at Walmart. Now I'm on my sixth pair of glasses.

When I first knew I was going to wear glasses I felt kind of excited because I would be able to see, but I didn't want them to be big, thick, and heavy. The lenses I have are pretty thin, even though they're very powerful; when my friends try on my glasses they say, "Gosh you must be blind!" because they're so strong. I have to wear them everywhere, because I can't see a thing without them. The only time they're not on is when I go to sleep.

When I was in sixth grade, there was this cute boy in school, and he didn't have glasses. I thought *Oh no, I have these brown glasses, I hope I don't stick out like a geek*. He came up to me about the Valentine's Day dance, and he was about to ask me something. Then he changed his mind. He said, "I never had a girl with glasses." And I said, "There's nothing different about me, it's just I need glasses." He asked why I couldn't get contacts and I told him that my mom won't let me right now. We didn't go to the dance together, but I went to the dance anyway with a couple of my friends and danced with some other boys. Now I hear that he transferred to another school, and you know what? He got reading glasses himself! That serves him right.

Mostly, good things happen from wearing glasses. And they look kind of cool. People tell me that I look prettier with my glasses on—and smarter. Like, I'm in the school orchestra, and when we went to play a concert at another school some of the kids there said, "Gosh, you must make high honors or something, you look so smart!" I do make honor roll anyway, but when people see glasses they just think you're so intelligent.

Teeth

Smiles are made of thirty-two teeth that start to grow when we're still babies, and are replaced by a permanent set by the time we reach adulthood. Each tooth is composed of an outer layer of calcified enamel, also called the *crown*, and an inner layer of *dentin*. The *root* is below the gum surface and lies in a socket connected to the jaw bone.

Dental Care

Brushing and flossing are your two best defenses against tooth decay—and frequent, sometimes painful visits to the dentist. Here are brushing and flossing tips for good dental hygiene:

- Get in the habit of brushing at least two times a day, once when you wake up and again before going to bed. If you snack on sweets between meals, be sure to brush right afterwards.

- Use dental floss that slides easily between teeth. Floss comes in various flavors, widths, and waxed or unwaxed ribbons. To use, pull off a string about ten to twelve inches long, wrap one end around your right index finger and the other end around your left. With your thumbs, gently wedge the floss between your upper and lower teeth in a back and forth motion. Don't jam the floss between your teeth because it can damage your gums. Rinse.

- Using a soft toothbrush and fluoride toothpaste, gently brush in small circular motions and short back and forth motions. Don't scrub hard back and forth or up and down on your gums because this can cause them to recede and expose the roots of your teeth. After brushing your teeth, brush your tongue and rinse.

- If you like to use a mouthwash, be sure to use one that has little or no alcohol, because high alcohol content can cause mouth sores. Most mouthwashes only give you temporarily fresh breath and most do nothing to help remove plaque. Few things get rid of bad breath except regular brushing, flossing, and dental cleaning (once or twice a year). You may want to try a swish of warm water and salt.

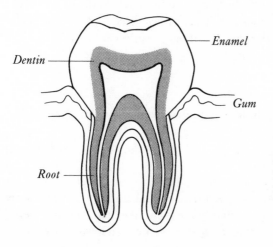

Show them you care. Brush your teeth twice a day, and floss once a day.

- Visit your dentist for checkups and cleaning every six months. If you have chronic problems, your visits should be two times or more annually.
- Avoid candy and sticky sweets. Aside from being junk food, chewy and sticky sweets cling to your teeth and cause cavities. Get in the habit of snacking on fruits, vegetables, popcorn, nuts and seeds, yogurt, or other snacks that are also good for you.

Dental Problems

There are a lot of dental problems that could easily be avoided if you're willing to take care of your teeth daily. However, others may require a consultation with your dentist.

CAVITIES

Cavities are caused by bacteria colonies called plaque forming on your teeth. The longer plaque has to hang out, the more at risk your teeth are for decay. Sugar is plaque's best friend because they team up to form an acid that erodes tooth enamel and lets bacteria into the tooth. The best defense against these oral outlaws: brush and floss.

If you do have a cavity, don't delay going to the dentist or a little tooth decay could turn into a big pain in the mouth.

BAD BREATH

Halitosis is a fancy clinical term for bad breath and is one of the biggest sources of embarrassment. Bad breath is usually caused by not cleaning gums and teeth properly, and can generally be fixed by flossing, brushing, and swishing with mouthwash twice a day. Getting a checkup and cleaning every six months to be sure all the plaque buildup gets washed away can also help. Smoking also causes bad breath, so unless you want to smell like an ashtray, don't do it. Sometimes bad breath doesn't come from the mouth at all, but from stomach or digestive problems. Either way, if your halitosis persists, discuss it with your doctor.

"I've gotten so used to the braces that I don't know how I'm gonna look when they come off."

BILON, 13, ST. PETERSBURG, FLORIDA

When I was ten years old my mom told me I needed braces because my teeth were overlapping—coming out in front and stuff. I used to suck my finger when I was younger and that made them like that. I always knew that someday I would need to have braces. Part of me even looked forward to it.

Sometimes I felt like when I talked no one listened to me because of my funny-looking, overlapping teeth. I guess I thought that if I looked better then people would pay more attention to me.

I also thought they might even look pretty. I had a choice of colors, so I selected pink. Mine are silver underneath with pink over the silver.

I've now had braces on for three years. The only bad thing that's ever happened with my braces was one time when I bumped my lip and it got stuck to my braces. It was bleeding a lot, and I got scared. When I got home, my mom lifted my lip and got it unstuck. It hurt for about a half hour, and then I felt fine.

I've gotten so used to the braces that I don't know how I'm gonna look when they come off. But I'm looking forward to it. My advice to other kids who need braces is don't be afraid. You might feel a little different, but everybody has something that's a little different about them.

THE HAZARDS OF PUMPING UP THE VOLUME

Did you know that once you lose your hearing it never comes back? The ears are very sensitive organs, so you may want to think twice the next time you listen to music with the sound turned all the way up, or go to a concert and stand right next to the speakers.

How do you know if your hearing is fading? Here are the two big signs:

- When you take off your earphones, get out of your car, or turn off the stereo in your room, you hear ringing, buzzing, or whistling in your ears.
- After a concert, sounds seem temporarily muffled or softer. Repeated exposure to loud noise can make this shift permanent.

Preventing the problem is simple: turn down the volume, stand away from the speakers, and wear earplugs to reduce the noise. Beeswax earplugs are your best option.

Where to Turn

Recommended Reading

500 Beauty Solutions, Beth Barrick-Hickey, Source Books Inc., 1993.

Don't Go to the Cosmetics Counter Without Me: An Eye-Opening Guide to Brand Name Cosmetics, Paula Begoun and Mariam Bulmer, eds., Beginning Press (Seattle), 1994.

Good Hair, Lonnice Bonner, Crown Books, 1994. Combination "how to" beauty book and hilarious autobiography that celebrates Black hair.

The New Medically Based No-Nonsense Beauty Book, Deborah Chase, Avon Books, 1990.

The New Teenage Body Book, Kathy McCoy, Ph.D., and Charles Wibbelsman, M.D., Berkley Publications, 1992. This book has an excellent chapter on plastic surgery, plus chapters on skin, hair, eye, and teeth care.

Take Care of Your Skin, Elaine Brumberg, HarperPerennial, 1989.

True Beauty: Secrets of Radiant Beauty for Women of Every Age & Color, Beverly Johnson, Warner Books, 1994. By the black supermodel.

A Woman's Skin, David Stoll, M.D., Rutgers University Press, 1994.

Women of Color: The Multicultural Fashion Guide, Darlene Mathis, Ballantine, 1994.

Support Groups and Organizations

Skin

The American Academy of Dermatology, Communication Dept., P.O. Box 4014, Schaumburg, IL 60168-4014; (708) 330-0230. Write for a free pamphlet on a specific skin condition (acne, psoriasis). Must include a business-size self-addressed stamped envelope. Also, pamphlet specifically on black skin care.

The American Skin Association, Inc., 150 E. 58th St., 32nd Fl., New York, NY 10155-0002; (212) 753-8260. ASA is primarily a resource for addresses and phone numbers of organizations that deal with specific skin conditions.

The Skin Cancer Foundation, 245 Fifth Ave., Suite 2402, New York, NY 10016; (212) 725-5176. The SCF offers pamphlets, brochures and other informational materials having to due with skin cancer.

Solutions, 530 East Eighth St., Suite 103, Oakland, CA 94606; (510) 893-7546. This clinic provides skin-care information especially helpful for women of color.

Hair

National Alopecia Areata Foundation, P.O. Box 150760, San Rafael, CA 94915-0760; (415) 456-4644. For hair loss.

The Tricholtillomania Learning Center, 1215 Mission St., Suite 2, Santa Cruz, CA 95060; (408) 457-1004. For those who twist, twirl, or tug at hair.

Teeth

The American Dental Association, 211 E. Chicago Ave., Chicago, IL 60611; (312) 440-2593 (the number for referrals) or (800) 947-4746. Call the 800 number for free pamphlets on a number of dental issues such as

"Caring for Teeth and Gums," "Basic Flossing," "Tooth Decay," "Diet and Dental Health," "Smokeless Tobacco—Think Before You Chew."

American Dental Hygienists Association, Suite 3400, 444 N. Michigan Avenue, Chicago, IL 60611; (312) 440-8900. Request booklet, *An Ounce of Prevention*, that explains simple techniques to prevent periodontal disease, send self-addressed stamped envelope (#10) to above address.

The National Dental Association, 5506 Connecticut Ave. NW, suite 24, Washington, DC 20015; (202) 244-7555. The NDA provides brochures on basic dental care and can provide referral to a local chapter that will offer a list of dentists in your area.

Eyes

Better Vision Institute, 1800 N. Kent St., Suite 904, Rosslyn, VA 22209; (703) 243-1508. For information on prevention, detection, and treatment of eye diseases.

National Eye Institute, Information Office, 31 Center Drive, MSC 2510, Building 31, Room 6A32, Bethesda, MD 20892; (301) 496-5248. This agency distributes information on eye problems.

Prevent Blindness America, 500 E. Remington Rd., Schaumburg, IL 60173; (800) 331-2020 or (708) 843-2020. Provides free information on eye health and safety topics.

Hotlines

Center for Sight: (800) 221-3004. Provides information on a broad range of eye health and safety topics.

Ear Foundation: (800) 545-4327. Committed to the goal of better hearing and balance through education programs and support services. Provides literature, including newsletters.

Hearing Helpline: (800) 327-9355. Provides information on better hearing and preventing deafness. Materials are mailed upon request.

CHAPTER 3

GOOD INSIDES:
HEALTHY EATING, EXERCISE, AND AVOIDING SUBSTANCE ABUSE

Eating healthy foods; keeping fit; avoiding cigarettes, drugs, and too much drinking: if you do these things, you'll live for a long time and lower your risk of contracting heart disease, cancer, diabetes, and other diseases that our grandparents and great-grandparents have had to deal with. But even in the here and now, taking care of yourself is important. Listen up: if you treat your body right, you'll have more strength and energy, get sick less often, maintain a comfortable weight, have healthier skin and hair, and just feel better overall.

Healthy Eating

There are three easy rules to healthy eating basics: moderation, variety, and balance. Eating in moderation basically means eat what you like, but without eating too much of any one kind of food. By eating a variety of foods—primarily plant foods, such as vegetables, fruits, and grains—you'll be sure to get enough daily nutrients from each food group (see the food pyramid). And balance means eating foods that provide vitamins, minerals, carbohydrates, protein, and other nutrients as well as small amounts of fats and sugars.

Eating Right Every Day

Most nutrition experts tell us that we need to eat three well-balanced meals a day—that means three meals plus a few healthy, not too fatty snacks. The food pyramid is a good guide, but here are a few more tips to lifelong healthy eating:

THE FOOD PYRAMID

This food pyramid suggests the best way to balance your daily diet. Most of your diet should come from foods at the bottom of the pyramid.

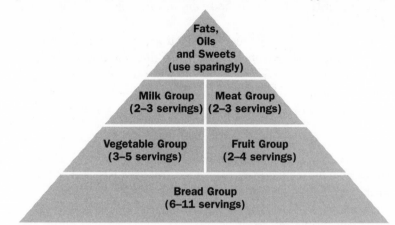

Food Group	Serving size
Fats, Oils and Sweets	Keep all cookies, cakes, sodas, fried foods or foods high in fat to a minimum.
Milk Group	1 serving = 1 cup of cheese, milk, yogurt, or other milk product. Nonfat or low-fat are best.
Meat Group	1 serving = 2 oz. cooked lean meat, poultry, or fish, 1 egg, 3/4 cup of beans or peas, or 2 tablespoons peanut butter.
Vegetable Group	1 serving = 1/2 cup cooked or 1 cup of juice. Dark green veggies such as spinach and broccoli are best.
Fruit Group	1 serving = 1 piece of fruit or 1 cup of juice. Deep yellow fruits are best (papayas, mangoes, apricots).
Bread Group	1 serving = 1 slice of bread, 1 oz. of cold cereal, or 3/4 cup of pasta.

- Eat foods that are low in fat, saturated fat, and cholesterol. The government advises that less than 30 percent of calories should come from fat, but ideally only 20 to 25 percent of what you eat each day should be fat. Remember that one gram of fat equals 9 calories.
- Eat plenty of vegetables, fruits, and grains. More than half of what we eat should be complex carbohydrates, including starchy foods. They help us maintain a healthy weight and make us feel full without all the fat.

- Don't overdo the sugar. Sugar is packed with calories, sweetness, and no nutrition. Filling up on soda and candy may give you a quick energy rush, but will soon leave you feeling hungry and tired. Keep in mind that the sugar your body doesn't use right away is stored as fat.
- Watch the salt. We only need a small amount of sodium to stay healthy. Since what we need is already in the foods we eat, there's no need to add more salt to food at meals or while cooking.
- Choose low-fat or nonfat dairy products and seasonings or spreads like ketchup and mustard, which have very little fat.

WHERE'S THE FAT?

- dairy products, including cheese, whole milk, and ice cream;
- most meats except for lean cuts;
- hamburgers;
- fried foods like French fries;
- and pizza (because of the cheese).

What's a Calorie?

Calories are the fuel that our bodies burn in order to sustain themselves, and are found in all foods. They're like the wood that keeps a fire burning. The body needs a certain number of them each day to sustain weight, very roughly desirable weight times twelve. In other words, if you weigh 120 pounds, you need approximately 1440 calories each day to stay at your 120 pounds. Add your activity level to this: if you exercise more or are very active, you'll need more calories.

Different foods contain different amounts of calories. Fatty, sugary foods contain more, fruits and vegetables contain less, and water has none, which explains why the following three foods all equal about 220 calories:

one slice of pepperoni pizza (high in fat)
one jelly donut (high in sugar)
7 carrots

Picking the Right Stuff

It's tempting to run into a convenience store and grab a bag of chips to stave off the hunger. But it's better to choose healthier alternatives, foods that will energize you rather than weigh you down. For example, instead of the chips, try a bag of low-salt pretzels or air-popped popcorn. Here are some tips for facing the snack food challenge.

READING THE FINE PRINT

Food packaging can be confusing, with all those percentages, grams, and ingredients nobody can pronounce. To take some of the mystery out of reading food labels, here is an example of a macaroni and cheese package:

NUTRITION GUIDE

Serving Size	½ cup (114g)	Calories 260 (Calories from fat 120)

Servings per Container 4

Per Serving	% Daily Value	Daily Value	
Fat (13g)	17%	Less than	75 g*
Saturated Fat (5g)	20%	Less than	25 g*
Cholesterol (30mg)	10%	Less than	300 mg
Sodium (660 mg)	28%	Less than	2,4000 mg

Per Serving	% Daily Value	Daily Value
Carbohydrate (31g)	10%	352 g
Complex Carbohydrate (26g)		
Sugar (5g)		
Dietary Fiber (0g)	0%	25 g
Protein (5g)		50 g

Vitamins & Minerals	% Daily Value		
Vitamin A 4%	Vitamin C 2%	Calcium 12%	Iron 4%

*For a 2350 calorie diet, Your daily value may be higher or lower, depending on your calorie intake.

SERVING SIZE — Start here to see what amount of food the information below refers to. Sometimes a product seems healthy until you realize the serving size is about half of what you planned on eating. The serving size here is ½ cup or 114 grams (the "g" stands for grams, and "mg" stands for milligrams).

% DAILY VALUE — This refers to the suggested percentage of nutrients you need every day, based on a 2,350-calorie diet. (Most young women require far fewer calories than this.) For example, this serving contains 12 percent of the daily recommended calcium. Keep in mind that even if an item seems high in one nutrient, it could still be high in fat and sodium.

FAT — Avoid foods high in fat, especially if they're high in saturated fat. These include palm and coconut oil and animal fat (like butter). If a label reads "low-fat," the food can't have more than 3 grams per serving. For any serving size under 50 grams (in this case the serving size is 114 grams) there must be less than 3 grams per serving.

SODIUM — If an item has more than 500 milligrams of sodium per serving, don't buy it. Some foods high in sodium don't taste salty but can still overload you on sodium.

*OTHER TIPS — If the ingredients on the label are really long and hard to pronounce, they're probably additives and preservatives, and you're better off without them.

MUNCHIES

Nothing's wrong with snacking, especially if you're constantly on the run or participating in sports—or both. But don't choose junk. Here are the best snack choices:

- fruits, like apricots, apples, cherries. grapefurits, mangoes, melons, nectarines, papayas, peaches, strawberries, tangerines
- veggies, like broccoli, carrots, cabbage, celery, peppers, radishes, spinach, sweet potatoes, tomatoes, zucchini
- no- or low-fat dairy products, like yogurt, milk, or cheese
- proteins, like nuts, tofu, and beans

FAST FOOD

Fast food doesn't have to be unhealthy. Use these tips to choose smart:

- Keep it simple. "Jumbos" and "doubles" of anything will weigh you down, trigger weight gain, and could lead to health problems in later years. Stick with the single-deckers and don't add extras like bacon and cheese. A plain burger with lettuce, tomato, and other vegetables on a whole-grain bun is a good bet.
- Better than a burger, substitute a chicken or fish sandwich. These choices are lower in fat and calories—unless the fish or chicken has been dipped in batter and fried. Instead, choose skinless white meat chicken and a fish filet that hasn't been fried.
- Take it easy on the sauces. Many fast food chains now have low-fat mayonnaise, which makes a good substitute for "special" sauces and cheese. Why not try a little bit of mustard, an extra tomato, and a pickle.
- Try to resist fries, because most are cooked in beef fat (saturated fat, which is the worst kind). Instead order a baked potato with butter on the side or at least get a small rather than large order.
- To cut fat and calories, choose vegetable instead of meat toppings for pizza. And don't order extra cheese.
- Order nonfat or low-fat frozen yogurt rather than a milk shake or ice cream. Although most frozen yogurt is loaded with sugar, it's still lower in fat than the alternatives. Topping yogurt with fresh fruit gives you added nutrition.

Compare the calories and fat grams of these to make better fast-food choices:

FAST FOOD CHOICES

Compare the food choices on the right with those on the left. The foods on the left offer better nutrition and a lot less fat and fewer calories. Removing the skin from chicken and eliminating olives from pizza would reduce fat and calories even more.

Kentucky Fried Chicken:

	Fat Grams	Calories		Fat Grams	Calories
Original recipe chicken breast (3 oz.)	14	260	Extra crispy chicken thigh (4 oz.)	31	414
Mashed potatoes and gravy (3 oz.)	2	71	French fries (2 oz.)	12	244
Corn on the cob (2 oz.)	2	90	Total	43	658
Total	18	421			

Domino's Pizza:

	Fat Grams	Calories		Fat Grams	Calories
12" Hand-tossed veggie pizza with mushrooms, green peppers, onions, and olives (2 slices)	10	360	12" Deep-dish pepperoni pizza	29	621

(Information provided by KFC Corporation and Domino's Pizza, Inc.)

SALAD BARS

Going to a salad bar is a great alternative to fast food. But choose wisely or you'll still be loading up on calories and fat.

- Pick leafy greens and lettuces. The darker the better, like spinach and romaine, because they have more vitamins than other lettuces.
- Eat as many fresh vegetables as you'd like. Asparagus, broccoli, carrots, cauliflower, celery, cucumbers, green beans, mushrooms, onions, peas, peppers, radishes, red cabbage, tomatoes, zucchini are all great choices.
- Put low-fat or noncreamy dressings on the side. Rather than drenching salads in dressing, use them as needed.

"I know eating right is good for me, and I also know it's going to help me from getting diabetes like my grandfather."

LIZETTE, 15, RIO GRANDE CITY, TEXAS

I usually eat what my mom buys and brings in the house. It used to be chips, chocolate chip cookies and soda between meals. For breakfast I'd make tacos with *huevos* [eggs] and *papas* [potatoes]. For lunch I'd eat at the cafeteria, but mostly at the snack bar, which was hamburgers and chili fries and a soda. Dinner was usually something like hamburgers or fried chicken and ice cream for dessert.

When my grandfather died of diabetes, my mom decided to join a local wellness program that gave information to women about how to eat healthier. I noticed that she started to change the foods she bought. Instead of whole milk it's 1 percent, our chips are baked tostitos, and we don't buy soda, cookies, or ice cream any more. Instead we have fruit and yogurt for snacks now.

After her classes my mom would come home with recipes, and she'd try them out to see what we liked. While she was cooking I'd watch her and learn the new way to cook. Before when I used to make dinner for myself I'd cook chicken-fried steak with batter-covered meat and fries. Now I usually have vegetables with baked chicken or boiled without the skin or lean cuts of beef. And we make rice without the oil. For snacks we usually eat fruit or no snacks. At school I just eat at the cafeteria, because they have healthy foods like vegetables and enchiladas cooked without a lot of fat. We use bread or corn tortillas instead of flour tortillas, which are higher in fat, and we drink water or juice; I barely drink sodas any more. And for dessert we now have nonfat frozen yogurt instead of ice cream.

Shopping's different too. Before we used to put anything we wanted in the basket. Now we watch what we put in. We're looking at the calories and the foods have to have less fat. We also look for the amount of salt and preservatives.

At first I didn't like all the changes. It was hard. But now I know eating right is good for me, and I also know it's going to keep me from getting diabetes like my grandfather. I've been doing this for over a year, and I think the changes will be permanent. I think this is better than dieting because I eat the same, but have fewer fats. And I still get to eat the kinds of foods that I like. I've lost weight, about fifteen pounds. It feels great. Before I wouldn't go walking, but now I will. Eating right made me want to exercise because it made me feel good about myself.

Losing Weight/Gaining Weight

Is your weight causing you health problems? Are you uncomfortable in your body? Do you feel too large, do you get out of breath easily and have to struggle up a flight of steps? Or are you so thin that you feel weak and tired? (For more on body weight and image, see Chapter 1.)

If you need to put on weight or take it off, here's what you need to know.

To gain:
- Don't skip meals. Make sure you're getting at least three full meals a day, including a good breakfast. Also pay attention to your hunger and don't put off eating.
- Eat healthy snacks between meals. Just because you need to gain weight, doesn't mean you should load up on junk food. Just eat more meals and snacks and larger portions—of healthy choices, such as carbohydrates—rice, beans, peas, pasta, grains, and potatoes.
- Exercise at least three times a week. Exercise will help build muscles, which add weight and bulk, but not fat. Weight training, either on machines or with hand weights, is your best bet.

To lose:
- Don't diet or use diet pills. New research shows that diets don't work because your body knows how many calories you need to maintain weight and will readjust to a new, slower rate of burning calories. Once you go off the diet, your body will burn calories at the slower rate and you'll end up *gaining* weight—even though you're eating the same as before the diet!
- A better choice, cut the fat out of your meals. That means less meat, butter, ice cream, cheese, fried foods, processed and fast foods. Substitute fruits, vegetables, fish, and lean meat.
- Even if you still eat the same amount of food, you can lose weight by exercising. Most days of the week, you'll need to do twenty to thirty minutes of an activity that gets your heart pumping: soccer, basketball, tennis, jogging, brisk walking, in-line skating, or swimming, to name a few options.
- Keep track of what and when you eat. For three or four days, write down what and when you eat. You'll start to see patterns that can help you, like eating more in the morning, eating out of nervousness (such as before a test), or eating lots of chips and soda. Modify your habits by eating a good breakfast in the morning if that's when you're hungriest, munching on carrots, apples, or a plain bagel before a big exam, and carrying healthy snacks like dried fruit, unbuttered popcorn, and juice to satisfy afternoon hunger.

- Eat three meals a day. Skipping breakfast or lunch to save on calories is the same as dieting. Starving for several hours will only make you hungrier and more likely to eat junk uncontrollably.

- Don't stuff yourself. Be in tune with your body and aware of when enough is enough.

- Eat what you like. Don't try to eat food you hate just to lose weight. The goal is to eat what you like, but to prepare it in the most healthy way. If all you like are hamburgers and fries, it's time to start experimenting with new foods. If you have a sweet tooth, indulge in an occasional treat once a week so you don't feel deprived.

THINKING ABOUT VEGGING OUT?

More and more people have stopped eating meat, some for health reasons—meat is usually high in fat, and can contain the hormones and antibiotics that are fed to animals—others for ethical reasons, such as the belief that animals should not be used for food. Studies show that vegetarians are less likely to suffer from serious illnesses such as heart disease, and cutting meat out of the diet can aid weight loss.

There are several different types of vegetarians, so if you're considering vegetarianism, you can start gradually and stop anywhere along the way.

Semi-vegetarian: eats chicken, turkey, and fish, but no red meat.
Lacto-ovo-vegetarian: no meat of any kind, but eats eggs and dairy products.
Lacto-vegetarian: no meat, no eggs, but still eats dairy products.
Ovo-vegetarian: no meat, no dairy products, but eats eggs.
Vegan (pronounced vee-gan): strict vegetarians who eat only fruit, vegetables, grains, and legumes, but no meat, no eggs, no dairy products.

Exercise

There is one activity that can extend your life, relieve stress, fight headache and back pain, help control weight, increase circulation, strengthen muscles and bones, keep you out of the doctor's office, and make you feel energized. Plus, you only have to do that one thing twenty to thirty minutes, five to six times a week, and it's free and fun. It's called exercise—walking, running, skating, swimming, biking, playing sports—and everyone should be doing it in order to stay healthy and feel great.

What Is Fitness?

Fitness is a mixture of strength, flexibility, and stamina.

- Strength means being able to lift heavy things, whether they're weights, bags of groceries, or your own body as you run up a steep hill. Muscles get stronger when they contract against resistance—pushing a barbell, doing pushups, or running up flights of stairs.
- Flexibility describes the ability to bend, stoop, and stretch without straining joints and muscles. You can increase flexibility with stretching and yoga exercises.
- Stamina, or endurance, is the ability to work longer and faster without stopping. This is the most important part of fitness, because it is aerobic activity that keeps our hearts and lungs strong and healthy. Activities like walking, running, in-line skating, playing tennis or basketball, or dancing at a brisk pace for twenty to thirty minutes all increase endurance.

The National Federation Handbook lists the top high school girls sports:
- basketball;
- track and field;
- volleyball;
- softball.

WHY EXERCISE?

Here's what the experts have to say about fitness:

- **A Melpomene Institute study found physical activity improves self-confidence, assertiveness, emotional stability, independence, and self-control.**
- **This same study revealed that girls with good physical skills felt competent and confident to try new things.**
- **In a Women's Sports Foundation study, Hispanic female athletes were more likely to score well on achievement tests, stay in high school, and attend college.**
- **Kids are more attentive to homework and other activities with strength training than without it, reports *Med Sci Exercise Journal*.**
- **Girls who are active in sports grow up with more confidence, self-esteem, and pride in their physical and social selves, says a Miller Lite report.**

- A Snyder & Kilven study found that female athletes have a more positive body image than nonathletes.
- According to the Study of Stanford and the Schools, girls who participate in sports tend to have higher grades.
- Two hours a week of exercise can lower a girl's risk of ever getting breast cancer, reports *USA Today*.
- Exercise reduces stress, anxiety, and depression, reports *Sports Medicine*.

"When I was younger and wasn't into sports I was critical of myself and always wondering what's wrong with me. But now I've found something I am good at and that makes me feel good about myself."

SONJA, 16, SCOTTSDALE, ARIZONA

We moved to Scottsdale when I was in seventh grade, and I started playing basketball. Being on the team made it easier to meet people being at a new school, because I'd hang out with the other players after school. That really helped me since I'm not very outgoing outside of sports. I get to show my true colors when I'm on the court, like being aggressive, loud. I'm usually mild-mannered at school, just there to learn, but then when I play basketball I'm there to play and let all my emotions out.

Team sports are great. You get to trust one another and work for a common goal, kind of like a family with your teammates helping you, cheering you on. When you make a basket it's for the whole team's benefit and everybody's happy.

Being on a team has also helped me in self-discipline, like setting goals and reaching them, setting my own pace, knowing my limitations. I know I can't hang out with the wrong crowd or get caught up in drugs and smoking because it would reflect badly on me and affect my playing ability. And playing is an incentive to do well in school: you have to have good grades to play on the team or to get college scholarships.

Outside of school, sports has helped me become a better person because I feel good about myself, and I'm not afraid of doing my own thing. It's made me very self-confident. When I was younger and wasn't into sports I was critical of myself and always wondering what's wrong with me. But now I've found something I am good at and that makes me feel good about myself. Like at the mall if I'm by myself and everyone is hanging out with their friends, it doesn't bother me. I don't feel inferior or like I'm missing out because there's a time to be with my friends and a time to be alone.

As far as my health, I'm not hurt a lot or sick often because I'm always active. I have a healthy appetite but I don't gain weight. I know that when I get older I'll always be active and not have to worry about getting obese. And I plan on going into engineering and I think having played on a team will help me in my career. Going to practice every day and going through the drills has taught me that when I put my mind to something I can meet my goals.

Abusing Our Bodies

Why?

It's hard to say why some people treat their bodies like shrines and others like garbage cans. The experts offer some reasons why some young people drink too much, smoke and use drugs:

- Stress: family problems, changing schools, pressure to do well in school.
- Boredom: wanting to have fun, but with few outlets.
- Depression: feeling isolated or alone, hopeless about the future and wanting to escape.
- Curiosity: not everyone who takes drugs is a heavy user, and many quit after the first try. But studies show that experimenting with pot and alcohol can lead to harder drugs. For example, the Center on Addiction and Substance Abuse reports that if a person has smoked marijuana more than one hundred times, the likelihood of using cocaine goes up 70 percent.
- Fitting in: being popular is a key desire for most of us. Unfortunately some take risks against their own judgment in order to hang with the cool clique.
- Learned behavior: some young people who watch their parents dealing with their problems by taking drugs may follow their example during difficult times.
- Lack of self-esteem: people who don't feel good about themselves are more likely to do things that are harmful. Most drug users and drinkers will admit they do it to fill up an empty feeling inside or to try to appear cool.
- Feeling unsure about sexuality: young people dealing with same-sex attractions may be drawn to drinking and drugs in order to ease fear and confusion.

Substance abuse—drinking and drugging—can destroy your life and your future. And according to a recent study, substance abuse is on the rise among young people. Though many are tempted to experiment, it's hard to know beforehand who will and who won't get hooked. Someone who abuses alcohol or drugs can't control their use. They need more and more drinks and drugs to achieve a high. The use of the substance leads to problems such as difficulties in school, loss of job, trouble with family, friends, and teachers. Of course no one starts taking drugs thinking she will get addicted, but when it happens, it's a long road back.

"I was always really quiet and shy and didn't have a lot of friends. That was one of the main reasons I started drinking; I was lonely."

TAMMA, 18, SALT LAKE CITY, UTAH

Since I was young, we moved around a lot. I always felt out of place, like I didn't fit in anywhere. I had a desire to belong somewhere and to feel like there was something I was good at. I was always really quiet and shy and didn't have a lot of friends. That was one of the main reasons I started drinking; I was lonely.

I made a decision when my family moved that when I started at the new school I didn't want to be lonely anymore. Drinking was an easy thing to fall into. It felt dangerous, fun, like I was living on the edge, and people accepted me. It was the cool thing to do. And it was a way to connect with people. They approached me and then I tried to be like them, by dressing like them and fitting in.

I first started drinking at thirteen. The first time I got drunk it was frightening and exciting and new, rebellious, sneaky. Then it got to the point where I was drinking more than I should have. I loved to drink and looked forward to the next time that I drank. I needed it because it was an escape for me.

When I was sixteen I started abusing prescription drugs and smoking pot. It went along with the drinking, first by taking diet pills that my friends and I would buy at the store. After a while we liked it so much we'd steal from our parents and from stores. My friends didn't pay attention to any sort of responsibility. We had fun together, but there was no real closeness or sharing. The objective was to get high. On the weekend there was no question that we'd get beer and go get drunk.

When I look back I see that I was getting progressively desensitized to the things I had thought were bad or wrong. I had a breakdown in my moral system. It crept up on me, and I found I was doing things I never thought I'd do, like stealing and being verbally abusive to my mother. I kept my grades up as justification that I was still a good kid and I was still OK. But the rest of me was lost and I was just searching for an answer I couldn't find anywhere.

It was really confusing and frightening. I felt horrible about myself. I didn't like myself at all. I started mutilating myself and always thinking about suicide. I looked around and wondered "What am I doing?"

Finally my whole family started to be afraid for my life, because I threatened suicide, ran away from home, and had scars all over from mutilating my body. So my mom put me in rehab.

Rehab was a big slap in the face. I had to take responsibility for everything that I had done and clean up the messes I had made. Before my relationship with my family had been really tense, but when we got down to real stuff, we realized times are hard and we could work through it. The hardest part for me was letting go of old cycles, like compromising myself in order to be accepted. I used to not show who I was, be really fake so people would like me.

Even though I've been in recovery for two years and I struggle every day, I'm doing better now than I ever have. I really like who I am, I like being alone with myself going on walks or reading. I've learned how to maintain my calm when a storm comes along by accepting myself and not trying to control everything. I also maintain honest relationships. I go to Alcoholics Anonymous and work as a peer counselor in the rehab center where I was. It's really rewarding. Overall I learned that there's a life lesson in everything, in taking care of myself and letting myself live. I am a survivor and can do whatever I want. I don't feel sorry for myself and I have the power to change my situation.

Does a Friend Have a Problem?

You may not have a problem with drugs or alcohol, but you may know someone who does. If you or a friend have been going through some changes lately and find it more difficult to cope without a drink, pill, smoke, or whatever drug, pay attention to these warning signs:

Your friend:
- Pours a drink/takes a drug as a reaction to a problem. Does she say, "I'm so depressed/sad/pissed off/stressed out, I need a joint?"
- Frequently drinks or takes drugs as a way of "celebrating."
- Drinks until she's totally bombed or gets completely stoned on drugs.
- Starts ditching school to go hang out and "party" or sleep in because of a bad hangover.
- Drives while drunk or high.
- Constantly fights with her parents about taking drugs or drinking.
- Lies about what she does with her time and money.

- Asks for money or steals to support her drug or drinking habit.
- Doesn't look good and acts strange. Has she lost a lot of weight, does she cough all the time or reek of alcohol? Does she act paranoid, get angry or violent, or secretive and aloof?
- Has she ever been arrested for driving while drunk or high?
- Withdraws from friends who don't use and starts hanging out with the "wrong" crowd.

If you think your friend has a problem, speak to her frankly and encourage her to get help. See the resource guide at the end of this chapter for more information.

Smoking

Cigarette smoking is so addictive that almost half of all teens who even try cigarettes go on to smoke every day, says the U.S. Surgeon General's Report. And according to the American Medical Association, 2,000 teenage girls start smoking *every day*.

The most common reasons we start are to:
- express independence and freedom from parents and authority;
- look sexually attractive;
- stay slim;
- hide strong emotions like anger, fear, or hurt;
- feel powerful;
- have a reliable "friend" (the cigarette) for comfort, pleasure, or escape;
- seem older and able to make our own decisions;
- take risks or challenge the rules.

We don't have to look too far to discover where the notion that cigarettes could help us become more sexually attractive, slimmer, independent, or anything else listed above comes from. Most teen and fashion rags have ads that try to burn these images into our brains.

Most smokers don't consider the serious, dangerous health consequences of cigarettes. Many make the mistake of thinking that smoking won't really hurt the body. But cigarettes are highly addictive, so once someone starts, it's very hard to quit. And smoking is a direct cause of lung cancer in nearly all cases (in fact 45,000 women each year die of lung cancer caused just by smoking!), as well as other health problems including heart disease and asthma. Plus, although some people think smoking is sexy, it's really very nasty. It makes your breath, fingers, and clothes stink, and your skin look gray.

If you want to quit smoking, the best thing to do is to get into a program that includes a support group. (See resource list at the end of this chapter for more information.)

· · · · · · · · · · · · · · · · **SMOKING AND RACE** · · · · · · · · · · · · · · · · ·

Did you know:

- According to Women and Girls Against Tobacco, smoking kills approximately 1,000 African Americans a week from smoking-related disease.
- A study that appeared in the *American Journal of Public Health* on smoking and Hispanic women who live in the U.S., found that the more assimilated into mainstream culture Hispanic women become, the more likely they are to start smoking.
- In a study by the California Department of Health Services, Japanese women (15 percent) and Korean women (14 percent) smoked more than their Filipino (9 percent) and Chinese (5 percent) sisters.
- Vietnamese women smoke one-third less than all U.S. women, says the Asian American Health Forum.
- The American Lung Association reports that at 39 percent, Native Americans have the highest smoking rates in the country.

· ·

· **WHAT ARE YOU GONNA DO ABOUT IT?**

WOMEN AND GIRLS AGAINST TOBACCO

What is Women and Girls Against Tobacco? A group of angry women who are spreading the word that smoking sucks.

The group organizes letter-writing campaigns against women's magazines that carry cigarette advertisements, as well as women's organizations, such as the League of Women Voters, that are sponsored by tobacco companies. The idea isn't to attack women's groups and publications, but to convince them to get money from sources outside of the tobacco industry.

Carliss Bodely, fourteen, belongs to the Jasira Warriors, a leadership advocacy program sponsored by Girls Inc. in Oakland, California, for girls twelve to nineteen years old. She is spearheading events and activities at her school. "I'm responsible for getting people together, recruiting at the schools, writing letters, and deciding what speakers to invite," says Carliss. Recently the Warriors began a letter-writing campaign to appeal to Bay Area city council members to attend an awareness conference for community support against tobacco. The group also works within the Oakland community and members have educated over one hundred merchants who sell cigarettes to minors.

Carliss says she got interested in the program when other Warriors came to her school. "I don't smoke, but I wanted to learn what's in them and how they're made so I can help more girls my age stay off them with positive messages and information." She thinks of one person in particular, "My cousin smokes, and I always tell her that she's just helping tobacco companies stay in business. Besides, being a Warrior is a better alternative to hanging out after school and smoking."

For more information contact Women and Girls Against Tobacco, 2001 Addison St., Suite 200, Berkeley, CA 94704-1103; (510) 841-6434.

Alcohol

According to a study by the U.S. Department of Health and Human Services called *Monitoring the Future*, seven out of eight high school students have had a drink by senior year. In fact, even though it's generally illegal to sell alcohol to anyone under twenty-one, it's widely available, which means it gets abused more than any other substance, especially by young people.

As with smoking, advertisers try to make drinking look glamorous, exciting, and sexy. In addition, there are many alcohol manufacturers that market their products to communities of color using rap lyrics or celebrities that appeal mainly to young people. They use words like "power" or "force" in slogans and brand names, words that send messages linking drinking and aggression with self-esteem.

In truth, those who drink the most have the lowest self-esteem and least hope for the future. The *Monitoring the Future* study notes that students who don't have plans to go to college are more likely to binge drink (five or more drinks in a row at once) than those who are college-bound. Contrary to the ads, drinking in excess doesn't make people feel better about themselves; it only compounds problems.

ALCOHOL BY NUMBERS

- A survey by the U.S. Department of Health and Human Services indicates that most binge drinkers drink when they're upset, bored, alone, or wanting to escape.
- Among high school seniors, binge drinking is highest among whites (32 percent), followed by Latinos (31 percent), and blacks (11 percent) in the *Monitoring the Future* study.
- According to an Alcoholics Anonymous survey, over 30,000 members are under twenty-one.

HOW TO TALK A FRIEND OUT OF DRIVING DRUNK

Don't drive drunk and don't let a friend get behind the wheel while intoxicated. If you're going to a party where you know there'll be drinking, plan ahead:

1. Know who you're going with. If you know who's driving it's easier to get an idea of what the night will be like.
2. Know how you're getting there.
3. Know how you're getting home. This is especially true if you're going on a date. If this is a first time date, make plans to call a friend during the evening to "check in." And have a Plan B to get home with taxi money, a parent, or friend to call to pick you up, or a friend at the party if things get out of hand.

Whether or not you are driving with a friend, it's *never* a good idea to just walk away from a drunk driver. As a sober person you have a responsibility to try to keep that driver off the road. This is no small task, but it's better than the alternative. According to Mothers Against Drunk Driving, more than 17,000 people die each year due to intoxicated drivers, and about 1,700 of these are teens. There are a few strategies that Students Against Driving Drunk advise:

- Talk to your friend with respect and caring. Confrontation, judgment, and yelling won't work. Which works better on you, when someone screams at you, or when someone appeals to you as a friend?

- Don't say:
  "Michelle, you're too drunk to drive. Give me the keys." This will only make her defensive and want to prove that she can "handle it."

- Do say:
  "What a wild party, huh Michelle?" Get her involved and interested. Then express concern.

  "You know, it would be a shame if something were to happen to you. I mean, I'd really feel bad." She will probably tell you she's fine and nothing will happen to her.

  "Well, I've only had soda all night, so I'm cool to drive. It might be easier if you gave me the keys." You can also offer other options like calling a taxi or spending the night somewhere.

- Get the best person for the job. If you don't think you're being heard, get someone else involved or a group of people. They may be able to physically block her from getting into her car—whoever or whatever it takes.

• Don't give up. Few things are more frustrating than trying to reason with a drunk person. But try to fight the urge to walk away with a "Fine, I don't care what happens to you" attitude. You're saving lives, and with your distractions, buying time at least until she begins to sober up. Coffee and blasting the tunes don't work.

• Keep your goal in mind. Not just the life of the drunk driver could be saved, but also the lives of other sober drivers who might come in fatal contact with her. When you succeed, you can pat yourself on the back for having kept someone's mom or little sister alive.

For more information on preventing drunk driving or to start a chapter at your middle school, high school, or college, contact Students Against Driving Drunk, Box 800, Marlboro, MA 01752; (508) 481-3568.

Drug Use

• Studies by Partnership for a Drug-Free America show that African American teens have the lowest rate of drug use in the nation.
• Almost 7 percent of high school seniors used LSD and 25 percent smoked marijuana, reports *Monitoring the Future*. The organization also found that use of inhalants was highest among eighth graders.
• Females have lower rates of drinking and drug use than males.

Truth and Consequences: What Drugs Do to the Body

This chart will give you some idea of how popular drugs can make you feel in the long and short run. However, it doesn't list cravings, withdrawal symptoms, or adverse side effects that come from using street drugs. Nor does it mention how little it takes of some drugs to become addicted. If you're thinking of experimenting, read this carefully. Drugs affect everyone differently, depending on tolerance, state of mind, and expectations. Just because your friends say they're having a good time, doesn't guarantee you will.

Drug	Short-term Effects	Long-term Effects
Alcohol	Slowed motor responses, dizziness, nausea, aggressive behavior, depression, feeling silly or giddy, feeling uninhibited	Memory loss, stomach ulcers, hallucinations, permanent loss of brain cells, heart disease, failed liver, decreased immune system, sterility, cancer

Drug	Short-term Effects	Long-term Effects
Marijuana	Hallucinations, feeling giddy or silly, hunger, paranoia, nervousness	Permanent memory loss, lung cancer, sterility in women, apathy, mood swings, depression
Cocaine	Stimulation, euphoria, depression, weight loss	Depression, paranoia, severe mood swings, collapsed nasal passages, seizures, heart failure
Crack	Stimulation, euphoria, depression, weight loss, aggressive behavior	Depression, paranoia, loss of appetite, hallucinations, heart failure, lung disease
Heroin	Euphoria, sense of peacefulness, nausea, vomiting, drowsiness	Skin abscesses, weight loss, loss of appetite, failing immune system, convulsions, coma, high risk of getting AIDS and hepatitis
PCP	Bizarre behavior, disorientation, body numbness, depression, temporary psychosis, impaired sense of space and time	Memory and concentration loss, loss of sensory perception and judgment, coma, speech difficulties, loss of motor skills, catatonic syndrome (user becomes mute, disoriented, and makes repetitive motions)
Inhalants (glue, paint)	Dizziness, heart palpitations, difficulty breathing, headache, abdominal pain, hallucinations, nausea, involuntary passing of urine and feces	Severe mood swings, numb hands and feet, loss of sense of smell, brain and nervous system damage, sudden death
MDMA ("ecstasy")	Stimulation, sense of peacefulness, loss of appetite, jaw clenching and teeth grinding, headaches, nausea, depression, chills, heart palpitations (greater for females)	Personality changes, sleep disturbance, extreme anxiety, panic, depression, seizures, severe attacks for sufferers of asthma, permanent brain damage, Parkinson muscle tremors
LSD ("acid")	Distortion of time and spatial distance, difficulty thinking clearly, mood swings, impaired judgment, confusion, panic, hallucinations, temporary psychosis	Continued hallucinations, chronic anxiety, panic, or depression, distorted sense of touch, distance, and hearing
Mushrooms, Peyote, and Mescaline	Distortion of time and spatial distance, hallucinations, stimulation, extreme anxiety, depression, confusion, distorted sense of what's real or fantasy	Internal infections, tetanus, hepatitis, prolonged psychotic episodes, mental illness

Drug	Short-term Effects	Long-term Effects
Methampheta- mines ("speed," "ice")	Stimulation, euphoria, impaired judgment, impulsive behavior, nervousness	Mood swings, restlessness, sleeplessness, paranoia, tempo- rary psychosis, brain damage, heart failure, convulsions

STEPS TOWARD RECOVERY

If you think you may have a drug problem, take these three key steps:

1. Admit that you have a problem and make a commitment to do something.

2. Tell someone who can help, either a support group or referral service for information and treatment.

3. Tell your family and friends that you know you have a problem. They can be an important support network for you, which is essential when you're trying to kick an addiction.

Where to Turn

Recommended Reading

The New Teenage Body Book, Kathy McCoy, Ph.D., and Charles Wibbelsman, M.D., Perigee Books, 1992. This book has chapters discussing healthful eating, exercise, and drug abuse.

Teenage Health Care, Gail Slap, M.D., and Martha Jablow, Pocket Books, 1994. A comprehensive medical guide for teens and their parents, including chapters on exercise, nutrition, and alcohol, tobacco and drug use.

For eating and exercise

Eat Smart: A Guide to Good Health For Kids, Dale Figtree, New Win Publishing, Inc., 1992.

Fat to Fit Without Dieting, Jeanne Rhodes, Contemporary Books, 1990.

The Healthy Woman, Alice Feinstein, Rodale Press, 1994.

How to Be a Reasonably Thin Teenage Girl, Bonnie Lukes, Atheneum, 1986.

Living Without Dieting, John Foreyt and Ken Goodrick, Warner Books, 1994.

Stop the Insanity, Susan Powter, Simon & Schuster, 1993. By the fitness guru who lost many, many pounds.

A Teen's Guide to Going Vegetarian, Judy Krizmanic, Puffin Books, 1994.

For substance abuse

Alcoholism: The Facts, Donald Goodwin, Oxford University Press, 1994.

Drinking, Driving and Drugs, Jean M. Knox, Chelsea House Publishing, 1991. Examines in depth the ways in which alcohol and other drugs impair the coordination and judgment essential to safe driving.

No Ifs, Ands or Butts: A Smoker's Guide to Quitting, Harlan Krumholz and Robert Phillips, Avery Publishing Group Inc., 1993.

What You Can Believe About Drugs, Susan Cohen and Daniel Cohen, Dell Publishing, 1993.

Support Groups and Organizations

For exercise

Aerobics and Fitness Association of America, 15250 Ventura Blvd., Suite 200, Sherman Oaks, CA 91403; (800) 233-4886. AFAA answers questions regarding safe and effective exercise programs and practices.

Arthur Ashe Athletic Association, 355 Lexington Ave., 16th Fl., New York, NY 10017; (212) 953-3100. Founded by Arthur Ashe in 1990, AAAA is a support and resource organization for Black athletes.

The Black Women in Sport Foundation, P.O. Box 2610, Philadelphia, PA 19130; (215) 763-6609. This nonprofit group encourages and promotes the involvement of black women in sports and now offers mentoring programs in golf and tennis in cities throughout the country.

Melpomene Institute for Women's Health Research, 1010 University Ave., St. Paul, MN 55104; (612) 642-1951. Helps women and girls link physical activity and self-esteem through seminars, publications, and videos. They have information packets on body image, eating disorders, exercise and menstrual function, as well as exercise and pregnancy.

President's Council on Physical Fitness and Sports, 701 Pennsylvania Ave. NW, Suite 250, Washington, DC 20004; (202) 272-3430. The Council offers a variety of testing, recognition, and incentive programs for individuals, institutions, and organizations. Materials on exercise and physical fitness available for all ages.

Teen Connections, sponsored by Girls Inc., P.O. Box 2813, Rapid City, SD 57709; (605) 341-5010. In the "Body by Me" programs, teens participate in a physical fitness, education, and nutrition program at least twice a week. The teens work with a professional to decide how they can improve their health.

Women's Sports Foundation, Eisenhower Park, East Meadow, NY 11554; (516) 542-4700 or (800) 227-3988. Provides informational packets on eating disorders, physical fitness, pregnancy and exercise, drugs and the female athlete.

YWCA, 726 Broadway, New York, NY 10003; (800) YWCA-US1. Call the national office or check the Yellow Pages for the YWCA in your area.

Nutrition

American Dietetic Association, 216 W. Jackson Blvd., Suite 800, Chicago, IL 60606–6995; (800) 366-1655 or (312) 899-0040. Call toll-free number to speak to a dietitian about healthy eating or to request nutrition brochures. They will also answer questions about going vegetarian.

Center for Science in the Public Interest, 1875 Connecticut Ave., NW, Suite 300, Washington, DC 20009; (202) 332-9110 or (800) 237-4874. Write for publications and posters that discuss nutritional issues.

Indian Health Service, Communications Office, Parklawn Building, Room 6-35, 5600 Fishers Lane, Rockville, MD 20857; (301) 443-3593. Focuses on Native American health issues, including nutrition.

Office of Minority Health Resource Center, P.O. Box 37337, Washington, DC 20013-7337; (800) 444-6472. OMH maintains information, resources and publications on health-specific topics that target African American, Asian American, Hispanic/Latino, Native American and Pacific Islander people. Indicate that you are interested in nutrition and exercise.

U.S. Food and Drug Administration, Office of Consumer Affairs, 5600 Fishers Lane, Room 16-85, Rockville, MD 20857; (301) 443-5006. Provides publications specifically for teens on topics ranging from nutrition and eating disorders to acne and cosmetics.

Vegetarian Resource Group, P.O. Box 1463, Baltimore, MD 21203; (410) 366-VEGE. For a free brochure on nutrition for teenagers, send a self-addressed stamped envelope.

Substance Abuse

Alcoholics Anonymous World Services, 475 Riverside Dr., New York, NY 10115; (212) 870-3400. AA is a fellowship of women and men who share their experiences, strength, and hope to solve their common problem and help each other recover from addiction. No fees or dues for membership.

American Cancer Society, 19 West 56th Street, New York, NY 10019; (800) ACS-2345. Check your local chapter or toll-free number for information about "Fresh Start," a program to help smokers quit. ACS also provides a brochure called "Smart Move: A Stop Smoking Guide."

The American Council for Drug Education, 136 E. 64 St., New York, NY 10021; (212) 758-8060. Call to receive a catalogue on books, posters and videos.

American Lung Association, 1740 Broadway, New York, NY 10019; (800) LUNG-USA or (212) 315-8700. Two self-help manuals to ask for: *Freedom from Smoking in 20 Days* and *A Lifetime of Freedom from Smoking.*

Black Alcohol/Drug Service Information Center (BASIC), 1501 Locust St., Suite 1100, St. Louis, MO 63103; (314) 621-9009. BASIC offers a variety of (outpatient) services to help combat alcohol and drug problems in the black community.

Caritas House, Administrative Offices, 166 Pawtucket Avenue, Pawtucket, RI 02860; (401) 722-4644. Caritas House offers a substance abuse program for teen girls.

Cocaine Anonymous World Service Office, P.O. Box 2000, Los Angeles, CA 90049; (800) 347-8998. Cocaine Anonymous is a fellowship of men and women who meet across the country to kick drug habits and help others. There are no dues or fees for CA membership.

Girls Incorporated, 30 East 33rd Street, New York, NY 10016; (212) 689-3700. Girls Inc. offers a program called "Friendly PEERsuasion" that teaches teens to educate each other about avoiding the hazards of alcohol, tobacco, and other drugs. It is the only substance abuse prevention program that specifically targets girls.

Institute on Black Chemical Abuse/African-American Family Services, 2616 Nicollet Ave. S., Minneapolis, MN 55408; (612) 871-7878. Provides books, articles, and videos on prevention and treatment of alcoholism and drug abuse.

"Just Say No" International, 2101 Webster St., Suite 1300, Oakland, CA 94612; (800) 258-2766. "Just Say No" International has a Youth Power Program that empowers young people to discover and make use of their inherent strengths to help themselves and their peers succeed and avoid substance abuse.

Narcotics Anonymous, P.O. Box 9999, Van Nuys, CA 91409; (818) 780-3951. A nonprofit fellowship of men and women who are recovering from drugs; no fees for membership.

National Black Alcoholism Council, 1629 K Street NW, Suite 802, Washington, DC 20006; (202) 296-2696. A national resource center.

National Clearinghouse for Alcohol and Drug Information, P.O. Box 2345, Rockville, MD 20847-2345; (301) 468-2600 or (800) 729-6686. Request pamphlets on various drugs or get a referral to organizations.

National Coalition of Hispanic Health and Human Services Organizations, 1501 16th St. NW, Washington, DC 20036; (202) 387-5000. The Coalition currently offers an inhalants substance abuse program in which tenth grade students speak to fifth grade students about the hazards of inhaling glue, markers, and other such substances.

National Council on Alcoholism and Drug Dependence, 12 W. 21st St., New York, NY 10010; (212) 206-6770 or (800) NCA-CALL. Toll-free number offers local referrals and general information about alcoholism and other drug dependency.

National Families in Action, 2296 Henderson Mill Road, Suite 300, Atlanta, GA 30345; (404) 934-6364. A substance abuse information center.

National Family Partnership, 11159 B South Towne Square, St. Louis, MO 63123; (314) 845-1933. NFP offers a youth drug-prevention training program, called Code Red, for junior and senior high school students as well as videos, pamplets, and other drug prevention information.

Nicotine Anonymous World Services Office, P.O. Box 5177, San Francisco, CA 94159; (415) 750-0328. A self-help group founded in the twelve-step tradition, centered around nicotine addiction. Literature is available.

SADD (Students Against Driving Drunk), P.O. Box 800, Marlboro, MA 01752; (508) 481-3568. The only student-based, activist organization dealing with underage drinking, drug abuse, and death due to drinking and driving.

Women and Girls Against Tobacco, 2001 Addison Street, Suite 200, Berkeley, CA 94704-1103; (510) 841-6434. A project dedicated to raising consciousness about the tobacco industry's targeting of women and young girls. Call for fact sheet, poster and other information.

Women for Sobriety, P.O. Box 618, Quakertown, PA 18951; (800) 333-1606. The first and only self-help program for women with addictions. It has self-help groups all across the country that meet weekly.

Women's Alcohol and Drug Education Project, Women's Action Alliance, 370 Lexington Avenue, Suite 603, New York, NY 10017; (212) 532-8330. Provides drug and alcohol prevention education.

Hotlines

For exercise and diet

American Dietetic Association Nutrition Hotline: (800) 366-1655.

YMCA: (800) 872-9622. Provides information about YMCA services and locations of Ys in residential areas.

For alcohol and substance abuse

Al-Anon/Alateen: (800) 344-2666.

Alcohol/Drug Abuse Referral Hotline: (800) ALC-OHOL (24 hours).

Alcohol and Drug Helpline: (800) 821-4357.

American Council on Alcoholism: (800) 527-5344 (24 hours).

National Cocaine Hotline: (800) COCAINE (24 hours).

Youth Crisis Hotline: (800) HIT-HOME (448-4663).

CHAPTER 4

WHAT YOU SHOULD KNOW ABOUT HEALTH CARE

Who is the number one expert on your body? A brain surgeon, gynecologist, or research scientist? None of the above! *You* are your own expert when it comes to the body you live in twenty-four hours a day, seven days a week. Although doctors and researchers can offer invaluable information about how the body works and the care it needs, individuals know their own bodies best.

In your expert capacity, it's very important to pay attention to the signals your body sends. For example, partying too hard and staying up too late generally leads to exhaustion. That's the body's way of saying "take it easy." The body may also send more subtle messages, so it's important that you listen closely to your intuition—your inner feelings—so that you can be aware of when something is wrong.

Staying on top of health means taking care of yourself by eating right, getting enough sleep, and avoiding the "bad stuff" (like cigarettes and drugs). It also requires you to get a checkup if something feels wrong and get gynecological care if you're sexually active. The following is some practical advice on getting the care you need.

Getting Care

Deciding what kind of care you need can be tough. First you have to consider how you're feeling, and then decide whether you need help. Your next decision will be who to see for care. Most young women have several options: school-based or school-linked clinics, private doctors, clinic or emergency room. You and your family will make the decision based on your own needs as well as on how much money your family has to spend. But here we'd like to say a more detailed word about the school-based clinic option. If you have access to one, it can be a free source of sensitive, quality care.

For example, check out these stats: according to a fact sheet published by Advocates for Youth, school-based and school-linked health centers are important to students because:

- Students in New York City who used them missed fewer days of school than those who didn't.
- Students in North Carolina who used them were more likely to stay in school and graduate than those who didn't.
- Among students in Oregon, there was less binge drinking and sexual activity in districts with school-based clinics.

What Are School-based or School-linked Clinics?

These clinics are designed specifically for teens and are based either in or near schools. Services are free, and providers deal with several types of primary medical care, like general exams and physicals, treating injuries and chronic illnesses (such as asthma), as well as reproductive and gynecological care. Providers can diagnose and treat health problems, which may include writing prescriptions. School clinics also have mental health services, which provide individual, family, and crisis counseling, and may have a social services department to help teens understand what social entitlement programs are available.

Unlike school-based clinics, school-linked clinics aren't limited by school or parental restrictions, and the staff has more freedom in the services they provide, for example dispensing birth control. But because they aren't on campus, school-linked clinics can be more of a hassle to get to.

According to Linda Juszczak, nurse practitioner at the Far Rockaway High School Clinic in Queens, New York, most girls who come in seek gynecological care for procedures like pregnancy testing and routine pelvic exams. Though there's an equal number of girls and guys coming into the clinic, girls are more likely to use the mental health services to help them deal with depression, family problems, and issues surrounding violence. "Most kids who come in to the clinic either don't have health insurance or don't have enough and therefore won't get routine medical care otherwise," says Juszczak. Because the services are right on campus and free to students, Far Rockaway's clinic has 1,000 out of 1,700 students registered.

"I can go to the clinic to talk to my counselor, Dee. We'll sit there and have discussions on my friends, problems I have, and any trouble in school."

ANGELINA, 16, QUEENS, NEW YORK

I started going to the clinic in school in my junior high. Now I go to the one in my high school. It's located right inside of the building, in its own little section. We even have doctors who come into the school. They all have their own offices and their own equipment. They have medicine they can give you then and there, for girls who don't have Medicaid or medical coverage from their parents.

I go in for gynecological exams, pregnancy tests, and when I'm sick, like with an ear infection or sore throat. I have other friends who use the clinic, and sometimes we just go there to talk.

The clinic is better than going to a home doctor because it's cheaper, and because sometimes the home doctor has to tell your parents things. But at the school clinic it's confidential. It doesn't really matter for me because everything that happens there, my mother knows about. But a lot of other girls like it because of that.

We also have counseling, like social workers, for the girls who have kids. There are also these groups where all girls get together and talk about their problems. Some go to talk about their boyfriend problems or their family problems or they just tell how, you know, some girls hurt inside, and they want to run away or something like that.

I go there to talk to my counselor, Dee. We'll sit there and have discussions on my friends, problems I have, and any trouble in school. And I talk about times when I just don't get along with my teachers. Dee calms me down and helps me express myself.

When to Say Good-bye to the "Baby Doctor"

Regardless of where you get your care, once you reach the late teens, you'll need to start thinking about whether or not you've outgrown the pediatrician. Though they specialize in children's health, pediatricians can provide care up to the late teens. By then, however, you'll probably be more than ready to move beyond the waiting room Dr. Seuss books and screaming kiddies. At the very least, you should begin seeing a gynecologist at eighteen or when you become sexually active, whichever comes first.

You may need to go earlier than this, because even if you're only thinking about having sex, you'll need to speak to a doctor about contraception and alternatives to sexual intercourse *before* you have your first sexual experience. Some young women see pediatricians as distant relatives and are too embarrassed to talk about growing sexual feelings that may begin before the teen years.

Some pediatricians will refer their patients to gynecologists at an appropriate age, but you or your parents will probably have to take the steps to switch. If you're tight with your mom or another female relative, she may be able to help find a new doctor. Otherwise, call the agencies listed in the resource guide at the end of this chapter for referrals.

When It Matters If They're Black or White . . . or Brown, or a Woman

Most of us feel comfortable with what's familiar. That may explain why many women feel more comfortable when examined by a female doctor or nurse rather than by a male. Studies show that women are more likely to discuss emotional issues with female health care professionals than with males. Another study notes that female doctors spend more time with their patients compared to male doctors. Because communication is key to getting good health care, many women actively seek women doctors.

Women may also prefer a female practitioner because they believe that she understands their problems better because she's been through the same things. Getting monthly periods and giving birth are truly women-only issues. Plus some women are too intimidated to expose themselves to a male doctor, especially if they've suffered sexual abuse by a man.

The question of race and ethnicity is equally important. Just as some people feel better understood by a woman doctor, they may also feel more at home with someone from their own community. Research shows that black people believe that white doctors treat them differently than they treat white patients, and feel that white doctors don't ask enough questions or give good explanations about their condition, diagnosis, and treatment.

Whether it's fact or perception that people of different races get different treatment doesn't matter. If you don't trust your doctor, you won't have a good relationship with her or him, and this can lead to more frequent and worse medical problems.

Keep in mind, though, that just because a doctor is a woman and is the same race, doesn't guarantee that she'll be a good listener or more understanding. If gender and race are important issues, pay attention to your feelings and choose a doctor that suits you. Above all else, pick a provider you can talk to, who you trust and who listens to you.

What to Expect From a Medical Provider

A lot of teens are used to being led by the hand to the doctor's office. There's also the expectation that either parents or the health care provider will explain what's wrong and why it occurred, and discuss what to do about it and how to keep it from happening again. But as many women have painfully discovered, that doesn't always happen. That's why you must demand more than a bunch of commands and an occasional prescription from medical professionals. And that assertiveness should start with your very first "adult" visit to the doctor.

Dr. Alvin Goldfarb, executive director of the North American Society for Pediatric and Adolescent Gynecology, sees young women every day who have had bad experiences. So he devised a set of rules that neatly spell out what to expect from any doctor or health care provider:

- Respect: to be treated with dignity, concern, and politeness and never to be made to feel bad, stupid, or guilty about your body and health.
- Empowerment: to feel in control of your body and know that you are ultimately responsible for your well-being.
- Joint decision-making: to be able to work with the provider with the understanding that you are the expert on your own body. You want the provider to be a partner so that together you can make decisions about your health.
- Education: each appointment should be treated as an opportunity to learn—from the provider—about your body and how to maintain good health.
- Confidentiality: what is discussed in the office stays between the two of you, unless it is a life-threatening situation.
- Trust: to be able to talk freely about what is affecting you and share what you need physically and emotionally.

If you aren't getting any one of these, you have the right to reject your health care provider. Keep in mind that you may have to demand these things from your doctor, rather than sit back and hope to get what you need.

But you also have to do your part when preparing for an appointment. Here are the two most important things to do that will show any provider that you are serious about your health care:

1. Know your history. Your personal and family medical history is really helpful for doctors and professionals, because illnesses as well as good health tend to run in the genes. If you can find out the specifics on the health of your grandmothers on both sides, it'll tell your medical provider a lot.

2. Have tons of questions. Write down even the eensiest symptoms or sensations that you've had, whether they're related to a current illness or not. Then ask the practitioner everything you want to know about your body and health.

Once the doctor knows about you and your family medical history, she'll have you undress and put on one of those mod hospital gowns (paper if you're really lucky) and begin the exam. There are two kinds that she will probably give, the physical exam and the pelvic exam.

PHYSICAL EXAM

Checking in with the doctor once every twelve to eighteen months is a good idea if you're in good health. But if you have any problems or questions, it's important to call or schedule an appointment just in case. For a routine physical, the doctor will go through the basics:

- Height and weight: to make sure you're growing at a healthy rate.
- Blood pressure: the Velcro armband and pump can tell the health care provider about your blood pressure—if it's too high or too low.
- Heart rate: with a stethoscope placed on your chest and back, the provider will check for any abnormal heartbeats or problems with your lungs.
- Eyes, ears, nose, and throat: the provider will flash a beam of light in all the openings in your head, to check for anything unusual, such as an infection.
- Abdomen: your provider will use her or his hands to press your midsection to see if there are any problems with your organs.
- Walking: it's not about poise, this is a check for any problems with balance or gait.
- Arteries in neck, groin, knees, and feet: to be sure the blood is circulating properly and to look for any swollen lymph glands.
- Breast exam: to be sure there are no abnormal lumps or discharge from the nipple.
- Anything that hurts: when your provider asks if anything hurts or feels weird, tell her exactly where and how it feels.
- Urine sample: this is the pee-in-a-cup test that's sent off to a lab to check for infections that show up in urine.
- Blood sample: the doctor or nurse will draw a couple of tubes of blood and send them to a lab to be tested for the blood cells, cholesterol levels, and blood sugar, as well as diseases like leukemia or illnesses of the liver and kidney.

PELVIC EXAM

This exam focuses on a woman's reproductive organs. Once you become sexually active (or when you turn eighteen), you'll need one regularly. Many clinics, private doctors, and women's health centers perform these exams, and you need one before getting birth control.

For a pelvic exam, the provider will have you slide to the edge of the examining table and lie back with your feet up in two u-shaped foot rests

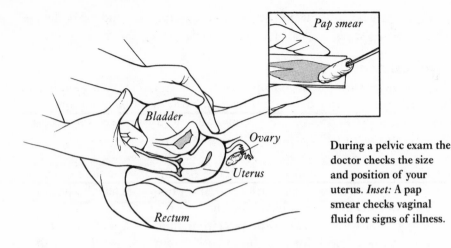

Pap smear

Bladder

Ovary

Uterus

Rectum

During a pelvic exam the doctor checks the size and position of your uterus. *Inset:* A pap smear checks vaginal fluid for signs of illness.

called stirrups. This position allows for maximum visibility of your genital area and allows the provider to easily feel around your pelvic region.

There are three parts to the exam:

1. The genital exam: an examination of your external genitals, like your vulva and urethra, to see if there's any swelling, cysts, genital warts, or unusual skin changes.

2. The vaginal exam: the provider will insert a long metal or plastic instrument that looks sort of like a curling iron, called a speculum (SPEC-you-lum), into your vagina. While it's inside, she or he will open it up and look for any inflammation or problems in the vagina, on the cervix, or with your discharge. With the speculum still open she or he will use a long cotton swab, spatula, or brush and wipe it gently on your cervix and cervical opening. The discharge will be put on a glass slide that will be sent to the lab to test for abnormalities.

She or he will then do a manual exam by putting two fingers inside your vagina to the cervix and one hand on top of your lower abdomen to feel around your uterus. This will be a check of the size and position of your uterus and to see if there are any cysts.

3. The rectal exam: probably the least fun part of a gynecological exam, the provider puts her or his finger in your rectum to get another angle on the backside of your uterus. This is also a check for hemorrhoids or any other abnormalities. Even though this exam doesn't hurt, it may feel weird. Just remember that it's over quickly.

Once the exam is done the practitioner will probably have a talk about what she or he has found, though you may be getting the information all along, too. This is the time to fire away any questions you might have. Ask for a pen and paper to write down what she's saying so you can remember.

* *

If you're sexually active or intend to be soon, getting a vaccination for hepatitis B is essential. The shots are given at three separate times, but are the best protection against this highly contagious disease. Like HIV, hep B is spread through oral, vaginal, and anal contact (even kissing), or through unclean needles. Up to 200,000 Americans each year get hep B, a liver disease that can be fatal or affect some people for life. For more info call the National Foundation for Infectious Diseases' Hepatitis B Hotline at (800) HEP-B-873.

* *

What's Up, Doc? Top Ten Questions to Ask Your Doctor

1. Can we have some time alone in your office?
By the time you reach about eleven years old or get your first period, health care providers should encourage you to have a private session away from Mom to discuss anything your heart desires. Take advantage of this time to ask some of those questions you may be too embarrassed to discuss with your parents.

2. If I tell you something, will you keep it between us?
Unless it's an emergency, doctors should work to build your trust by keeping what you tell them strictly confidential. In most states you have a legal right for your provider not to reveal any information regarding sexually transmitted infections and drug and alcohol use or treatment to anyone, including the 'rents.

3. Can you give me birth control without my parents saying it's OK?
By law you can get contraception without Mom and Dad granting permission, but not always from a private doctor. If you can't get it from your provider, you can ask for a referral to a family planning clinic that will, and should, keep the matter private. However, your provider may encourage you to discuss it with your parents, which you should consider.

4. Could you explain what you just said in plain English (or Spanish or French or Chinese or Swahili)?
Just because doctors have had to memorize all those fancy bacterial names doesn't make them smarter than you. All doctors should be able to translate medicine into understandable terms for you. If for any reason

something isn't clear, ask. You are responsible for your body. The doctor is only there to help.

5. What are you doing?

Don't be a wimp when it comes to getting the physician to tell you every single thing she or he is doing (or about to do) to your body and why. You should understand every part of the exam—from the time you walk in until you leave.

6. What am I taking this medication for?

It doesn't pay to be shy when it comes to prescriptions. Putting anything in your body without knowing why isn't safe. And "because the doctor said so" isn't a good enough reason either. If a practitioner writes any prescription for you, you should know the following:

- What it is.
- Why she or he's giving it to you.
- What it's for.
- How and for how long you should take it.
- What the side effects and risks of taking it are.
- Whether there are any alternatives.

7. You told me something the last time I was in here, but I read a magazine article that said just the opposite. Who's right?

It's important to stay informed about health without relying solely on your provider. Likewise, as the saying goes, you can't always believe what you read. When you get conflicting information, ask for clarification.

8. Is it serious?

If a doctor thinks you may have a problem that's more serious than she or he can treat, or if you need another doctor's opinion, you may be sent to a specialist. Or you or your parents may feel that you want another opinion about treating a severe condition. In either case, get some referrals either from your current doctor or from organizations such as the American Medical Association in Chicago.

9. Can I call you?

Most doctors can be reached by phone either during office hours or after hours. Find out what days yours is available or if you can speak to another provider (such as another doc, a nurse or a physician assistant). For emergency calls, almost all doctors have pagers or can be reached immediately. If your physician is unavailable, she or he should have a replacement doctor who can help.

10. When should I come back?

Depending on your health, your provider will recommend a time to set up your next appointment. If you're in tip-top shape, it'll probably be in a year. For illnesses or chronic conditions, you may have to check in every few weeks or months. But don't wait until she or he makes the next date. Take the initiative to set up the appointment yourself and keep it.

"I've learned that as long as I stay calm about the asthma, everyone else keeps calm, too."

NATASHA, 17, MOUNT VERNON, NEW YORK

Asthma is when your lungs become swollen and tight and fill with mucus, making it difficult to breathe. I was diagnosed with it when I was about two years old. I wasn't actually aware that I had asthma until I was about five. I woke up in the middle of the night and couldn't breathe, so my mother took me to the hospital.

When my parents got divorced, my condition got worse. I don't think a month went by that she didn't have to come to school and get me because of asthma problems. It made me feel different from the others when they put chairs together for me to lie on to wait for my mother.

I take medication to control my asthma, but only as needed, like when I'm getting a cold, because that can turn into asthma. Or when I'm doing strenuous activities, like running around, increasing my heart rate. Then I feel my lungs tightening up, and I need to take something.

Asthma doesn't interfere with my daily life, unless I get into some horse-play with my friends or something like that. But when it does, it's serious. Most asthmatics know what triggers their attacks. Like I know that spring and fall are my worst seasons, because those are allergy seasons. I have to be sure to keep my neck and chest and back covered and warm, otherwise, for some reason, I can get an asthma attack so easily. This happens mostly during colder weather or during changes in weather.

Lately, my attacks have been less frequent, like two or three months apart. They used to be almost every month. The doctors say it's probably going away. But they've been saying that since I was little, so I don't really know.

My advice to people with asthma: don't let it get in the way of things you do, and don't use it as an excuse to hold you back. Many teachers, once they know you have asthma, want to count you out of everything, even things you know you can do. They're so afraid of dealing with it that they panic. Once, a teacher almost called an ambulance for me, when all I needed was some cool, fresh air. So you should try to keep a cool head. I've learned that as long as I stay calm about the asthma, everyone else keeps calm, too.

TAKING CARE OF THE TWINS: HOW TO DO A BREAST SELF-EXAM

If you're like many people, you may know someone who has or had breast cancer. All experts agree that finding a breast lump early can save your life.

If anyone in your family has ever had breast cancer, you should learn how to do a self-exam ASAP. By age twenty everyone should be doing breast exams once a month. According to the American Cancer Society, most breast lumps are detected by women themselves, and most are *not* cancer. If you feel uncomfortable touching yourself, think of it as a health procedure, like checking your mouth for cavities. Here's how:

- Check your breasts just after your period (because the breasts may be more lumpy right before or during your period), or if you have irregular periods, once a month on the same day.
- Lie down with a pillow under your right shoulder and put your right arm behind your head.
- Using the tips of your first three fingers (not your thumb) of your left hand, press firmly on your breasts in one of three ways:

  In a circle around the whole breast.
  Up and down the whole breast.
  From the nipple out in straight lines.

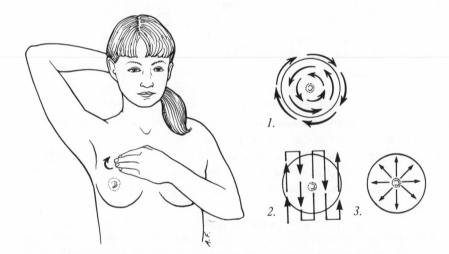

Now's the time to learn how to examine your breasts. You can check them by moving your fingers in a circle (1), up and down (2), or from the nipple out (3).

- Use whichever way you like, as long as you check your whole breast and your underarm.
- Switch the pillow to the other side and do the same on your left breast. You can also do an exam in the shower standing up.
- If you find any changes in how your breasts feel (any lumps) or the way they look (dimpling in the skin, changes in your nipples, redness, or swelling), *call your health care provider.*

The more exams you do, the better you'll know your breasts. Considering that the American Cancer Society says that 92 percent of women who contract cancer while it's still in the breast survive, regular exams could save your life.

WORKING IN MEDICINE

Have you ever considered a career in health care, such as becoming a physician, psychiatrist, nurse, midwife, or physician assistant? Maybe you should think about it. Many of those in the field report that it's rewarding and a good way to make a living. Because of the major advances in technology and medicine, training in medicine has become more involved and sometimes very expensive (one year of med school costs between $8,200 and $22,300). While many jobs in health care are dominated by women (such as nursing), the majority of doctors are men. Still, that's changing; in fact, by the year 2010, one in three doctors will be a woman.

About physicians, the American Medical Association reports:

- Most women doctors are in pediatrics, family practice, psychiatry, gynecology, internal medicine, or pathology. Women are still underrepresented in surgery, research, and medical teaching.
- Seventy-five percent of female physicians are married, and 85 percent of those women have children.
- Women gynecologists earned an average of $183,000 in 1993, compared to $211,000 for men.

"I'm interested in health care, because I want to make a difference."

GENEVIEVE, 17, BLADENSBURG, MARYLAND

I was born in the Philippines, and from very young, I knew that I wanted to be in the medical profession. My mom is a nurse, and her mom was a nurse during World War II, so I would be the third generation of nurses in my family.

In my school there are two courses offered in the health care field: medical assistant for juniors and seniors, and nursing assistant for seniors. In addition we have a health class and physical education. Other than that, the rest of my day is regular high school. Some of my other classes are art, journalism, and advanced placement English.

At the end of this year I'll be getting my certification for nursing assistant and will work in a hospital while I'm in college. I hope to go to the University of Maryland in College Park for prenursing, and then proceed to the University of Maryland in Baltimore County, which has one of the best nursing programs in the country. During the two years in prenursing you take classes like biology, chemistry, anatomy, physiology, and so on, as preparation for the two-year nursing program. I think you get internships with hospitals in your last two years.

Nursing is more demanding than many other academic careers, and it means really sticking to the books. A visiting graduate from our nursing assistant program who is now at Howard University told us that out of the fifty-two students in her class, only twelve are passing. She spends most of her time studying. But if it means something to you, then you sacrifice. Like anything else, if you want the best, you've got to work for it.

I'm interested in nursing, because I want to make a difference. I would like to be a source of strength and support for others, to take care of people, to make their lives better. By lifting yourself up to another level, you become a better person. I want to be the best I can in whatever I do.

And there are financial benefits. Starting salaries in nursing are about $30,000 a year right now. My mom has been a nurse for eighteen years, so she makes twice that much. Nursing assistants are paid at least $8 an hour—but it's a lot better than flipping burgers for $4.25!

WHAT ARE YOU GONNA DO ABOUT IT?

TEENS FOR TEENS IN BIRMINGHAM, ALABAMA

"I never knew it could be this hard and this much fun," says Meredith Lilly, a fifteen-year-old intern of the Teens for Teens program in Birmingham, Alabama. For the past five summers she's either been a student or a teacher in the program, which educates young women aged thirteen to eighteen about fitness, eating right, peer pressure, crime, sexuality, drugs, self-esteem, date rape, violence, and teen pregnancy. The trick is always coming up with a fun way to get each lesson across. "Some days we exercise by walking around the gym track, and then one of the students brings a snack made from a healthy recipe book, like ant logs made with celery, peanut butter, and cinnamon," says Meredith.

Other tactics include making up skits for touchy situations in which the girls have to discover tactful ways to communicate. One skit was about how to tell a girl she has a "hygiene problem" without hurting her feelings. "Instead of just yelling out 'you stink' and picking on her, we had another girl pull her aside privately and say 'I'm not trying to hurt your feelings, but you have a hygiene problem,'" explains Meredith.

At the end of the summer, Teens for Teens throws a health fair and invites all the girls from the center and their parents. "We also put up posters and fliers in hospitals and clinics, and make phone calls to get experts to come in and talk about all kinds of stuff," Meredith says. A dentist brought in free toothbrushes and talked about dental hygiene, a doctor from a children's hospital discussed not being scared when going to the doctor, and a career specialist gave out information on different careers in the medical field.

LaQuita Bender, a fifteen-year-old leader in a neighboring center, had her group produce their own exercise music video. "Each of us added our own step to the routine and then we pieced it all together by the beats. It took us two weeks, and then we put on matching shorts, shirts, white socks, and tennis shoes and videotaped it," recalls LaQuita. "We showed it at the health fair, and at the end everyone applauded."

For more information about Teens for Teens contact Bernice Humphrey at (317) 634-7546. Similar programs are located in Rapid City, South Dakota, South Bronx, New York, and Seattle, Washington.

Where to Turn

Recommended Reading

All About Eve: The Complete Guide to Women's Health and Well-Being, Tracy Chuthorian Semler, HarperPerennial, 1995.

The Alternative Health & Medicine Encyclopedia: The Authoritative Guide to Holistic and Nontraditional Health Practices, James Marti, Visible Ink, 1995. This practical, easy-to-read guide gives you the latest facts and expert opinions on health issues including acupuncture, yoga, and botanical herbs, with a chapter devoted to health problems specific to women.

Before You Call the Doctor: Safe, Effective Self-Care for Over 300 Common Medical Problems, Anne Simons, M.D., Bobbie Hasselbrig, and Michael Castleman, Ballantine Books, 1992. A thorough, medically safe self-care guide that covers home care for hundreds of ailments including anemia, fatigue, and urinary tract infections, with a whole chapter on women's health including menstrual cramps, PMS, uterine fibroids, and yeast infections.

Body & Soul: The Black Women's Guide to Physical Health and Emotional Well-Being, Linda Villarosa (ed.), HarperPerennial, 1994.

Every Woman's Body: Everything You Need to Know to Make Informed Choices About Your Health, Diana Korte, Fawcett Columbine, 1994. This is an excellent resource for women to educate themselves about their health care. This book covers everything from menstruation, urinary tract infections, and uterine fibroids, to lupus, endometriosis, and AIDS.

Indian Herbalogy of North America, Alma R. Hutchens, Random House, 1991. A pioneering work that has served as a bible to herbalists throughout the world, it is an encyclopedic guide to more than two hundred medicinal plants found in North America, with descriptions of each plant's appearance and uses, and directions for methods of use and dosage.

Smart Questions to Ask Your Doctor, Dorothy Leeds with Jon M. Strauss, M.D., HarperCollins, 1992. This comprehensive guide will help you ask the right questions so you can participate in your own health decisions. Includes questions about choosing a doctor, tests and exams, diagnosis, treatment, and second opinions.

Understanding Your Body: Every Woman's Guide to Gynecology and Health, Felicia H. Stewart, M.D., Felicia Guest, Gary Stewart, M.D., and Robert Hatcher, M.D., Bantam Books, 1987. This comprehensive guide to women's gynecological health includes everyday health care, including how to do a breast self-exam, what's involved in a pelvic examination, what to expect from a doctor's office, tests and procedures.

The Teenage Body Book, Kathy McCoy and Charles Wibbelsman, Simon & Schuster, 1984. Includes a chapter devoted to special medical needs such as urinary tract infections, anemia, asthma, diabetes, and epilepsy. Also has a chapter about how to get the medical help you need, including how to choose a doctor, communicating with your doctor (with a list of questions a doctor is likely to ask you), as well as a detailed explanation of what a doctor does during a physical exam. The end of the book contains an excellent list of Adolescent Clinics throughout the U.S.

Support Groups and Organizations
Health Organizations
Hispanic Health Council, 195 Main Street, #3A, Hartford, CT 06106;

(203) 527-0856. Offers health programs, including one on substance abuse, and a clinic.

Indian Health Service (IHS), Room 6-35, Parklawn Building, 5600 Fishers Lane, Rockville, MD 20857; 301-443-3593. IHS provides a comprehensive health services delivery system directly and through tribally operated health programs to federally recognized American Indians and Alaskan natives. They have special initiatives in areas such as injury control, alcoholism, diabetes, and mental health.

National Asian Women's Health Organization, 440 Grand Avenue, Suite 208, Oakland, CA 94610; (510) 208-3171. Through its programs, research, education, advocacy, and policy, NAWHO strives to address the interconnections of mental, emotional, physical, sexual, social, and spiritual health that impact the overall well-being of Asian women and girls. They provide an Asian Women's Health Fact Sheet.

National Black Women's Health Project, 1237 Ralph David Abernathy Boulevard SW, Atlanta, GA 30310; (404) 758-9590 or (800) 275-2947. Provides information on black women's health issues. The yearly conference features special programs for teens.

National Women's Health Network, 514 10th Street NW, Suite 400, Washington, DC 20004; (202) 347-1140. Makes a large number of information packets available to the public, including "Young Women's Health Issues," which covers a wide range of topics such as self-esteem, contraception, substance abuse. For more information, write to above address and request their order form.

Native American Women's Health Education Resource Center, P.O. Box 572, Lake Andes, SD 57356; (605) 487-7072. Provides information on birth control, HIV, and other reproductive health issues.

Office of Minority Health Resource Center, P.O. Box 37337, Washington, DC 20013-7337; (800) 444-6472. OMH provides *Closing the Gap*, a newsletter that focuses on minority health issues. Topics include "Adolescent Health," "Diabetes," "Women's Health." Their staff can locate minority organizations or community programs, as well as provide the names of experts in your specific geographical area.

Organizacion Nacional de la Salud de la Mujer Latina/National Latina Health Organization, P.O. Box 7567, Oakland, CA 94601; (510) 534-1362. Formed to raise Latina consciousness about health and health problems, La Organizacion offers a series of bilingual classes and workshops on a wide range of health issues. The Health Advocacy desk acts as a resource and referral to Latinas for a vast array of health issues.

Smart Kids, P.O. Box 44, Kingsport, TN 37662; (615) 245-0135. Smart Kids offers "Teen Health," a holistic health promotion and disease prevention program for thirteen to seventeen year olds, offered weekly in the community's five public housing developments.

Society For Adolescent Medicine, 19401 E. 40 Highway, Independence, MO 64055; (816) 224-8010. Send a self-addressed stamped envelope for a list of adolescent clinics, physicians, and other health care professionals in your area. If you have a specific question the society may be able to answer it directly or refer you to someone who can.

Women's Health Action and Mobilization (WHAM), 515 Eighth Avenue, New York, NY 10018; (212) 560-7177. Activist women's health organization.

CHAPTER 5

SEX ED 101

Leaving childhood for adolescence and adolescence for adulthood is full of physical and emotional transformations, some that are welcomed and others that aren't. Most of the changes that take place relate to a heightened awareness of the body and feelings. At this time it may seem as if biology has taken over.

The best way to keep from feeling completely thrown off by the changes is to be informed about what's happening. Remaining clueless about your body only leads to added stress. Information will enable you to see your maturation as part of a life-long process. It's also the first step in taking responsibility for your own well-being, one big part of growing up.

The whole point of puberty is that the body is shifting gears into womanhood at high speed. But it doesn't happen at the same pace for everyone. That's why you may be developing curves way ahead or way behind your friends. The same goes for starting your period. You may begin monthly menstrual bleeding before you've officially entered the teens or after the teen years have ended. The best way to predict when your own changes will occur is to ask your mom about her puberty.

Naming All the Parts

Most of us are more comfortable talking in slang when referring to anything sexual, either the act of sex or the sexual organs. It may feel easier to call the genitals by a silly name given to us during toddlerhood or by a harsh one overheard in the school hallways. Most of us find words like "vagina" or "penis" too clinical and embarrassing, but without knowing your body parts and how they work, you can't expect to know how to take care of yourself. Imagine calling your mouth "the black hole" or "talkbox" and being too squeamish to discuss brushing your teeth. A lot more people would have

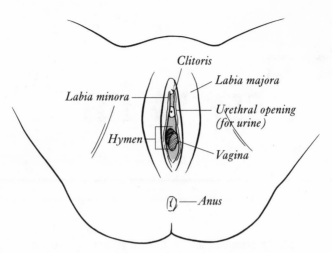

Don't be afraid to look. You need to be as familiar with your genitals as you are with other parts of your body.

cavities and bad breath. The genitals are no different and deserve just as much serious attention and information as any other body part.

The best way to get to know the parts of the body is by looking at them. You can study an illustration or, even better, you can check out your own body using a small mirror. This might feel a little strange at first, but relax, this is the best way you can learn about *you*.

The Outer Genitals

Start at the top of the genital region where your pubic hair begins (or will begin), just below your stomach area. Underneath your pubic hair is a round bone called the *mons*. If you've begun to develop, you may notice that your pubic hair extends below the mons and surrounds your genitals on both sides. These protective flaps, called *outer lips* (or *labia majora*), are soft, fleshy, and covered with pubic hair. Inside the outer lips is another set of lips called the *inner lips* (or *labia minora*). Every woman's vaginal lips have a unique shape. Your inner lips may be longer than your outer, they may have several folds, or they may be pale or dark in color.

Between your inner lips, where they come together closest to your mons area is a protective fold of skin, called the *clitoral hood*. If you pull this back, you will expose a small, round organ about the size of a pea. This is your *clitoris* (KLIT-oh-ris), the most important organ for women's sexual pleasure. In fact, unlike any other human organ, the sole purpose of a woman's clitoris is to provide sexual pleasure.

Just below your clitoris you will see a small opening, your *urethra* (you-

REE-thra), which is where urine passes. If you continue downward, below your urethra, you will see a larger opening, which is your *vagina*. Your vaginal opening may still be covered by your *hymen*, a stretch of skin. Some young women don't have a hymen, and others have already stretched it open during physical activity or tampon use. Contrary to myth, all virgins do not have unbroken hymens. Between your vagina and *anus* is a region called the *perineum* (per-IN-ee-um). The anus is actually the opening of your *rectum*, where bowel movements pass through the body.

The Reproductive Organs

The reproductive organs are hard to see without special instruments that doctors use. This illustration gives a good idea of what's where.

VAGINA: The vaginal opening connects our inside and outside organs. The canal is a moist, elastic passageway that measures three to five inches in length. It's amazingly stretchable: it can accommodate a tampon or allow a baby to come through. The vagina is also an incredibly clean organ. With the help of secretions, it flushes out dead cells much like our nose produces mucus. This fluid, which can be clear or whitish depending on the time of the month, is known as discharge. Though some vaginal discharge has a slight smell (some describe it as fishy or spicy), it should not have a strong odor, be green or yellow, cause itching or burning, or have clumps or blood (if it's not during

Fallopian tubes
Ovaries
Uterus
Vagina

The female reproductive system includes the uterus, which is no bigger than a fist but expands to fit a growing fetus.

your period). Any of these are symptoms of medical problems and should be discussed with a doctor.

CERVIX: At the upper-most end of the vagina is the cervix. If you feel with your finger, it's a rounded bump with a small dimple in the middle (called the *os*). The cervix is the lower part of the uterus, and the os is the hole through which sperm can enter. To protect the inside organs from bacteria, the os has a thin covering of mucus. Like the vagina, the cervix and the os greatly expand to accommodate a baby passing through.

UTERUS: On the other side of the cervix is the uterus. Like the other female reproductive organs, the uterus has dual functions. During the nine months of pregnancy it houses the fetus. Once a month during menstruation, it holds then sheds the endometrial lining if there is no fetus. The uterus is a muscular organ only about the size of a fist, but its elasticity allows it to grow large enough to hold a fully developed fetus then go back to normal size.

FALLOPIAN TUBES: The two arm-like appendages on both sides of the uterus are fallopian tubes. The tissue at the ends of the tubes help move the egg from one of the two ovaries into the tubes once a month during ovulation. If the egg is fertilized by sperm, it will go to the uterus and develop into a fetus. If not, it will disintegrate and leave the body during menstruation.

OVARIES: The ovaries are responsible for producing and housing unfertilized eggs. There are two ovaries, each supported by ligaments attached to the uterus. Both have thousands of follicles that release a mature egg into alternating fallopian tubes each month.

HIS BODY

The male reproductive equipment is made up of three parts:

TESTICLES: These produce the hormone testosterone, which is needed for creating sperm cells. The testicles are covered by the *scrotum*, the two-sectioned sac that hangs behind the penis.

SPERM DUCTS: During the journey from the testicles to the penis, sperm passes through various areas of the male reproductive system. Once the sperm are produced, they pass through the *epididymis*, which are coiled over each testicle, to the *vas deferens*, located in the lower abdomen. From there they make a loop around the bladder and are stored in the *ejaculatory duct*.

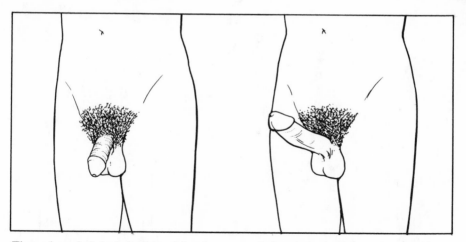

The male genitals include the testicles, the two sacs below the penis. The penis on the left is soft, but when sexually aroused it fills with blood and becomes hard or erect (like the penis on the right).

PENIS: The penis is made of spongy tissue, blood vessels, and nerves. Unlike women, who have separate openings for urinating and for reproducing, men's urethras are the only opening in the penis, through which both semen and urine pass. When a male is excited into orgasm, he ejaculates a white fluid called *semen* through his penis. The penis squirts out about a tablespoon of semen, which contains about 400 million sperm (they're microscopic, of course).

Going Through Changes

During puberty—the set of physical changes that take place during the teen years—your body will alter dramatically. It may not feel like a big deal from day to day, but your body at age twenty will look *very* different from the way it looked at ten. Everyone goes through the same set of changes but not necessarily at the same age. See page 92 for what you can expect—and (roughly) when.

Other Changes

At different times within the five stages of puberty you may notice other changes, such as:

- Perspiration. With the growth of underarm hair and flooding hormones, your body will begin to produce a new, "adult" smell under your arms. If the smell bothers you, deodorant may make it more tolerable.

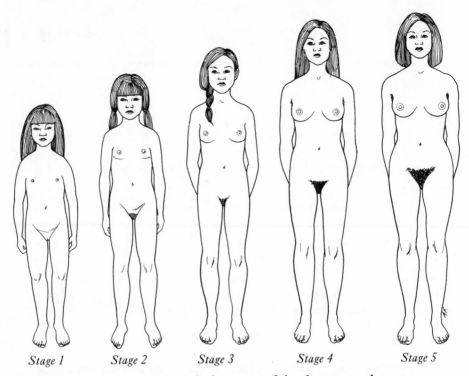

| Stage 1 | Stage 2 | Stage 3 | Stage 4 | Stage 5 |

Every young woman goes through the stages of development at her own pace.

STAGE ONE (ages 8 to 11) This is a quiet stage, as not much activity takes place outside the body. But inside the ovaries are maturing and your brain has stimulated the release of hormones.

STAGE TWO (ages 8 to 14) Breast buds are the most obvious marker for the beginning of this stage. You'll notice your once flat-as-a-pancake chest transform into noticeable nipples that might bring you (wanted or unwanted) attention. Sometimes the small breasts get tender and the area around the nipple, called the *areola* (ar-ee-OH-la), darkens. In a less visible spot, your first pubic hairs will begin to sprout.

At the same time you will probably get taller, and your hips, thighs and behind may begin to fill out. No need for alarm. You're supposed to increase in body weight and body fat at this time. Without a certain amount of increased body fat, you won't develop properly.

STAGE THREE (ages 9 to 15) Your breasts and pubic hair continue to grow, and you may also continue on your up-and-out growing jag. Your increased hormones cause your vagina to grow and to begin producing discharge. This discharge is a natural cleansing process and not a sign of being "dirty" or "gross."

STAGE FOUR (ages 10 to 16) Your body will begin to have a more mature look. For instance, your areolas will become full and lift a little from the breast, pubic hair feels coarse and grows in a triangular patch, and underarm hair makes its first appearance. The biggest change is happening internally. Your ovaries are growing and may even begin to produce eggs. Some girls get their first menstrual period during this stage.

STAGE FIVE (ages 12 to 19) You're at the end of puberty at this point. Your breasts are their full size, your pubic hair has filled in (sometimes growing on the inside upper thighs), and you've basically stopped growing. If you hadn't started your period, it will begin during this stage—a monthly fact of life for the next thirty or forty years or so, as your ovaries regularly produce eggs.

- Pimples. With the increase of certain hormones, you may start to get small eruptions on your face, chest, and back. If you're lucky this will only be a passing stage, but for some of us acne lasts throughout adulthood. (Read more about acne in Chapter 2.)

- Growth in height, hips, and bottom. Don't bug out about putting some pounds on. It's supposed to happen. To lessen the shock, stay active and eat right. (Find out how in Chapter 3.)

- Strong emotions. Don't underestimate the power of hormone surges. Although you have enough reasons for your feelings to be all over the place without them, hormones can greatly contribute to the intensity of feelings (ecstatic instead of just happy one minute, then totally depressed the next).

Do you slouch your shoulders to hide your height? Well even if you hate being so tall now, you'll love it later. Recent research at the University of Helsinki found that height works to women's advantage because they're perceived to have more authority. So, straighten up and take charge!

Getting Your Period

Every young woman has a different reaction to getting her first period. Some dread the day, while others are bursting with anticipation. And then there are those who fall somewhere in between, knowing it's inevitable and taking it as just another part of growing up.

Attitudes about menstruation are generally shaped by moms and other women. However, a lot of mothers and grandmothers grew up with the notion that to get your period was "a curse" and the whole process is "disgusting." Even the tampon ads have picked up on these attitudes, trying to make us believe that their products will keep us from feeling embarrassed about strong odors or overflowing sanitary pads. The truth is that menstruating is a natural, normal part of being a woman.

What Is Menstruation?

In a strictly biological sense, menstruating gives women a monthly opportunity to create offspring. Considering that the world record for the number of babies born to one woman is sixty-four (many of them multiple births), it's obviously impossible to get pregnant every month. None the less, our bodies go through a monthly cycle that lasts generally between twenty and thirty-five days—with the average being twenty-eight days.

Most young women are only aware of their menstrual cycles during the approximately five days when bleeding occurs. However the menstrual bleeding is only one part of the overall cycle. The first day of the cycle begins with the first day of menstrual bleeding, and the day before bleeding begins the following month signals the end.

Here's what's going on during the menstrual cycle:

DAY 1: The first day of menstrual bleeding marks the beginning of the cycle. Estrogen and progesterone hormone levels drop, which causes the lining of the uterus to shed. It may also make you feel tired or not have much energy. The lining (called the *endometrium*) is mixed with blood, vaginal secretions, and mucus, which together make up the menstrual blood. Though it may feel like you're gushing blood, the amount of blood that flows is really only four to six tablespoons. Some women experience cramping that lasts one or two days, because the uterus is contracting.

DAY 2–5: On average, the menstrual period lasts about five days, with the first two being the heaviest flow and the last three the lightest. But the amount of time may vary. Yours may last for as little as two days or as many as eight days.

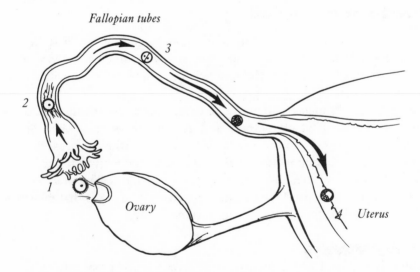

Fallopian tubes

Ovary

Uterus

Each month the ovary releases one egg, and the follicles of the fallopian tube sweep it up (1). Once in the tube, the egg has a six-day trip down the tube to the uterus. If it meets with sperm (2), it can become fertilized (3). If it is fertilized, the egg attaches itself to the lining of the uterus (4), where it will grow into a fetus. If not, it is absorbed by the body and the lining of the uterus sheds as the menstrual period.

DAY 6–14: Once your period is over, the body works overtime producing hormones. This is so that the pituitary gland (in the base of your brain) will release a follicle-stimulating hormone (FSH) to get your eggs to grow in the ovary. At the same time your uterine lining is getting ready to receive another egg. One follicle will get to produce eggs, and those evolving eggs begin to produce estrogen. All this rush in hormones may cause you to feel energetic and basically in a good mood.

DAY 15–16: This point is called the midcycle, and some pretty amazing stuff is going on. For instance, one egg (an *ovum*) is called from the ovary with the help of progesterone and estrogen to begin the trip through the fallopian tube. (Remember only one egg from one ovary is released each month.) This process is known as *ovulation* (ov-you-LAY-shun), and is the easiest time of the month to get pregnant if the egg is fertilized by sperm. An egg takes up to six days to reach the uterus, and during this time the egg is ripe for conception. Having sex days before or during this time without a contraceptive is incredibly risky, because sperm can live for several days in the vagina before they die. Not everyone's periods are regular, nor can everyone calculate the exact day of ovulation. So, basically—unless you're *extremely* in touch with your body and your cycle—no time of the month is safe without birth control.

During ovulation you may get a few cramps (sometimes on the side from which the egg was released), you may notice a little bit of blood in your underwear (spotting), and your discharge will be thinner. Right after ovulation, your temperature rises.

DAY 17–28: The egg bursts from the ovary, turns yellow, and continues down to the uterus. It pumps out more of the hormone progesterone, and you'll notice that your vaginal discharge is thicker. Because it's not fertilized, the egg will be absorbed into the body, and hormone levels will begin to decline. The endometrium starts to break down and the uterus fills with blood and tissue. While your body is preparing to begin another cycle, you may feel bloated, have tender breasts, or undergo emotional changes (depression, tension, arousal). Once you start your period, your uterus begins to contract, starting the flow of menstrual blood.

Preparing for the "Big Day"

Getting your period for the first time can be weird. Many women have distinct memories of *that day*, whether it was relief that the whole waiting ordeal was over with and it wasn't such a big deal after all, or it was a complete shock because it wasn't what was expected. For those who haven't started having periods, there is still anticipation of when, where, and how it will happen.

To give some hints about the when, Dr. Jean Emans, co-chief of Adolescent Medicine at Children's Hospital in Boston, Massachusetts, says to expect it about two to two and a half years after first breast development. Though not everyone fits this rule of thumb, chest-sprouting is just about the best indicator, aside from the actual bleeding, of course. Women who've had their periods for a while often develop mood swings, bloating, or cramping—premenstrual syndrome (PMS)—but young women in their teens don't usually begin the first menstrual cycle with PMS side effects.

The best way to prepare for your first period and to avoid possible embarrassment is to have a plan. To avoid surprises, think of it like a fire drill. Here's Dr. Emans' advice:

• Know what products you want to use.
• Practice how to use them.
• Keep them around the house, locker, pocketbook, backpack, jacket, sock, gym bag, or wherever you can get to them when you need them.
• Know where you can get to them in case you don't have any or run out, such as in a nurse's office, bathroom, good pal, or teacher.

Rehearsing and having a plan are two ways to get ready for the experience without freaking out. Getting someone to walk you through, Mom, sis, a buddy with experience, whoever is available, will also make it not as strange. Luckily many moms are hip enough to talk about their experiences in the open, so that's where we get info.

But even when you have someone to talk to, you still may feel embarrassed, self-conscious, upset, or afraid about making the transition into biological womanhood. Antronette K. Yancey, M.D., M.P.H., a preventive medicine specialist and adjunct assistant professor at UCLA, has some tips on ways to deal with the emotional upheaval:

• Talk to a friend. Whether it's with someone you trust who hasn't gotten her first period, or if you need to talk to someone older, maybe even an adult, get it off your chest. Sharing your feelings is one of the best ways of dealing with them.
• Write down your feelings. If you're completely worried that you'll be the first and only one of your friends to get your period, write about it. It's a great release and helps you get a perspective.

- Exercise. It not only keeps you in shape (which you may be concerned about now that your body is totally changing), exercise also is a proven mood-lifter and anxiety-buster.
- Read books or look at videos. Some good choices are *Period*, a book by JoAnne Gardner-Louland and others, and the video "On Becoming a Woman: Mothers and Daughters Talking Together," put out by the National Black Women's Health Project (call 800-ASK-BWHP). Take a look at the list at the end of this chapter for more suggestions.

"Starting my period was no problem, because I knew what was going to happen, what to do, and I could talk to someone about it."

STACY, 13, RAPID CITY, SOUTH DAKOTA

When I was twelve, my mom talked to me about how I was going to develop, like about my breasts, my pubic area, and my menstruation. She told me that my period could be heavy or light like blood on my underwear, and that there's nothing to be scared of, nothing wrong with me. I was really worried about starting my period, so I was glad that we talked.

My mom also explained to me that she wanted me to know what was going to happen, because her mom never told her about menstruating, so she was scared the first time. She told me that she never told her mom when her period began, and she hid her underwear under her bed. Her mom didn't find out until a week later, so she had to go to her big sister for help. She's Rosebud Sioux Indian, and I think it made her feel different from everybody else. She talked to her tribe counselor about her period, but the counselor didn't know a lot about it. So she had to go to her grandmother. I think it was very scary for her, so that's why I'm sure it's good for Native Americans to know about themselves and what's going to happen as they mature.

Two years ago two weeks into school in my eighth hour my period finally began. I kinda thought I wet my pants, so I asked to use the restroom. When I got to the bathroom and realized it was my period, I just laughed and thought "Oh my God, it finally came." I was kind of excited when it finally came, but kind of not. And I was scared that maybe it went through my jeans. I was embarrassed that somebody might have seen it. But it wasn't very heavy at all and just went onto my underwear.

I went to the nurse's office and got a pad. After school I went to the Girls' Club and told one of the staff members what happened and she understood me perfectly. She was happy that I knew something about it and wasn't feeling down. She got me a starter kit and explained everything in it.

Then I called my mom and told her. I wondered whether she wouldn't be ready for me to change, and I also wondered whether *I* wasn't ready to change into an adolescent from a child either. She got all hyper and said, "My little girl's a woman now." I was so embarrassed.

Now that I've had my period for over a year, I definitely feel different; I know I feel older. I thought my periods would be really painful but they're not. The only time it really bothers me is in the summer because I do a lot of swimming and I'm not using tampons yet. So I can't swim sometimes.

Starting my period was no problem, because I knew what was going to happen, what to do, and I could talk to someone about it. My advice to anyone else is to just let whatever happens happen and to talk to friends and family, because it makes a big difference.

So Many Choices

Just a couple of decades ago there wasn't the variety in "sanitary products" that there is today. Now the only problem is deciding which product and which brand to choose.

PADS: Although the old-fashioned kind that hooks onto an elastic waistband is still available, most napkins are pressed into panties and kept in place with an adhesive strip. It's best to experiment with products to discover what you like. The only rule is that a pad is changed every few hours to prevent infection or illness. (If you sleep with a pad, change it when you awaken.) Also, some women are allergic to scented products and can get irritated.

TAMPONS: Tampons are small white cylinders of synthetic or cotton material that are placed in the vagina. They are inserted with a plastic or cardboard (better for the environment) applicator or a finger, and are removed by pulling an attached string that stays outside the vagina. Though some young women aren't comfortable with the idea, tampons can be used from the very first menstrual period. They come in different sizes—junior, regular, medium, and super—depending on your flow and comfort.

TAMPONS: GETTING THEM IN AND OUT

It's important to read instructions on how to insert the tampon, though here are some tips to help:

- Know where your vagina is located. This may seem basic, but some women mistake their urethra or rectum for the vagina and experience pain in inserting.
- If you find it difficult to get the tampon in, apply a small amount of K-Y Jelly to the tip to slide it in.

Many girls start with sanitary napkins *(top)*, then progress to tampons *(bottom)*. Some use both; others alternate. Use which ever feels comfortable to you.

- You should not experience pain. Don't jab or cram the tampon in. Try to relax and get the hang of it. If it still hurts, try inserting the tampon a little higher, above the vaginal opening muscles, or try a smaller size. If the instructions say to put the tampon in at an angle, try inserting it the way their illustrations show.
- Try different positions. Some women insert tampons while sitting on the toilet, but others prefer standing up with one leg on the toilet seat.
- When taking out a tampon, be gentle. Sometimes the string can be hard to find, hiding in the labia folds or up in the vagina. Don't freak out. Tampons can easily be taken out with your fingers if you can't find the string.
- And, by the way, it's impossible for a tampon to get "lost" while inside you because it has nowhere to go except the vaginal canal (the opening to your uterus is too tiny). Nor can a tampon just fall out. They are designed to be held in place by the walls of your vagina and have to be removed to come out.
- A word of caution: Be sure to change your tampon every three to four hours and never use an absorbency that's more than you need (for example, using super on light days). By following these precautions you can avoid any risk of illness, including Toxic Shock Syndrome (TSS). Scientists believe that tampons left in too long breed bacteria, which can lead to TSS. Symptoms of TSS are sudden fever of 102 or more, vomiting, diarrhea, flu-like symptoms, fainting, dizziness, or a red rash especially on hands and feet. If you experience these symptoms, immediately remove the tampon and call a doctor. Though it's not common, TSS can be fatal.

"WOMEN'S PROBLEMS"

Premenstrual syndrome (PMS) A pattern of physical and emotional changes that some women notice generally a week before menstruation.

SYMPTOMS: Bloating, weight gain, water retention, breast tenderness, swelling in hands and feet, sleepiness, nausea, vomiting, diarrhea, constipation, acne, respiratory problems, or food cravings, depression, irritability, anxiety, stress, tension, mood swings, inability to concentrate.

TREATMENT: Most women don't suffer severely from PMS, but come to recognize some of their symptoms and to understand when they come up. For those who have intolerable PMS, some take birth control pills, progesterone, or vitamin B_6. There is no cure for PMS, but doctors recommend exercising at least three times a week, drinking eight glasses of water a day, and avoiding caffeine.

Amenorrhea (a–men–or–EE–a) Not getting a period, whether menstruation has begun or not.

SYMPTOMS: Never having had a period; missing one or several periods.

TREATMENT: A doctor will prescribe hormones if there is a hormonal problem, but most cases of amenorrhea don't need treatment. Those who have never had a period can probably expect one soon, but should see a health care professional to verify that there are no hormonal problems. Young women who have regular or irregular periods but have missed one or more could be exercising at a very high level (elite runners and swimmers often stop menstruating during heavy training), or undereating. Both stunt production of estrogen, the "female" hormone. Another reason for ceased periods is pregnancy. Any woman with amenorrhea who is not already pregnant is still at risk of getting pregnant. Also any woman in doubt about a pregnancy should get it confirmed as soon as possible.

Dysmenorrhea (dis–men–or–EE–a) Having a painful or difficult period.

SYMPTOMS: Pain or cramping in the lower abdomen, back, thighs, or hips during menstruation. Also nausea, vomiting, diarrhea, or body aches.

TREATMENT: Most women who have pain or cramps during periods can get relief from over-the-counter drugs like ibuprofen or aspirin. Exercise can also ease the problem. If periods become really out of control, it may be a sign of a larger problem, so talk to your medical provider.

Sexually transmitted infections (STIs) Also sometimes called venereal disease (VD), include infections like gonorrhea, chlamydia, syphilis, herpes, genital warts, HIV. (Read about HIV and AIDS in Chapter 6.) They are spread from one person to another through sexual intercourse and oral or anal contact, and are very common among teenagers and young adults.

SYMPTOMS: Sores, lumps, bumps, lice, or warts on genitals; genital or anal itching; discharge from vagina or anus; burning during urination; sore throat; swollen lymph glands or fever; pains in the groin or lower abdomen; skin rashes on soles of feet or palms of hands.

TREATMENT: The best treatment for STIs is prevention. This means abstaining from genital contact or using a condom (which is helpful but not a guarantee against STIs). Lots of women (and men) don't have any symptoms with STIs, so a screen for them should be part of a regular checkup. Without treatment, STIs can lead to greater problems, such as pelvic inflammatory disease and infertility. Anyone with an STI is obligated to tell all of her sexual partners so that they may receive treatment. A practitioner may prescribe antibiotics to kill the disease.

Yeast Infection This is a type of vaginitis which is fairly common; it is irritating but not serious.

SYMPTOMS: Itching, cottage cheese-type vaginal discharge.

TREATMENT: Yeast infections are often caused by pregnancy, diabetes, taking antibiotics or the pill, or an iron-deficiency. There are over-the-counter medications that cure the infection, but it's best to talk to a doctor about symptoms before taking them. Some women mistakenly believe they have yeast infections when it's actually something more serious.

Bladder or Urinary Tract Infection Sexual activity or improper wiping after a bowel movement are the most common causes of this infection, which is bacteria in the bladder.

SYMPTOMS: Frequent and immediate need to urinate; burning during urination; pressure in lower abdomen; blood or strong odor in urine.

TREATMENT: Bladder infections aren't dangerous, but if left untreated can lead to kidney complications. After taking a urine sample and bacterial culture, a doctor will prescribe antibiotics to kill the bacteria. Some women have found that drinking lots of cranberry juice is also helpful, though probably not as effective as medication. To prevent the infections from recurring, drink water and urinate before and after sex, and always wipe away from the vagina, from front to back, after a bowel movement.

Feminine Sprays and Douches

Because the vagina is a self-cleaning organ, it's usually unnecessary to do any extra deodorizing beyond regular washing with soap and water. In fact, most doctors advise against using genital sprays because they're unnecessary and can cause irritation. Many doctors also do not recommend regular douching because it can upset the delicate chemical balance of vaginal secretions and actually cause serious infections. Douching more than once a week is especially harmful. If you do douche once in a while, take the natural route and use a water and mild vinegar solution. If you notice any strong odors or abnormal discharge tell your mom or talk to a physician. A doctor may prescribe a special douching solution if it's required. Otherwise, don't get snowed by the ads that try to make you feel worried about having a peculiar smell "down there."

• •

In a study published by the *Journal of Pediatrics*:

- Eighty-nine percent of girls use pads for their first period, 7 percent use tampons, and 4 percent use both.
- The average age that young women first use tampons is fourteen.
- Most girls start using tampons because they're involved in sports, want the convenience, can't stand using pads, and are influenced by their friends. Most girls use pads because that's what their moms gave them.

• •

Ten Puberty Questions Too Embarrassing to Ask Mom

Moms and sisters can be great resources for most body weirdness questions. But some people may either be too shy or not on close enough terms with their family members to talk about the real nitty-gritty stuff that feeds into that nightmare world of "I'm the creepiest looking person alive." To help us out of our personal hells, Dr. Lauren Budow, an adolescent medical specialist at Coney Island Hospital in New York who's really down-to-earth, gives some comforting answers to our favorite worries.

1. **My underarms stink. Do everyone's pits smell this funky? What can I do to avoid taking out the whole school?**

First of all, understand where the odor comes from. As your hormones increase, you'll begin to sweat more under your arms. The hormones will also cause underarm hair (called *axillary hair*) to grow. When you sweat, bacteria combines with the moisture and gets trapped. This causes the odor. To avoid it, bathe and use deodorant daily. Some young women also like to shave or use a depilatory on their underarm hair, which isn't necessary because hair itself doesn't cause odor. If the idea of underarm shaving appeals to you, talk it over with Mom. Be careful about putting on deodorant right after shaving because your skin could be irritated and deodorant might sting.

2. **My period is really schizo. Sometimes I get it once a month, then it skips a month, and sometimes it doesn't come at all. What's up?**

Your body's just getting used to having periods. Usually for the first two years after your first period (called *menarche* [men-ARE-key]) your periods won't be regular. If you're sexually active and you've missed more than one period, definitely go to the doctor for a pregnancy test. Also, if you're bleeding frequently, like two or three times a month for more than a week, call the doctor because you may be losing too much blood. This can lead to anemia, where you feel tired, dizzy, and look pale. To regulate their periods, some girls have to be put on hormone or birth control pills for three to six months and then taken off to see if their periods are regular.

3. I feel awful when I get my period. My stomach and back hurt and sometimes I throw up. My friends say I'm just exaggerating to get attention, and that that's how it is for women. Isn't there anything I can do?

Definitely. Your symptoms are real for you and many women who suffer from dysmenorrhea, or painful periods. The stomach pain is actually your uterus contracting from a flood of chemicals called prostaglandins. The backache and vomiting are from hormones. Fortunately you don't have to suffer and there are many things you can do. To ease the cramps, try a heating pad, hot water bottle, or bath to relax uterine muscles. Also try over-the-counter drugs like ibuprofen. If this doesn't work, your doctor can prescribe stronger medication. Because there are so many remedies available, you shouldn't miss school or miss out on any fun because of your period.

4. Will I still be a virgin if I use tampons?

Yes. Tampons and virginity have nothing to do with each other. You're a virgin until you have sex, some people would say until you have intercourse and a male's penis goes into your vagina. Inserting a tampon into your vagina isn't considered having intercourse, and therefore has no bearing on your virginity. Some young women worry that inserting a tampon before they've ever had sex will tear the tissue at the opening of the vagina called the hymen. But tampons are small enough that most of the time they can be used without tearing the hymen. Feel free to use them before you're sexually active, like many young women do.

5. It seems like I'm the last one of all my friends to start developing. They're all wearing bras and having their periods. I'm really psyched to join them, but will I have to wait until I'm in college?

Probably not. Puberty is a series of physical and emotional changes that begin at different times for all of us, usually between nine and twelve years old for girls. Ask your mom when she started her period, because late-bloomers usually follow in their mom's footsteps. Also you need a certain amount of body fat to get your first period. If you're athletic or have an eating disorder, you may still develop, but you might not get your period for a while. Talking your feelings out will probably help you feel better. Remember, regardless of how late, you will eventually develop. If not by age eighteen, see a health care practitioner.

6. My grandma says not to wash my hair, take a bath, or walk barefoot when I'm on my period. Should I follow her advice?

Following her advice won't have any effect on your period. Almost all cultures have some rules, ceremonies, or myths surrounding women getting their periods. This probably started as a way to explain the previously unknown and mysterious process of menstruation, and some of the folklore still survives today with our elders. Rather than just dismiss her suggestions, use them as an opportunity to talk to your grandma about how life was for her growing up. You might learn something interesting about your heritage and get closer to your grandma too.

7. I heard my friend's sister say that once you have your period you're ready to have a baby. What's that mean?

While it's true that once you have your period you're biologically able to produce and carry a fetus, it doesn't mean that you're *ready* to. Being ready means having the physical, emotional, and financial capacity to care for a child. Other things have to be taken into consideration, like your age. Going through a pregnancy during adolescence affects your physical development, and can cause malnutrition. Because of the stress that a fetus puts on maturing young women, babies born to teens are often low birth weight and premature. Emotionally you haven't gone through any of the tests you need to figure out who you are, what you need, and how to take care of yourself. Having a baby too early limits your emotional growth, not to mention your freedom, or chances at a good education and job. It's better to wait until you can give your baby and yourself the best future possible.

8. Either my mirror is warped or my breasts really are two different sizes. What the heck is going on?

When you start puberty, one breast usually develops before the other, sometimes as early as six months before. Even once they're fully developed, there's still a slight difference in size, with the right one usually bigger than the left. Some girls have major differences between breast sizes at the end of puberty, though it's rare. If you do and you find it really bothers you, there are two things you can do. One is to get padding for the smaller breast and wear it in your bra. The other is more drastic because it involves getting surgery to either reduce the larger breast or enlarge the smaller breast to even them out. Only consider this last alternative after a serious chat with your parents and a doctor.

9. My friends call me "Big Foot" because I wear a size 9 shoe, but I'm still really short, and my butt's getting big. I feel like a troll, but with better hair. Is there anything I can do?

It'll be hard, but try to relax as much as you can. This is a transitory stage. During puberty your hands and feet grow first, then your arms and legs, then your torso. Your hips will probably grow before your breasts, making them look huge when they're not. Even though you may seem out of proportion now, eventually it will all fit together nicely. Don't diet! It's normal to feel abnormal, and dieting will only interfere with your nutrition and growth, and if you don't have enough body fat, it will also prevent you from getting your period. Just as you feel self-conscious, your friends do too. Pick clothes that enhance your best features, which may mean giving up a favorite shirt or dress in place of a more flattering one that makes you feel better. And exercise to promote muscle growth and toning.

10. I know what goes on with girls during puberty. What's the deal with guys?

Though it may be less obvious, boys are going through changes too. Hormone changes cause their pubic, axillary, and facial hair to grow, their testicles and penis grow, their voices to change, acne to develop, and increased perspiration. Most guys start maturing two years later than girls, around eleven to fourteen years old, but as they do, their muscle mass increases, their shoulders broaden, and they get a big growth spurt. Many boys also have their first "wet dream" in mid- to late puberty. Wet dreams happen when a guy has an erection and ejaculates in his sleep, all outside his control. Just like us, guys have their own puberty horror stories, such as feeling that their penises are too small or that they don't have enough pubic hair or getting erections in public. We all have to find ways to cope during this awkward time.

Let's Talk about Sex

Obviously, sex is about more than just making babies, and making the decision whether or not to have it can be extremely difficult. (The discussion here covers mostly the physical aspects of sex; for a full-scale discussion about deciding when to have sex or not, see Chapter 11.) And it's also more than having intercourse (when a male puts his penis in a female's vagina). This is only a small part of sex, and not necessarily the best.

People have sex for a variety of reasons. First, most of us do it because it feels good. Like being in love, making love should be pleasurable, not painful, uncomfortable, or frightening. Often, along with pleasurable physical sensations, come emotions such as intimacy and closeness as well as a release of tension.

Perhaps the most important part of sex has nothing to do with technique. Which part goes where comes second to what's going on in the mind. So much of what is exciting and stimulating has to do with respect, trust, and good communication with a partner.

Though the movies make it look easy, sex isn't something everyone's born knowing how to do. Being sexual comes naturally, but knowing exactly what brings pleasure comes from experimenting. And everyone is different, with individual likes and dislikes. Like any learning process, it takes time, experience, and creativity. That's why rushing into intercourse just for the heck of it can turn out to be a less than earth-shattering ordeal.

What Happens During Sex?

Though any part of the body can be sensitive to touch, some areas are more responsive than others, such as: the lips and mouth, ears and neck, hands and feet, breasts and nipples, clitoris (incidentally, this is the only part of the human anatomy designed solely to give pleasure!).

Knowing that there are alternatives to intercourse can open up a whole new world of sensual feelings. It allows for pleasure that doesn't lead to pregnancy or disease. Actually, many sexually experienced women put intercourse toward the bottom of their Having Good and Safe Sex list. Because they have a broad range of things they like, they aren't hung up on intercourse for a fulfilling experience.

Keep in mind that if you do choose to explore your sexuality with a partner, it's always best to set limits before getting into something heavy, so that you feel comfortable that things won't go too far. Communicate your feelings clearly to your partner—"I like kissing you, and for now, that's as far as I want to take it." You can *always* change your mind once you get into it— either to go further or to stop—but it's important to let your partner know your limits.

WHAT'S SO BAD ABOUT MASTURBATION?

Masturbate and you will:
> get sick
> go crazy
> lose interest in sex with someone else
> get addicted
> act perverted
> become lonely and desperate

Not true—any of it! Some uptight people have made such a big deal out of masturbation. But when you think about it, what's so scary or dangerous about touching your own body? There are no negative side effects to masturbation—except, of course, guilt, if you believe you're doing something wrong. Although masturbation has gotten a bad rep, it's actually a good way to get to know your body and how it responds. In fact, at least as you're first exploring your sensual self, it may be better to touch yourself, than to have someone else touch you. Why?

- No risk of contracting a disease such as HIV or other sexually transmitted infections.
- No chance of getting pregnant.
- It's a good way to learn what is pleasurable and to explore how to have orgasms.
- It's under your control; you can decide how far to go.
- No one will be spreading embarrassing rumors the next day at school, because nobody else will know.

Besides, think about this: why is it OK for someone else to touch (or, at the extreme, abuse) your body, but taboo for you to touch yourself, even in a pleasurable way?

What's Going on Inside Our Bodies During Sex?

Sex can be both exciting and scary. To get an idea of exactly what goes on inside the body during sexual arousal, here's a blow by blow:

Excitement

HER: A tingling or tightening feeling around the genital area as it fills with blood. The clitoris becomes swollen and sensitive, and the vaginal walls secrete fluid to lubricate the vagina.

HIM: His genital area fills with blood as his penis goes from being soft and limp to erect. His penis will grow in length and width, his testicles elevate, and his breathing and heart rate increase. As with the size of women's breasts, the size of a man's penis has no bearing on his sexual functioning.

Plateau

HER: Muscles tense. The genitals become engorged with blood, the vagina is very wet and swollen, and the clitoris elevates. Breathing and heart rate increase. It may feel as though the senses are going haywire; orgasm is approaching.

HIM: His heart rate and breathing increase too as his genitals become engorged with blood. His testicles elevate. The opening at the tip of his penis (urethra) enlarges and seminal fluid (a clear liquid that can contain sperm) may come out.

Orgasmic

HER: During orgasm or climax (or "coming"), the muscles around the vagina and the uterus contract rapidly. These contractions and others in the rest of the body, along with the release of chemicals in the brain called endorphins, cause a feeling of intense pleasure. The feeling can be described as a wave taking over, a warm feeling that goes throughout the entire body, or a release felt all over or in the genital area. While some orgasms are mild and others strong, most women can reach them only if their clitoris is stimulated.

HIM: His body contractions cause him to ejaculate (or squirt) semen from his penis. Most men describe their orgasms as centered in their genitals, and rarely experience the whole body sensations that women do.

Resolution

HER: The heart and pulse rate slow down back to normal and genitals return to normal size. Some women are able to become aroused again immediately after their first orgasm and may even be able to have another or several more.

HIM: His heart rate returns to normal, his penis becomes soft, and his testicles go down. Some men require more time than others between orgasms, but unlike women, they can't become immediately aroused into another orgasm.

Sex is:

Supposed to feel good
An intimate and private act
Something to wait until the right time for
Mutually pleasurable

Sex isn't:

A game where whoever scores the most wins
Just about orgasms
Always a sign that he loves you
Something that you owe to somebody else
Something that somebody makes you do
A reward for dinner or a gift

"With my younger daughters, I'm not embarrassed to tell them everything I know. I try to be open about it."

ALMA ROMO, 36, COSTA MESA, CALIFORNIA

I have four daughters—twelve, thirteen, twenty-two, and twenty-three. When the twenty-two and twenty-three-year-olds were younger I talked to them about sex and the dangers. At that time it was mostly about not getting pregnant. If I heard a case of a girl getting pregnant I would say that it was going to ruin her life and her education and that she was going to have to tend to her child and possibly not finish school or go to college. I also told my daughters that the girl would have a bad reputation. I was trying to scare them, so they wouldn't do something, you know?

But it didn't work. I guess I spoke to them only very briefly and I didn't make myself very clear. They both knew the risks and they still got pregnant. The oldest one is married, and the twenty-two-year-old is not. The younger one of the two is working part time, and she will be going to school. It's going to be a big sacrifice.

Now with the other girls, I'm telling them this is what happened with your sisters, and I don't want it to happen again. I'm trying to get the younger girls involved in a lot of things so they have a dream that they have to work towards. If they're doing a lot of activities, I hope they won't be involved with the guys so much. I don't want them to say "yes" to prove their love for them. They don't have boyfriends yet, and they're not getting phone calls. If they had boyfriends, I would know.

They're also taking classes on sex education at the Girls Incorporated center. They learn a lot of facts and a lot of information. In the class, they're learning to look more to abstinence, but also that if they are going to be having sex they have to be protected. That's the goal.

With my younger daughters, I'm not embarrassed to tell them everything I know. I try to be open about it. Sometimes parents are so ignorant about things. We think our kids are going to be twelve forever. For Hispanic parents like myself especially. In our culture, there are a lot of chaperons, people supervising. But what happens when you're not there? You think they're in school, but they could be somewhere else, having sex.

The most important thing now is to give girls so much self-esteem so that they'll just say "no." So they'll say, "No, my life is too important, I want to study, I want my college career."

"I'm glad I can talk to my mom about sex because she knows a lot and gives me better advice than anyone. She's a very cool mom."

TANYA ROMO, 12, COSTA MESA, CALIFORNIA

I first learned about sex from my mom when I was like ten or eleven. It's not really embarrassing because I don't even want to be near a guy. I don't go out on dates; my dad would kill me. My parents don't even let me put makeup on.

I'm very close to my mom, so there isn't really anything we can't talk about. I can't even be away from her for more than three days. I'm glad I can talk to my mom about sex because she knows a lot and gives me better advice than anyone. She's a very cool mom.

My friends can't talk to their moms about this. They talk to counselors or their aunts or something. They just don't communicate with their moms like I can. Girls who want to talk to their mom should just say, "Mom, I'd like to talk to you about something."

It helps me when I see my sisters, what they have to do with their kids.

They can't get nothing done. Even when I have to babysit or something I can't get homework or anything done. I look at my sisters and feel like the world comes to an end when you have all these little kids. All these little kids all over you—I wouldn't want that.

A lot of my friends are into boys, like they French kiss and stuff, but I don't even want that. I don't want to be thinking about a boy, I want to think about my homework. I want to go to college. I want to be a math teacher or a lawyer.

• According to the American Public Health Association, teens want to talk to their parents about sex, but half of the teens in the study said their parents have not provided enough information about sex. They also want to talk more openly with parents about sex.
• Ninety-eight percent of parents in an Alan Guttmacher Institute study said they need help in talking to their kids about sex.
• A poll by the Planned Parenthood Federation of America reveals that 62 percent of parents have discussed birth control with their kids.
• In a study published by *Family Planning Perspectives*, kids who take sex education classes in school are more likely to talk to their parents about pregnancy, than those that have no sex ed at all.
• The more parents talk to their kids about sex, the more they influence their kids' values and choices, says a study put out by *Adolescence*.
• In a Planned Parenthood Federation of America survey, parents usually talk to their daughters rather than sons about contraception.
• Moms are more likely to talk about sex with kids than are dads, says a *Demography* study.

WHAT ARE YOU GONNA DO ABOUT IT?

GROWING TOGETHER, DALLAS, TEXAS

There's nothing like having a hip mom to go to when "female" issues come up. That's why the Dallas chapter of Girls, Inc. devised a mother-daughter program that would get families talking about subjects that make most kids and parents clam up. Once a week for four weeks, moms and daughters like Monica and Melissa Rojas come to the center to learn new ways to discuss tough topics surrounding sex education. The goal of Growing Together is to get parents to 'fess up that they don't know everything about sex and often don't share what they do know with their daughters, and to get daughters to stop thinking of their parents as too out of it to talk to about sex.

"When I was younger, no one talked to us about stuff like this. We just had to learn it on our own," laments Melissa's mom, Monica.

The program deals with this problem by getting parents to talk about their puberty experiences and myths about their bodies and sexuality that they still hold on to. This lets moms see how important it is to get over the initial embarrassment of bringing up the "birds and the bees" and begin honest communication with their teen daughters.

"I signed up for Growing Together with Melissa because I thought it was a good idea for me and Melissa to be together," says Monica. "We were real open before, but I wanted to see how she would react around other kids."

For young women like Melissa, age twelve, Growing Together also gives practical information that neither mothers nor daughters have. "I learned about nutrition while I'm on my period, and to exercise if I get cramps," remembers Melissa. "And I learned about the different pads, for light and heavy days, and tampons."

Recently Melissa decided to give her mom the opportunity to put the program skills to work. "I just started my period at the beginning of last month, and my mom showed me which pads to use. I used to talk to my mom about this kind of stuff but not as much as I do now. It makes me feel closer to her."

For more information contact Growing Together, 3107 Cole Avenue, Dallas, TX 75204; (214) 979-9430.

Where to Turn

Recommended Reading

My Body, My Self: The What's Happening Workbook for Girls, Lynda Madaras with Area Madaras, New Market Press, 1993. The companion workbook to *What's Happening to My Body? Book For Girls*.

Changing Bodies, Changing Lives, Ruth Bell, Random House, 1987. From co-authors of *Our Bodies, Ourselves*.

Period, JoAnn Gardner-Loulan, Bonnie Lopez, and Marcia Quakenbush, Volcano Press, 1981.

The New Teenage Body Book, Kathy McCoy and Charles Wibbelsman, M.D., Berkley Publishers, 1992. This book tries to answer every body question you might have and gives helpful tips about all aspects of life and growing up.

The What's Happening to My Body? Book for Girls: The Growing Up Guide for Parents and Daughters, Lynda Madaras with Area Madaras, Newmarket Press, 1987.

Support Groups and Organizations

The Door, 555 Broome St., New York, NY 10013; (212) 941-9090. The Door offers programs for New York's youth between the ages of twelve and twenty, including sexual awareness programs, that discuss birth control and AIDS information and education.

Society For Adolescent Medicine, 1916 Copper Oaks Circle, Blue Springs, MO 64015; (816) 224-8010. The society can provide names of adolescent medicine specialists in your area.

CHAPTER 6

DOING THE RIGHT THING:
AVOIDING PREGNANCY, PREVENTING DISEASE

One of the changes that comes with puberty and menstruation is the ability to bear children. But just because you're capable, of course, doesn't mean you're ready or even want to. There are lots of ways to avoid having kids, including not having sex at all, using protection if you're sexually active, or ending a pregnancy before the fetus develops into a child. (Abortion is discussed in Chapter 7.) These are all viable options—ways of controlling reproductive freedom.

Reproductive freedom also means keeping protected against sexually transmitted infections, including HIV, the deadly virus that causes AIDS. With that in mind, acting responsibly either by abstaining from sexual intercourse or making sure your partner always uses a condom is absolutely essential.

Abstinence and Postponement

Bring up "sex" these days and you'll hear buzz words like abstinence and postponement that sound like part of a vocabulary homework assignment. Both words imply that having sex is best delayed until later, but abstinence and postponement have somewhat different meanings when it gets down to practice. And the command to "just say no" is difficult when faced with a sexual situation. (In fact, one survey reveals that 64 percent of all teens think that "just saying no" just doesn't cut it when trying to get teens to abstain from or postpone sex.) Read on for advice on how to make your own decisions about sex.

What Is Abstinence?

This usually means waiting until marriage or a committed long-term relationship to have sexual intercourse. People choose this option for a variety of reasons, including their religious beliefs or personal feelings about sex before marriage. Those who choose to abstain from sex may or may not have already had it for the first time.

Others take abstinence to mean not having sex for a period of time. For instance, a young woman may have already had sexual intercourse, but feels she'd like to wait a while before the next time, maybe until she's older, in a steady relationship or married.

What Is Postponement?

Like abstinence, postponement also means not having sex until a later date. However, postponement is considered a way to delay sexual intercourse until the right time, whether that means until a mature age or for a set amount of time within a relationship. It is more closely associated with "virgins," those who have never had sex. Postponement may be a better term than abstinence (which brings to mind nuns and priests), because it suggests finding our own personal limits. In an article in the June 1994 issue of *Essence* magazine, for example, writer Tara Roberts wonders "Am I the Last Virgin?" She notes that although Webster's dictionary defines a virgin as "free of impurity or stain; chaste; modest; unsullied," a book called *The Great Cosmic Mother* defines a virgin differently, as "a woman who is one-in-herself; not belonging to a man." Thus concludes Roberts: "I admit I feel lonely at times. But I want to wait for someone who is patient and will uphold my image of myself and my sexuality."

Regardless of the reasons, abstinence or postponement are important, viable options. According to Jo Gottfried, coordinator of the Willpower Won't Power program for junior high girls in Orange County, California, most teenage relationships don't last very long, so it may be good to wait until you're more sure about who you're dealing with before jumping into something as intimate as sex. "Young women have to learn how to deal with pressure from the media as well as from friends and boyfriends in order to make good decisions," she says. Here, Gottfried suggests ways to deal with the pressure:

- Don't believe the hype. Notice how advertisers on TV and in magazines sell products to girls. Think about how all the women, even business women, are sexualized. Be critical of these images and question how women are being used.
- Practice lines on your friends. With a few friends, discuss the corny pick-up lines guys use to get sex. Compare notes about how to han-

dle even the best of the sweet talkers. Question the sincerity of a guy who would rather badger you into sex than respect your feelings to not have it.

- Think ahead. Considering that most relationships during the teen years are short term, think about how you'd feel if you had sex with someone and broke up shortly afterwards. Many young women aren't ready to make tough emotional decisions—such as birth control, abortion, raising a child—until their late teens or even adulthood. That's why it's probably best to wait.

- Don't get drunk or high. Drinking a couple of beers or smoking pot often leads to risky or even dangerous situations. Guys rate drinking and taking drugs within the top three risk-taking behaviors for girls, which means they perceive a girl willing to get drunk or high as someone who's easy to convince to engage in sex. If you want to make sound decisions, do it with a clear head.

- Set limits ahead of time. Know before going into a situation how far you want to go with someone. And make sure your behavior is in sync with your decision. When telling someone what you do or don't want:

  1. Be direct and say exactly what you mean. ("I don't like it when you put your hand there.")

  2. Use a serious, confident tone of voice. "I mean it."

  3. If he doesn't stop, leave the room or the scene altogether.

  4. Practice what you may need to say beforehand until you get it. Some young women have a hard time not being "nice," but sometimes being nice means sacrificing your own feelings and doing things you don't really want to do. The best way to respect yourself is to respect your feelings.

Not having sex means different things to different people. For some it means not having sexual intercourse (when a male puts his penis in a vagina), while for others it means not going further than kissing and touching. You must define for yourself what it means and stick with whatever feels comfortable to you. Sex without vaginal, anal, or oral penetration is 100 percent effective in preventing pregnancy and the spread of sexually transmitted infections, including HIV, the virus that causes AIDS.

Sex is an act that requires responsibility and maturity. While some young women think they can handle it, others decide it's best to hold off until the right time. It's up to you to think critically about what you *really* want and how you feel, and to be brutally honest with yourself before making the difficult choice to "do it" or not to "do it." (For more on deciding when to have sex, see Chapter 11.)

- Most young men and women wait at least until their mid- to late teens before having sex.
- The vast majority of thirteen year olds, more than three-quarters of fourteen year olds, and 70 percent of fifteen year olds are not having sex yet.
- One in five teens don't have intercourse at all.

(Courtesy of the Alan Guttmacher Institute)

"For me, being abstinent is important because I have goals in my life."

CHRISTINE, 13, WASHINGTON, D.C.

I belong to a group called Best Friends that shows girls how to act like young ladies by teaching us about abstinence, drug abuse, and all the things we have to go through. At first I didn't realize that it was important to be in a group and get the information, but as I got older I realized how much it helped.

Not all my friends are in Best Friends, but some really need to know about abstinence because they're hanging in the streets without anyone to talk to. Some are getting pregnant. They talk to maybe an older sister or friend, not a parent or guardian, but friends might mislead you and tell you things that aren't true. You really need to get the right information about stuff like abstinence and get some guidance. Luckily, I'm really close with my mother and don't need it as much as some people. But having a support group is like having a second home and makes me feel more comfortable being by myself.

Instead of focusing on boys and sex, Best Friends teaches us to get good grades, go to college, and set standards and goals that we want to achieve. I'm different from the kids hanging out in the streets because I know that I'm not defined by other people, knowing that I have a choice, and that I have standards so that I don't have to be pressured into doing something I don't want to do. People that give in to having sex before they're ready give up their self-control.

For me being abstinent is important because I have goals in my life. I want to become a biologist, and there's no way I can do that if I'm having sexual encounters and getting pregnant. It's not gonna work. I don't want to have any sexual relations with anyone until I get married. Most girls in Best Friends say they'll wait until after high school. Right now it's not the most important thing to me. I don't think I could handle it. My emotions and hormones aren't ready for it. And all these diseases, you can't risk it. It's like throwing your life away because it's not safe any more.

Being in Best Friends lets us know we're not the only girls out there who decided not to have sex. It shows us that we can be somebody without doing what everybody else does. Being in a group lets you know there's someone else like you and you feel more comfortable hanging out with people like you.

My friends have been in situations where they've had to say no to guys. In Best Friends, we watch videos and see ways to say no when a guy says "If you loved me you'd have sex with me." And we say, "Well I must not love you because I have to love myself first and I'm not doing this." I have to love myself first before I can even try to love someone else. It makes me feel proud of myself when I can stand up to the pressure. But also sad when I find out that the person really doesn't care about me and just wants that one thing.

WHAT ARE YOU GONNA DO ABOUT IT?

POSTPONING SEXUAL INVOLVEMENT

The soap stars do it; the music video models do it; Madonna definitely does it. So why shouldn't everybody do it? "You have to be your own person with your own set of values and opinions when it comes to your body," says Sanita Richardson, veteran teen leader in the Postponing Sexual Involvement (PSI) program in Cincinnati, Ohio. This wise high school student teaches more than just-say-no skills to seventh graders who are about to bust into full hormonal teenhood and need solid examples of how to turn the pressure down. "I relate to the younger kids like a buddy, not a teacher," says Sanita. "All I teach is that it's their life. If they want to have sex, it's their choice. But if they're not sure, just wait."

Most of the middle-school kids that Sanita teaches get the message— but only after a couple of sessions of nervous tee-hees whenever the word "sex" comes up. Christa Miller, thirteen, and a graduate of Sanita's PSI class, recalls that by the third class they all got serious. "We learned about diseases, like gonorrhea. I wasn't aware of so many you can get from having sex," remarks Christa. "Sanita also taught me how to say no without hurting the guy's feelings by being direct and telling him 'I don't want to do this yet.' Because if you aren't direct he'll keep on pressuring." Has Christa had a chance to put her skills into action? "Actually I was in a situation and I told the guy no and I wasn't ready. He just said 'OK' and didn't try again. Before I had no clue what to say."

PSI classes have convinced Christa not to get sexually involved until she's married. "It's important to me that the first person I have sex with be someone who I truly love and who truly loves me. For me this means when I get married or we've been together a really long time."

For more information on the Postponing Sexual Involvement program, write: PSI c/o Hughes Center, 2515 Clifton Ave., Cincinnati, OH 45219; (513) 559-3014.

Birth Control

If you make the choice to be sexually active, you *must* also decide how you're going to prevent pregnancy and keep yourself free from sexually transmitted infections. It's important to know that some methods of birth control are better than others, depending on your needs. For example, while one young woman may be involved in a relationship and have sex frequently, another may not be presently involved in a relationship, but may need protection for an unexpected occasion. So, their needs are different.

Whether you're having sex now or not, it's still a good idea to know what's out there so that, when you become sexually active, you'll know what there is to choose from.

A study shows that 67 percent of teens think condoms should be given out at school.

This same study reveals that when adolescents don't use birth control 59 percent say it's because none was available.

The top three places teenagers get their contraception:

at a store: 74 percent
at the doctor's: 35 percent
at a clinic: 28 percent

Courtesy of the Sexuality Information and Education Council of the United States

Male Condom

How it works: A condom is made of latex (thin rubber), and is placed over an erect penis before sexual intercourse. It prevents sperm from entering the vagina.

Cost: About .25–$2.50 each.

Failure rate (estimated percentage of U.S. women experiencing an unintended pregnancy in one year of use): When used perfectly: 2 out of 100 women get pregnant. Typical use by the average couple: 16 out of 100 women get pregnant.

PROS

- Widely available and easy to find. You can buy them at convenience and drug stores.
- Don't cost much.
- Provide the best protection against sexually transmitted infections, including the AIDS virus, for both partners.
- No long-term health effects.

CONS

- Because they must be used by guys, you don't control them. Some men refuse to use them.
- Some people complain that they disrupt sexual activity and reduce enjoyment.
- Many people use them incorrectly. The failure rate for typical use is fairly high, and breakage during use is common.

TIPS TO USE IT CORRECTLY

Carefully take the condom out of the package. Squeeze the tip to remove air. (Excess air could cause the condom to break.) Place it onto the tip of his erect penis and roll it all the way down.

To remove the condom after sex, he should withdraw his penis while it is still hard. You or he should hold onto the rim of the condom as he pulls it out so nothing spills. Roll the condom off the penis, and discard it. Both of you should avoid further sexual contact until you have washed your sex organs and any other areas that came in contact with body fluids.

Never reuse a condom.

Keep condom away from extreme heat or cold and direct sunlight. Store in a cool, dry place, but not in a wallet or glove compartment. Remember to check the expiration date.

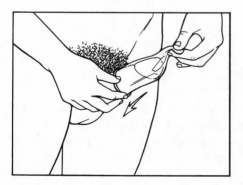

The male condom prevents pregnancy *and* disease, but it must be used correctly. While squeezing the tip, it must be rolled all the way down the erect penis.

- Be sure to use a latex condom. Avoid "natural" condoms made of sheep or lamb membrane. They are porous and can allow transmission of viruses, including HIV. Some people also believe that colored condoms break more often than the regular type.
- Condoms sometimes come in sizes. Make sure the condom fits his penis correctly.
- Don't use a condom that feels sticky or brittle or looks damaged.
- If you need to lubricate, choose a water-based lubricant such as K-Y Jelly, or a spermicidal gel or foam. Condoms also come prelubricated, and according to some, these tend to be less prone to breakage than the unlubricated kind. Never use oil-based lubricants such as petroleum jelly, baby oil, or shortening. They can weaken the latex and lead to breaks and tears.
- If the condom breaks and semen spills or leaks out, you and your partner should wash wherever you had sexual contact right away.
- For best results, use a condom with another form of birth control such as a diaphragm or the Pill. This way, you can better avoid pregnancy and protect against sexually transmitted infections.

Female Condom

How it works: This new device consists of a thin polyurethane (it's sort of like thin plastic) sheath with two flexible rings. One ring lies inside the closed end of the sheath and is used to insert the device and to hold it in place. The other ring remains outside the vagina after insertion. When the man inserts his penis into the woman's vagina, the sheath covers her labia and the tip of his penis. It is prelubricated and is sold over the counter in drug stores and pharmacies.

Cost: $2.75–$3.00 per condom (comes in a box of 3 or 6).

Failure rate (estimated percentage of U.S. women experiencing an unintended pregnancy in six months of use): When used perfectly: 2.6 percent. When used by the average couple: 12.4 percent.

PROS

- Completely controlled by the woman.
- You can buy them at convenience and drug stores without needing medical facilities or personnel.
- Failure rates are fairly low when used correctly.
- Because it is made of polyurethane, which is generally stronger than latex, it is more resistant to tears than the male condom.
- Helps prevent the transmission of sexually transmitted infections.
- No long-term health effects.

CONS

- Some people complain that they disrupt sexual activity and reduce enjoyment.
- Some women have complained that they are unattractive, uncomfortable, somewhat awkward to use, and difficult to insert.
- Expensive to use. They cost more than twice as much as the male condom.

TIPS TO USE IT CORRECTLY

To insert, squeeze the inner ring and insert it in a way similar to putting a tampon in. Push the inner ring up as far as it will go. The inner ring should be resting on the cervix, the sheath should fill the vaginal cavity and the outer ring should be resting on the labia, outside of the vagina.

Each female condom must be used only once and should be discarded like a condom.

Depo-Provera ("The Shot")

How it works: Depo-Provera, an injectable synthetic hormone, which was approved for use in the United States in 1992, is controversial. It has been available in other countries for many years. A synthetic form of the female hormone progesterone is shot into a woman's arm or buttock to suppress ovulation. It also thickens the cervical mucus to block sperm and makes the uterine lining unsuitable for implantation. A woman must receive the shot once every three months.

Cost: $30-$75 per shot plus doctor or clinic fees.

Failure rate (estimated percentage of U.S. women experiencing an unintended pregnancy in one year of use): When used perfectly: less than 1 percent. When used by the average couple: less than 1 percent.

PROS

- Highly effective and long-acting.
- Good for women who want to practice birth control discreetly but have little privacy.
- Easy to use. You don't have to take a pill or insert a device.
- Helps protect against iron deficiency anemia.

CONS

- Requires regular visits to a physician or clinic for injections.
- Some women experience side effects such as weight gain, menstrual irregularities, headaches, irritability, dizziness, and mood swings.

Other reported side effects: depression, hair loss, diminished sex drive and breast discharge.

- Not immediately reversible if side effects occur; it takes three or more months for effects to wear off.
- Studies show that Depo-Provera slightly increases the risk of breast cancer in women under thirty-five, and it may also increase the risk of developing cervical cancer.
- Does not protect against HIV or other sexually transmitted infections.

Who shouldn't use it: Women with acute liver disease, unexplained vaginal bleeding, breast cancer, or blood clots in the legs, lungs, or eye. A woman who suspects she's pregnant should not get the injection, which may cause low birth weight in babies.

The Controversy: Groups such as the National Black Women's Health Project (NBWHP) and the National Women's Health Network oppose Depo-Provera. Although the manufacturer insists that the drug is safe, studies show an increased risk of breast cancer in women under age thirty-five who use Depo-Provera. This may be an especially dangerous problem for women of color, who are more likely than other women to develop breast cancer at younger ages.

When using any of these contraceptive options, except the female condom, always also use a condom to prevent disease.

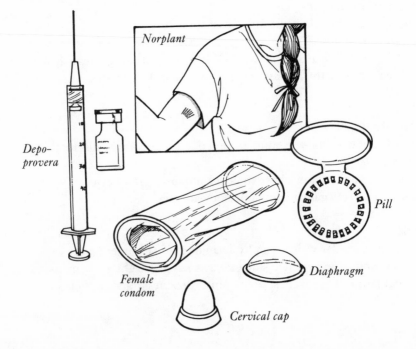

Norplant

Depo-provera

Pill

Female condom

Diaphragm

Cervical cap

Because Depo-Provera must be dispensed through the health care system, like Norplant, it can easily be administered inappropriately and coercively to poor women and women of color. Incidents of coercive use of the shot have been reported among Black women in South Africa and in Zimbabwe before independence. In the early eighties, African American women were part of the Depo-Provera trials in Atlanta. Some experts believe that many women who signed consent forms and received the shot may not have understood what they were signing or what they were getting.

Diaphragm

How it works: A woman inserts a round soft-rubber device with a flexible rim into her vagina to cover the cervix and form a barrier between the opening of the uterus and the sperm. Spermicide is placed in the diaphragm before insertion to kill any sperm that get past the barrier.

Cost: Between $13 and $25, plus doctor or clinic fees.

Failure rate (estimated percentage of U.S. women experiencing an unintended pregnancy in one year of use): When used perfectly: 6 percent. When used by the average couple: 18 percent.

PROS

- Entirely controlled by the woman. Unlike the condom, the diaphragm can be inserted in advance to avoid disrupting sexual activity.
- No long-term health problems.
- Practical for women who have infrequent intercourse.
- Can last for two years if cleaned and stored in a cool, dry place after each use.
- When used properly and with spermicide, may provide some protection against sexually transmitted infections. However, it should *not* be relied upon.

CONS

- Diaphragm must be properly fitted by health personnel.
- Users must be trained to ensure proper placement over the cervix and to recognize whether the diaphragm has become dislodged during intercourse.
- Cannot be totally relied upon to prevent sexually transmitted infections.

Who shouldn't use it: Women who are prone to urinary tract infections. The diaphragm may trigger them. Any woman who is allergic to rubber.

TIPS TO USE IT CORRECTLY

Be sure to have your health care practitioner explain how to insert the diaphragm. When you get home, follow instructions carefully.

Before inserting, place a teaspoonful of contraceptive cream or jelly into diaphragm, and spread a small amount around the edge with your fingertip.

You can insert the diaphragm up to six hours before intercourse, and it must be left in place at least six hours following intercourse, but not more than twenty-four hours. If sexual intercourse is repeated, insert additional spermicide into vagina.

To better avoid pregnancy and to prevent sexually transmitted infections, use with a condom.

If the size of the uterus changes, the diaphragm should be refitted. It may change following full-term pregnancy, abortion, or miscarriage beyond the first four months, pelvic surgery or weight change of ten pounds or more.

Intrauterine Devices (IUDs)

How it works: A physician inserts a small T-shaped plastic or metal device into the uterus; a string, which extends down into the vagina, is attached to the end of the device. An IUD can remain in place for up to eight years, depending on the type of device. How IUDs work is unclear; researchers speculate that the device inhibits the eggs from implanting on the uterine wall or blocks fertilization by the sperm. Two types are available in the United States: the Copper T380A, which can be used for four to eight years, and the Progestasert, which releases progesterone and might need to be replaced yearly. An IUD must be removed by a health professional.

Cost: About $150–$300 for exam, insertion, and follow–up visit.

Failure rate (estimated percentage of U.S. women experiencing an unintended pregnancy in one year of use): When used perfectly: less than 1 percent. When used by the average couple: 4 percent.

PROS

- Highly effective and easy to use.
- Reversible. Very appropriate for women who want a reversible method, but find other methods difficult to use.
- It can be inserted right after a baby is delivered or immediately following an abortion without negative health effects.
- Can be inserted after unprotected sex to prevent the implantation of the fertilized egg.

CONS

- Insertion and removal require access to trained health personnel with appropriate equipment and facilities.
- Insertion can sometimes be painful.
- May cause irregular or heavy bleeding, and occasionally severe cramping.
- The device can become expelled from the uterus without the woman knowing it.
- Provides no protection against sexually transmitted infections, including HIV.
- IUDs may increase the risk of developing pelvic inflammatory disease. At the time of insertion, microorganisms in the cervix or vagina may enter the uterus and cause infection. However, the risk falls as time passes.

Who shouldn't use it: Women who have unprotected sex with multiple partners are at high risk of contracting sexually transmitted infections and should not choose the IUD.

Norplant (Implants)

How it works: (Norplant is controversial; see "The Real Scoop on Norplant for Teens" below.) First the upper arm is numbed with a local anesthetic. Through a small incision, the health care practitioner inserts six thin, matchstick-sized Norplant capsules under the skin in an arc formation. Each capsule contains a synthetic hormone, progestin. Released at a slow, steady rate, it suppresses ovulation, thickens cervical mucus to block sperm, and makes the uterine lining unsuitable for implantation. The procedure takes about fifteen minutes and protection lasts for five years.

Cost: $500–$750 for the capsules and procedure.

Failure rate (estimated percentage of U.S. women experiencing an unintended pregnancy in one year of use): When used perfectly: less than 1 percent. When used by the average couple: less than 1 percent.

PROS

- Highly effective.
- Easy to use. You don't have to take a pill or insert a device.
- Reversible. Once the implants are removed, a woman can get pregnant. Or they can be removed if side effects occur.
- Good for women who have sex frequently, want a reversible method, but find other forms of birth control difficult to use, or lack a reliable source of contraceptive supplies.

CONS

- The majority of users report irregular bleeding, either spotting between periods or throughout the month. (Some women had enough bleeding to require a panty liner.) Other women report long periods, while others stop menstruating altogether. In most cases, the irregular bleeding disappears in a few months.
- Other reported side effects: headaches, sore breasts, enlarged ovaries, acne, moodiness, nausea, and slight weight gain or loss, gain or loss of facial hair.
- Although it's inexpensive in the long run, several hundred dollars is too much for some women to pay up front.
- Implants are less effective for large women, those weighing over 150 pounds.
- Cannot be removed by user, and removal is more difficult that insertion.
- Scar tissue may form around the implants, especially if they are inserted improperly. This can be a problem for those of us who have a tendency to form keloids.
- Does not protect against HIV or other sexually transmitted infections.
- Although five-year studies show no adverse effects on women, the long-term safety of Norplant (beyond five years) has not been determined. No one knows the effect on women and the children they bear after using Norplant.

Who shouldn't use it: Women with undiagnosed genital bleeding, known or suspected pregnancy, acute liver disease or tumors, known or suspected breast cancer. Women who smoke heavily are also advised against using Norplant. Women with health histories that include diabetes, high cholesterol, high blood pressure, cardiovascular disease, migraines, depression, epilepsy, gallbladder, or kidney disorders should consider Norplant use with extreme caution.

Signs that something might be wrong: Serious problems are rare but possible. These are the warning signs:

Vaginal bleeding that is heavier than your normal period.
Delayed menstruation after a long period of regular cycles.
Arm pain.
Severe lower abdominal pain.
Pus or bleeding at the implant site.
One of the implants seems to be coming out.

THE REAL SCOOP ON NORPLANT FOR TEENS

When Norplant came on to the scene in 1990, many young women couldn't wait to get the six capsules put into their arms. At the Laurence Paquin Middle/Secondary School in Baltimore for expectant women and teen mothers, which offers all types of contraception, students lined up eagerly to get their free "miracle" sticks so they could continue their education without worry of becoming pregnant again. In their company are thousands of other adolescents. According to Planned Parenthood, which makes Norplant available to teens at their clinics, about one-quarter of their Norplant users are nineteen years old and under.

But all is not paradise in Norplant-land. First of all, relying on any kind of birth control that doesn't protect against getting the HIV virus that causes AIDS is taking a *huge* risk. Though Norplant can prevent pregnancy, it can't save lives.

Another problem with Norplant is the side effects. Though the material that the manufacturer gives to users says that they include irregular menstrual cycles, headache, nervousness, nausea, and dizziness, there are current Norplant users who say that's just the tip of the iceberg. Women in various states, like Illinois, Florida, and Texas, have filed lawsuits against the manufacturer, Wyeth-Ayerst, saying that they were never told of some of the other more severe side effects. These young women suffered from short-term memory loss, drastic mood swings, and other discomforts before getting their birth control removed. In one Planned Parenthood study, 23 percent had the capsules removed because the side effects were intolerable. Part of the concern young women have is that little testing has been done to document the effects Norplant has on teens, especially the long-term effects down the road.

Removing the implants can also be a problem. Many women are discovering that getting the contraceptive taken out is difficult and sometimes painful. Unfortunately inexperienced doctors, who are trained to put the devices in but not take them out, cause bruising or scarring in some patients. Women of color who scar and keloid easily should be aware that both to insert and to remove Norplant requires the doctor to make a small cut in the upper arm.

Another big drawback for us struggling young women is that unless you've got a fat bank account, really cool parents, or access to free health care, Norplant is an expensive luxury. The birth control itself costs $365, plus $150 or more to get it implanted. That comes to an incredible $500 or more up front. Add that to the cost of buying condoms, not to mention the $100 to $200-plus it takes just to remove Norplant, we would have to have an after-school job just to afford contraception. Even more frustrating is knowing that women in developing countries can get Norplant for as low as $23!

A big, big minus to the whole Norplant issue is that it has been used against young women—especially those who are poor and/or black—in scary ways. Some states have passed bills forcing women, usually women of color, who are on government assistance, have committed crimes, or have a history of drug or child abuse to have Norplant inserted against their will. And in some cases teenagers are forced by their parents to wear it. Although these women want them removed because of the side effects, their wishes are ignored.

So if you're considering Norplant, like any other contraception, it's best to do your homework. Then weigh the pros and cons, and decide for yourself what suits you. Remember no contraceptive is perfect.

The Pill

How it works: A woman takes a small tablet containing synthetic hormones every day for either twenty-one or twenty-eight days. There are two types: combined oral contraceptives (birth control pills) and progestin-only oral contraceptives (minipills). The combined birth control pill contains estrogen and progestin to suppress ovulation, thicken cervical mucus to block passage of sperm, and thin the endometrial lining. The minipill contains only progestin.

Cost: About $15–$25 a month plus doctor or clinic fees.

Failure rate (estimated percentage of U.S. women experiencing an unintended pregnancy in one year of use): When used perfectly: less than 1 percent. When used by the average couple: 6 percent.

PROS
- Entirely controlled by the woman.
- Highly effective and reversible.
- Protects against cancer of the ovaries and uterus as well as ovarian cysts and benign breast cysts. It also reduces the risk of some pelvic infections and ectopic pregnancies.
- Causes lighter, regular periods and less cramping.
- Doesn't interrupt sex.

CONS
- Requires strict daily pill-taking.
- Requires a prescription and medical personnel.
- For women who smoke, it may increase the risk of blood clots.
- Some women experience a slight weight gain (it generally levels off or disappears after the first month), as well as spotting between periods, tender breasts. Less frequently, women complain of nausea and mood swings.

• Does not protect against sexually transmitted infections, including HIV.

Who shouldn't use it: The combined birth control pill contains estrogen, and taking estrogen is not recommended for women who have diabetes, high blood pressure, or are prone to headaches. Women who have problems with estrogen should not take the combined birth control pill, but can take the minipill. The combined birth control pill may also reduce the quantity of breast milk, especially if used within six weeks after delivery. The combined pill may also delay fertility for several months following discontinuation. Neither of these problems is associated with the minipill. However, the minipill is slightly less effective than the combined pill. Discuss the pros and cons of each pill with your doctor to determine which one is right for you.

TIPS TO USE IT CORRECTLY
You must take the pill regularly for it to work. It's best to take your pill at the same time each day so pill-taking becomes routine.

Spermicides
How it works: Foam, cream, jelly, or suppository is inserted into the vagina up to fifteen minutes before intercourse. Creates a barrier that kills sperm on contact and inhibits their movement up the vagina into the cervix.

Cost: About $8 for an applicator kit (foam or gel), $2–$4.50 for refills.

Failure rate (estimated percentage of U.S. women experiencing an unintended pregnancy in one year of use): When used perfectly: 3 percent. When used by the average couple: 30 percent.

PROS
• Completely controlled by the woman.
• Is widely available and easy to find. You can buy it at convenience and drug stores without needing medical facilities or personnel.
• Provides some protection against sexually transmitted infections.
• No long-term health effects.

CONS
• Extremely high rate of failure when used on average.
• Sometimes causes itching and burning. Some people don't like the mess and odor.
• Must wait fifteen minutes before intercourse takes place and lasts only an hour.

Who shouldn't use it: Listen up: Even though spermicides are cheap and easy to find, they are not a reliable form of birth control, nor do they provide adequate protection against sexually transmitted infections including HIV. A spermicide *must* be used with a condom.

Withdrawal (Coitus Interruptus)

How it works: The guy rapidly pulls his penis out of the vagina before he is about to ejaculate.

Cost: Free.

Failure rate (estimated percentage of U.S. women experiencing an unintended pregnancy in one year of use): When used perfectly: 4 percent. When used by the average couple: 24 percent.

PROS
• Requires no device or medical personnel.
• Can be done on the spot.
• Is free and requires no training.

CONS
• Has an extremely high failure rate. Accidents are easy, and pre-ejaculation fluid, which contains sperm and viruses, gets into the vagina.
• Doesn't protect against sexually transmitted infections that can be transmitted, for example, through sores.
• Interrupts lovemaking.

What you need to know: Forget it: Withdrawal is not an acceptable method of birth control.

THE BEST, THE GOOD, AND THE OK BIRTH CONTROL
· · · · · · · · · **METHODS FOR HIV/AIDS PREVENTION** · · · · · · · · ·

BEST: Abstain from penetration of any kind, because the only way to be absolutely, 100 percent certain of avoiding infection is to avoid exposure. That means a man's penis should not be inserted into the vagina, anus, or mouth, especially if it's not covered with a latex condom. This is the number one way to protect yourself.

GOOD: Condoms for men. For oral sex done to a man, anal sex, or vaginal sex, these are your best defense. They must be latex and should be used with the spermicide Nonoxynol-9, which kills HIV.

OK: Female condoms. These are only good for oral sex done to a woman or vaginal penetration. If your partner penetrates your mouth or anus, he must also wear a condom.

IN CASE OF EMERGENCY

The condom falls off or breaks, the diaphragm slips out, you forgot to take your pill, you got caught up in the moment and didn't use anything, or you were forced to have sex: these are all emergency situations that call for drastic measures to prevent pregnancy. Right now there is one available method called emergency contraceptive pills (ECPs) to help you deal in a crisis.

ECPs are really just a double-whammy dosage of the birth control pills Ovral. Here's how they work:

1. You have unprotected sex.
2. Within seventy-two hours you go to a clinic or doctor's office and get Ovral; you take two of them.
3. Twelve hours later, you have to take another dose of two.

Taking the pills either prevents the egg from getting fertilized or keeps the fertilized egg from implanting itself in the uterus. A lot of women feel nauseous, vomit, or have headaches as side effects because the dosage is so strong. That's also why this method is considered only in urgent cases. But it's a better alternative than getting pregnant and having to get an abortion or having an unwanted baby.

Pills and an exam cost about $60. Some college campus health centers give ECPs out for free or a small charge. Whatever you do, don't just take any birth control pill in high dosages to do the job. Ovral, its side effects, and its risks have been specifically studied for this purpose, and should only be taken under the supervision of a health care professional.

Another pill called RU-486, which is available in France and England, is now being tested here in the United States. It also acts as an emergency contraceptive, but with fewer side effects and is 95 to 97 percent effective (Ovral is about 75 percent effective). Depending on the Food and Drug Administration's approval, RU-486 could be made available within the next few years for contraception and for abortion (it not only prevents pregnancy, it can terminate pregnancy without surgery).

For more information about ECPs call Planned Parenthood at (800) 230-PLAN. If your doctor doesn't know about ECPs or will not prescribe them to you, contact Bridging the Gap Communications to order the book, *Emergency Contraception: The Nation's Best Kept Secret*, which contains a list of doctors in your state who make ECPs available at (800) 721-6990 or (404) 373-0530.

- Two-thirds of teenagers use some form of birth control the first time they have sex, usually a condom.
- Between 72 and 84 percent of teenage women and their partners use a contraceptive regularly.
- One-quarter of young women on the pill also use condoms.

(Alan Guttmacher Institute.)

"Before anything happened I wanted to make sure I was on birth control because I didn't want to be responsible for a child."

LISA, 18, MABLETON, GEORGIA

I started using the birth control pill about a year and a half ago, just before I turned seventeen. At that time, I was very involved with my boyfriend; I thought that I loved him. So before anything happened I wanted to make sure I was on birth control because I didn't want to be responsible for a child. I thought that it was very important that I took that kind of responsibility. I'm also concerned about disease. I mean I don't know, I've heard some pretty awful stories and that worries me. Like crabs and yucky things like that. It's really gross.

My older cousin Andrea—she's in her thirties and we were pretty close— was telling me that if I thought I was going any further that I should go ahead and take the next step and go on birth control. I thought about condoms, but there's a chance that it could break, something could happen and that's just too big a risk. I mean, they're good, and I use them to keep from getting other venereal diseases, but I can't like totally depend on that to keep from getting pregnant. When Andrea offered to take me to the clinic, I went.

I got on the pill and the first one I took gave me a humongous appetite. I would eat and eat, and I gained 15 pounds. I eventually asked my doctor about it and he put me on another pill that I'm much more happy with. With this new pill I don't have side effects—except that my period is very regular, and that's a good thing.

MYTHS ABOUT BIRTH CONTROL

Myth: You can't get pregnant your first time having sex, so you don't need to use birth control.

Fact: Any time a woman has unprotected sex, she risks getting pregnant. It's no different for first-timers. Half of all unintended teen pregnancies occur within the first six months of having sex for the first time!! Fortunately teens are becoming more responsible, according to an Alan Guttmacher Institute study, and 65 percent use contraception for first-time intercourse—usually a condom.

Myth: You can't get pregnant if he pulls out before he comes (ejaculates).
Fact: Withdrawal, or "pulling out" has one of the highest failure rates for birth control (about one in four women get pregnant with this method). A man's seminal fluid, which can come out before he ejaculates, carries sperm. Even if he has enough control to pull out just in the nick of time, his penis could still be close enough to the entrance of your vagina to shoot sperm inside. All it takes is one sperm to fertilize an egg.

Myth: You can't get pregnant if you have sex during your period without birth control.
Fact: To say it is more likely that you won't get pregnant if you have unprotected sex during menstruation is like saying it's more likely that a car will slam on its brakes if you walk out into the middle of traffic. Why risk it?!

Myth: If you know your fertile time of the month, you can have unprotected sex on all the days before and after that without getting pregnant.
Fact: Teenagers who use no contraception over a year have a 90 percent chance of getting pregnant, says the Guttmacher Institute. Most women cannot accurately chart their most fertile days when they have regular periods. Since teenage menstruation is often very irregular, and since adolescence is the most fertile time in some women's lives, it's almost impossible to know what days to avoid. And remember, sperm can live in the vagina for several days, so it's not just the fertile days that have to be watched for, it's several days before and after that. Be realistic, would you be able to resist temptation if things got hot and heavy on one of your "off" days?

Myth: You can't get pregnant if you have unprotected sex but don't have an orgasm.
Fact: Neither partner has to have an orgasm in order to get pregnant. If his seminal fluid has sperm, it could meet up with your egg and BAM, you're pregnant. But a man's orgasm does involve spurting mucho sperm-bearing ejaculation that makes fertilization much more likely. Some experts believe that women's orgasms also greatly increase the chance of getting pregnant because the contractions cause her uterus to be more receptive. So, although orgasm can enhance your chances, it doesn't make or break whether you will get pregnant.

Safe Sex to Stay Alive

Beyond pregnancy, being sexually active can also lead to a number of sexually transmitted infections (STIs), including HIV, the virus that causes AIDS. Given the reality of AIDS, having sex can literally be a matter of life or death. Although there are a number of infections—chlamydia, gonorrhea, and herpes—the section below focuses on HIV, the STI that's the most deadly. However, having sex safely insures protection against *all* STIs, including AIDS.

What Are HIV and AIDS?

AIDS stands for acquired immunodeficiency syndrome. It's not a single disease, but a series of illnesses that are caused by getting a virus called HIV (human immunodeficiency virus). Here's how HIV is transmitted:

- Through unprotected sex (not wearing a condom) during anal, oral, or vaginal intercourse with an infected person.
- By sharing needles with an infected person or being stuck with an infected needle. This can happen through shooting drugs into a vein or skin popping, tattooing, body piercing, or in a health care setting (for example, if a doctor punctures herself with an infected needle).
- An infected mother passing it to her baby during pregnancy, birth, or breastfeeding.
- From a blood transfusion with blood that's infected.

In short, the only way HIV is passed is by getting infected blood, semen, or vaginal fluid into the body.

HIV is *not* passed through:

- Casual contact (kissing, hugging, shaking hands, sitting next to an infected person).
- Using towels, plates or any other object that an infected person has touched, since the virus doesn't live outside the body more than a few seconds.
- Insects or insect bites, because they don't transmit HIV.
- Saliva, tears, or sweat. Though a small amount of HIV is in these fluids, it's so small that it can't be transmitted.

Being HIV-positive doesn't automatically mean a person has AIDS. Some people can actually live ten years or more with HIV before getting AIDS, which is the last stage of the virus. With AIDS, the body has little defense against various illnesses that it would otherwise be able to fight off.

Here is the progression of the disease:

1. The person gets infected.
2. The body puts up natural defenses, called antibodies, against the virus. During this stage, some people get flu-like symptoms as a reaction to the body trying to fight off the virus.
3. As HIV reproduces in the body, it breaks down the immune system.
4. Symptoms such as tiredness start to appear.
5. As the virus causes more damage to the immune system, the symptoms get worse, until it changes from HIV into what is called full-blown AIDS.

When women are infected with HIV, symptoms often begin as gynecological problems, such as pelvic inflammatory disease (PID), genital herpes, yeast infections that keep coming back, cervical cancer, and genital warts. Because these are common ailments that any woman can get—HIV-infected or not—some women who have these symptoms and *are* infected with HIV don't know it. Also, most of these problems are not part of the government's "official" definition of AIDS, so when women talk to a health care professional about these symptoms, even the doctor isn't clued in that the person is HIV-infected.

What's more, although most people infected with HIV are men who contracted the virus from another man or by using IV drugs, the numbers of HIV-infected women are growing rapidly. Did you know that:

• AIDS is the fourth leading cause of death among women aged twenty-five to forty-four.
• AIDS is the first leading cause of death among African American women aged twenty-five to forty-four.
• The proportion of AIDS cases among female adolescents has more than doubled from 14 percent to 32 percent since 1987.

Several factors contribute to these frightening statistics. The main cause: though women do contract HIV using intravenous (IV) drugs, most women who are infected contracted the virus from a man during sexual intercourse. It's important to note that it's much more likely for a woman to get HIV from an infected man during sexual intercourse than vice versa. (Vaginal secretions contain lower concentrations of the virus than blood or sperm.)

Because we are at greater risk of contracting HIV, all women need to be extra cautious about protecting ourselves—by either abstaining from sexual intercourse or having sex safely using a condom.

TOP FIVE MYTHS ABOUT AIDS

Most of us know by now that anyone can get AIDS. But still many of us believe in some of the AIDS myths like these:

Myth: Only gay men or drug users get it.

Fact: If that were true then heterosexuals—especially women—wouldn't be the fastest rising group infected with HIV, according to the Centers for Disease Control.

Myth: You can tell when someone has HIV.

Fact: Yeah, right. That's like saying you can look at someone and tell what her middle name is! People with HIV can look and feel perfectly healthy. The only way to know for sure if someone is infected is to take a blood test.

Myth: If you know your partner well, you'll know if he's infected.

Fact: So wrong. First no matter how well you know your partner, you can't know exactly what he did before he met you or who he slept with. And let's face it, some people are more concerned about their image than the truth. So you may not get an honest answer even if you ask all the right questions. Partners who have been married for decades have been known to contract HIV. Knowing someone isn't a protection against infection. Unless you've seen the results of a blood test, the only way to be safe is to abstain from intercourse or use a condom with Nonoxynol-9 every time you have oral, vaginal, or anal sex.

Myth: Asians don't get AIDS.

Fact: Because people tend to have stereotypical images of Asians as "model citizens" who do no wrong, they tend to get overlooked when it comes to discussing AIDS. While it's true that Asians only make up about less than one percent of all AIDS cases (compared to 49 percent for whites, 32 percent for Blacks, 17 percent for Latinos, and .2 percent for Native Americans), they have the fastest rate of growth for total AIDS cases, and are doubling every two years.

Says Quynh Dang, an HIV educator with the Multicultural AIDS Coalition in Boston: "Statistics on Asians with AIDS are misleading because we are not well documented. Because AIDS is such a stigma in the Asian community, some families, and even some doctors, would rather put cause of death as something else like cancer."

More facts to refute the myth:

- Many Asians leave the country before being documented.
- Though families are overwhelmingly supportive of relatives dying from AIDS, it's not openly discussed.
- Few clinics offer AIDS testing with health care professionals that speak Asian languages.
- The larger Asian community is unaccustomed to openly discussing sexuality, and people assume they are sexually conservative. But Asians, like every other ethnic group, practice the same risky behavior.
- Asians weren't even included in AIDS statistics until 1989.

Myth: There's no point in getting tested, because once you have HIV, you just get sick and die.

Fact: Many people who suspect they've been infected with HIV, don't get tested because they're scared to find out the truth. But for someone who is positive, it's much better to find out as early as possible. HIV is not a death sentence. There are early treatments, including changes in diet, that can prolong the life of an infected person.

While it's not necessary for everyone to be tested, anyone who answers yes to any of the following should seriously consider getting tested:

- Have you had unprotected sexual contact (oral, anal, or vaginal sex) under any circumstances?
- Have you shared needles with someone (for shooting drugs, skin popping, body piercing, or tattooing)?
- Are you pregnant?
- Do you suspect you put yourself at risk for HIV, and would you be relieved to know one way or the other if you're infected?
- If you suspect you put yourself at risk for HIV, and you found out you were positive, would you change your behavior? (Such as decide not to get pregnant.)

An HIV test should be taken at least six months after your last possible exposure to the virus. (It can take up to six months after someone was infected for the virus to show on a test.) That means if you had unprotected sex in January you should get tested in June.

There are two types of testing:

CONFIDENTIAL: This is typically done in a doctor's office or hospital, where the results of the test are kept in your medical records.

ANONYMOUS: This is usually done at a clinic, and you're only known as a number so only you know the results (unless you decide to share them with others).

If you do decide to get tested, be sure to get counseling beforehand about HIV, your risk, and what you would do if your results turn up positive. Also know that nobody can make you take a test, and your consent is required.

What Is Safe(r) Sex?

The only way to have completely safe sex is to avoid any exchange of bodily fluid (blood, semen, vaginal fluid) through intercourse and open cuts and sores. Sex with a condom is called safer sex because it still involves some small risk of getting a sexually transmitted infection, including HIV. The only way to be 100 percent safe is to not have sex. And, by the way, having safer sex will also keep you from getting pregnant.

But safer sex doesn't mean the end of intimacy or sexual pleasure. It does, however, require some thought and planning. Safer sex is:

- Dry kissing
- Hugging and massage
- Having sexual intercourse, anal or vaginal, with a condom.
- Having oral sex with a condom.
- Plus a whole range of other sensual activities that don't involve unprotected intercourse.

Dang suggests looking at wearing condoms like wearing seatbelts. "Some people wear seatbelts all the time, some only on the highway, and some people never wear them," she explains. "It's up to the individual to determine what amount of risk is acceptable."

To really consider how much risk you're willing to take, Dang suggests asking yourself a few questions:

- What do you want for your future?
- What would you do to get there?
- Would you be able to accomplish your goals if you got pregnant or became HIV positive?

How To Practice Safer Sex

If you've made the decision to have sex, please do it safely. Plan ahead—realistically not romantically. Dang warns that too many teens are caught up in the idea of the "perfect moment." But perfect moments exist only in movies, and hoping for them will only lead to disappointment—or worse.

"You won't know exactly what to do at every moment," she states, "and everything won't go perfectly."

So acquaint yourself ahead of time with safer sex protection, which includes condoms, spermicides, dental dams, and latex gloves. Dang thinks that going on a safer sex scavenger hunt is the best way to break the embarrassment barrier. Here's what you do:

1. Go to two or three drug stores and write down the price and brand of a few types of condoms, spermicides, etc.

2. Purchase the ones you think you'll use.

3. Take them home and start experimenting with them. Put a condom over your hand to see how much it stretches so that when he tells you "it's too tight" or "I don't have any feeling" you know the truth.

4. Compare notes with your friends who are also having sex.

5. Keep the condoms in a handy place.

6. Know how to unwrap the wrapper, apply the spermicide, and roll the condom on.

"I am not going to put myself in any kind of danger, because I love myself; I'm important."

SHARON, 16, TEANECK, NEW JERSEY

The first time I had sex I most definitely insisted that the guy use a condom. We had been together two years, and I didn't have to force him to use it, because he loves me. I feel that if a guy doesn't want to wear one then he's not respecting you. You don't get yourself into anything with anybody who's not going to respect you.

I make my partner use a condom mainly because you have to be safe. I even think your partner should use a condom *and* you should use a contraceptive. There are a lot of things going around now, and you have to be safe to live now in this society. I don't care who the person is—I don't care if it's Michael Jackson—I am not going to put myself in any kind of danger, because I love myself; I'm important.

A lot of my friends from age eleven to nineteen have gotten pregnant or gotten an STD, and they tell me about the situation. They say things like, "I was so into him, I just couldn't stop." I was like, "Look, you have to stop; just one time could change your whole life."

You have to make sure you're very careful about what's going on. There's a lot of men out here who will try to sweet talk you. You just have to ignore that stuff, because they will say they love you right up until it's time for you to have sex with them. As soon as you open up your legs for them, they don't want anything to do with you anymore. You have to be aware of those things.

Some guys try to slip their way in without a condom by saying it doesn't feel good to use one. What you have to do is stop the whole situation. And before you even get into the situation, you make sure that guy is going to use one. You don't just say OK, because you're putting yourself in danger. Even if it's getting hot and heavy, you have to put the brakes on completely, you have to be able to control yourself. If you're going to be woman enough to have sex you have to be able to control yourself. You have to be able to say, "Look, I'm not going to do this. I love myself."

My philosophy is that men come and go, but lives don't come and go. You don't have another chance on life, because once you get HIV, you're going to die eventually. I know it's hard for a girl to shut a guy down, but you have to; you have to say no. As my mom used to say, "Don't let your hormones get you in trouble. They will write you a check that you cannot cash."

TALKING BACK: WAYS TO GET HIM TO PUT ON A CONDOM

He: Condoms aren't romantic.

She: Just give me those condoms, and I'll show you how romantic they can be.

He: You don't trust me.

She: It's not a matter of trust, it's a matter of health.

He: I don't use condoms.

She: I don't have sex without a condom.

He: But I love you.

She: I love you too. But being in love can't protect us.

He: I *know* I'm clean; I haven't had sex with anyone in years.

She: Thanks for telling me, but let's use a condom anyway.

He: I can't feel a thing when I wear one.

She: I'm sorry if it makes you lose sensation. Maybe I can provide a little extra stimulation to make up.

He: I'll lose my erection by the time I get it on.

She: Here, let me help you.

He: Just this once.

She: Once is all it takes.

He: I don't have one.

She: I do.

He: What are you doing with that? Did you plan to seduce me?

She: I always carry one, because I care about myself. I made sure I had one tonight because I care about you.

He: I'm not using one. Forget it.

She: Let's put off having sex until we can work out our differences.

STUDENTS ORGANIZING STUDENTS (SOS) OF NEW YORK CITY

SOS is usually a cry for help, but in this case it's a call to action. The young women in SOS, or Students Organizing Students, are getting informed, taking charge, and hitting the streets. "Advocating for young women's health" (as their slogan says), SOSers are committed activists in all areas of women's health. For instance, they put out the latest information on contraception, hold workshops on gender discrimination, and demonstrate for women's right to choose abortion. But first they have to get prepared.

"In addition to research and advocacy," says SOS director of programs Anna Maria Nieves, "SOS programs give young people the awareness and leadership skills they need to become an active force in their communities." Young women get those skills by becoming SKILLees in the SKILLS program (SKILLS stands for Students Keeping Issues Linked Leadership Semester). Participants spend six hours a week for up to sixteen weeks either learning about specific issues in their communities or gathering community-organizing skills. "The program was designed to help low-income high school students, students of color, and women in particular believe in their power and to develop the tools and self-esteem to combat the problems that affect their health," explains Anna Maria.

SKILLS graduate Rosslyn Wuchinich, eighteen, and the president of the Women's Issues Group at Hunter High in New York City, found out about SOS at a pro-choice rally and looked them up in the phone book to find out about an internship. "I wanted to be with someone who worked in community organizing as a career and could teach me a lot," recalls Rosslyn. During her summer stint she worked as an intern and researched women and AIDS for a pamphlet to be distributed by SOS and completed her SKILLS training. "We mainly put together a pamphlet on teen pregnancy based on what we learned," says Rosslyn. "I got a general understanding of organizing and discipline, delegating, meeting deadlines, and coalition building with other groups who have similar goals."

A special SKILLS program called AWARE (Asian Women's Access to Resources and Education) was recently introduced for young Asian women because of their specific cultural needs. "AWARE is sort of like SKILLS but deals with Asian women's culture, like how people stereotype us as subservient," says fifteen-year-old Angela Tong, a sophomore in New York City. Another misconception that turned AWARE participant Angela around was believing that AIDS doesn't affect young Asian women. "Before, I was naive and didn't know how to protect myself. My parents are so traditional [Chinese] they'd never talk to me about this."

Since hooking up with AWARE, Angela believes that keeping matters such as contraception and HIV hush-hush doesn't work any more. "There's a crisis out there, and it's a touchy topic, but you have to talk about it to ensure there's a future."

For more information about chapters in New York City, Northampton (Massachusetts), and Atlanta, contact SOS at (212) 977-6710.

Where to Turn

Recommended Reading
Avoiding Pregnancy

Changing Bodies, Changing Lives, Ruth Bell, Random House, 1988. The chapter devoted to birth control and pregnancy explains in detail the various birth control options available and how to get them.

Girltalk: All The Stuff Your Sister Never Told You, Carol Weston, Harper-Perennial, 1992. In this book there is a section on birth control and pregnancy that confronts every girl's hang-ups, fears, and questions regarding these issues. The author even has some suggestions about what to say should your boyfriend complain about using a condom.

A Woman's Book of Choices: Abortion, Menstrual Extraction, RU-486, Rebecca Chalker and Carol Downer, Four Walls Eight Windows, 1992.

Avoiding Disease

100 Questions and Answers About AIDS: What You Need To Know Now, Michael Ford, Beech Tree, 1993.

Lynda Madaras Talks to Teens About AIDS, Lynda Madaras, Newmarket Press (New York), 1988.

Teens With AIDS Speak Out, Mary Kittredge, Julian Messner, Simon & Schuster, 1992. This book explains what AIDS is, how it spreads, and what teens have to say about an illness they know might end their lives.

Support Groups and Organizations
Avoiding Pregnancy

Advocates for Youth, 1025 Vermont Avenue NW, Suite 200, Washington, D.C. 20005; (202) 347-5700. Provides pamphlets for teens, by teens, on a number of topics including contraception.

The Alan Guttmacher Institute, 120 Wall Street, New York, NY 10005; (212) 248-1111. For statistics regarding birth control, pregnancy, and abortion.

Best Friends Foundation, 2000 N Street NW, Suite 201, Washington, DC 20036-2601; (202) 822-9266. The Best Friends Program offers a curriculum to help girls gain self-respect, make positive decisions, and support each other in postponing sex and rejecting drug use. Provides monthly group discussions, one-on-one mentoring, discussions with role models, weekly aerobics classes, and honors all the girls at the end-of-year recognition ceremony. Best Friends has been introduced into schools in Virginia, Wisconsin, New Jersey, Washington, and Maryland. If you're interested in having Best Friends join your school, write to above address or call.

Federation of Feminist Women's Health Centers, 633 East 11th Ave., Eugene, OR 97401; (503) 344-0966. The FWHC offers professional abortion services, pregnancy testing and counseling, innovative well-woman gynecological care, and birth control services. Phone counselors are available to answer a wide range of health questions and concerns, including abortion and birth control, and provide referrals for health services. Call for clinic in your area.

National Abortion And Reproductive Rights Action League (NARAL), 1156 15th Street NW, Suite 700, Washington, DC 20005; (202) 973-3000. The political arm of the grassroots pro-choice movement, NARAL also offers information about sex education, family planning, and freedom from coercive reproductive policies.

National Women's Health Network, 514 Tenth Street NW, Suite 400, Washington, DC 20004; (202) 347-1140. Can provide information about birth control methods.

Planned Parenthood Federation of America, 810 Seventh Ave., New York, NY 10019; (212) 541-7800 or (800) 829-7732. Planned Parenthood provides a wide range of services including birth control, pregnancy tests, abortions, and counseling. Call (800) 230-PLAN for a clinic in your area.

Teen Aid, Inc., 723 East Jackson, Spokane, WA 99207; (509) 482-2868. Teen Aid, Inc. has developed sex education materials that place sexuality in the context of commitment, responsibility, and family. Teen Aid, Inc. makes available pamphlets that present a strong message to teen girls to abstain until marriage.

Avoiding Disease

American Red Cross National Headquarters, 430 17th Street NW, Washington, DC 20006; (703) 206-7130. The American Red Cross sponsors an African-American HIV/AIDS Program that presents culturally affirming HIV/AIDS information to African-American youth. They also have a Hispanic HIV/AIDS program that emphasizes dialogue among youth and their families. For more information, contact your local Red Cross chapter or call the national office.

American Social Health Association, P.O. Box 13827, Research Triangle Park, NC 27709; (800) 227-8922. ASHA works to prevent and control all sexually transmitted infections. You can get a wide array of pamphlets on how to protect yourself against chlamydia, herpes, PID, HIV/AIDS, gonorrhea, a pamphlet written for teens, and one on how to talk to your doctor about sexual health.

Asian AIDS Project, 785 Market Street, Suite 420, San Francisco, CA 94103; (415) 227-0946. Provides posters, pamphlets, and booklets on AIDS (Cambodian, Chinese, Filipino, Japanese, Korean, Laotian, and Vietnamese) and a safe sex kit in a Chinese good luck envelope, which contains two condoms, Nonoxynol-9 lubricant, safe sex instructions in English and Chinese, and needle cleaning and condom use instructions in English with pictures.

Blacks Educating Blacks About Sexual Health Issues (BEBASHI), 1233 Locust Street, Suite 401, Philadelphia, PA 19107; (215) 546-4140. BEBASHI is a community based program which provides information and educational services about sexual health issues, particularly HIV infection and AIDS, to the African American and Hispanic communities. The Youth Program emphasizes sexual responsibility, decision making, and abstinence.

HEALTHWATCH, 3020 Glenwood Road, Brooklyn, NY 11210; (718) 434-5311. Provides accurate, relevant, culturally sensitive information, materials, and activities designed to decrease the risk of HIV infection for women and youth.

The Life Foundation, P.O. Box 88980, Honolulu, HI 96830-8980; (808) 971-2437. Provides a wide range of client services, including assistance with social benefit programs and referrals to community resources, a legal clinic, intervention services, education, public information, risk reduction, and prevention to Pacific Islanders and other people of color with HIV infection and AIDS.

Minority AIDS Project, 5149 West Jefferson Boulevard, Los Angeles, CA 90016; (213) 936-4949. MAP is the first community-based HIV/AIDS organization established and managed by people of color. It offers a wide range of services and programs including HIV anonymous testing, housing, support groups, counseling, youth employment and training program as well as "Say Sister" outreach to women of color.

Multicultural AIDS Coalition, Douglass Park, 801-B Tremont Street, Boston, MA 02118; (617) 442-1622. MAC's Community Resource Center contains materials covering a broad range of issues about HIV and AIDS, specifically for and about people of color.

The Names Project Foundation, 310 Townsend Street, Suite 310, San Francisco, CA 94107; (415) 882-5500. Young people who have had friends, family, or teachers die from AIDS can make a quilt panel in their honor to include in the gigantic 20,000-panel memorial quilt shown in cities throughout the U.S.

National Association of People With AIDS (NAPWA), 1413 K Street NW, Washington, DC 20005; (800) 92-NAPWA. NAPWA is a national "voice" for people in the United States infected and affected with HIV/AIDS. It offers HIV/AIDS prevention and treatment materials.

National Institute of Allergy and Infectious Diseases, Office of Communications, Building 31, Room 7A-50, Bethesda, MD 20892-2520; (301) 496-5717. The Institute provides information sheets on STDs including vaginal infections, HIV and AIDS, genital herpes, hepatitis, chlamydia, and pelvic inflammatory disease. (For information about clinical trials for HIV and AIDS, call the AIDS Clinical Trials Information Service: (800) TRIALS-A.)

National Native Americans AIDS Prevention Center, 2100 Lakeshore Avenue, Suite A, Oakland, CA 94606; (510) 444-2051. The Center can lead you to an enormous array of Native specific HIV/AIDS information, including books, brochures, posters, videotapes, and a list of organizations that offer special programs for Native Americans interested in AIDS prevention.

Novela Health Education, University of Washington 359932, 1001 Broadway, Suite 100, Seattle, Washington 98122; (800) 677-4799. Novela Health Education has pioneered the use of the "novela" (mini-drama) format since 1987 to present information about AIDS and STDs to Spanish-speaking people. The novela is available in print and in radio format.

Hotlines
Avoiding Disease

(800) 4-AIDS-KIT: AIDS Prevention Project Office offers a free FIRST AIDS KIT which will tell you all about AIDS and how not to get it.

ASHA Healthline: (800) 972-8500. American Social Health Association offers free publications about sexual health communication.

Herpes Resource Center: (800) 230-6039. The hotline answers questions about herpes and offers referrals for support groups. At this number you can also request free printed information about this infection.

National AIDS Hotline: (800) 342-2437 (English, 7 days/week, 24 hours/day); (800) 344-7432 (Spanish, 7 days/week, 24 hours/day). Hotlines serves as a primary resource for HIV and AIDS information, counseling and service referrals for the U.S. Counselors provide information on HIV infection, its prevention and transmission, testing and treatments.

National Native American AIDS Prevention Center: (800) 283-2437. Provides printed materials and information about AIDS and AIDS prevention in the Native American community.

National STD Hotline: (800) 227-8922. Provides free information about prevention of sexually transmitted infections and HIV testing and provides clinic referrals.

Project Inform Treatment Hotline: (800) 822-7422. Provides treatment information and referral for HIV-infected individuals. Information on clinical trials.

Youth Crisis Hotline: (800) HIT-HOME. Counseling and referrals for HIV and AIDS, substance abuse, homelessness, sexual abuse, pregnancy.

CHAPTER 7

BABIES ARE NICE, BUT...

Every year over 1 million teenagers get pregnant. And by age twenty-one, half of all teen girls will have become pregnant at least once. Most who do get pregnant will go on to become mothers. What does this mean?

For one, it's clear that most young women aren't using birth control correctly (or at all) every time they have intercourse. Even though the overwhelming majority don't want to get pregnant or don't plan on it, they either aren't facing up to the reality that it could happen to them or don't have enough information about how easy it is to get pregnant. Remember, half of all pregnancies happen within six months of the first experience with intercourse.

Pregnancy—whether it ends in abortion, adoption, or parenthood—signals a complete life change. A young woman who chooses to have and keep the baby finds her life tied up with two others, the father's and the child's. Think about it. Who was your last boyfriend? How long did that relationship last? And the one before that? Now imagine having to deal with an old boyfriend for the next twenty years, or the rest of your child's life. Or worse, having a baby with someone who abandons his responsibility altogether. Not a pretty picture in either case. This is what we risk for one night of unprotected sex—even just once.

The Biology of Making a Baby

It's very important to understand the process of conception and the nine months of pregnancy—whether you're planning to have a baby or to avoid having a baby, at least for now. The key point here is that we all came into the world the same way: a sperm-fertilized egg implanted itself in the lining of our mother's uterus and developed into a fetus. A sperm can fertilize an egg in one of several ways:

147

- If you have sexual intercourse with a male (when his penis is in your vagina), you don't use any birth control, and he ejaculates.

- If you have sexual intercourse with a male and he ejaculates, but your birth control method breaks or doesn't work.

- If a male ejaculates near the opening of your vagina and the sperm makes its way up (whether you're unprotected or your birth control fails).

- If you have intercourse with a male and he begins to ejaculate before he removes his penis (whether you're unprotected or your birth control fails you).

All it takes is one sperm to swim through the vaginal canal and uterus to meet the egg (released into the fallopian tube during ovulation). Once the sperm penetrates the egg, in the fallopian tube, the two cells merge into one, causing fertilization. The new cell, called a *zygote* (ZIE-goat), begins to produce new cells of its own, and when these new cells number sixteen, the zygote transforms into an *embryo* (EM-bree-oh). The embryo contains all the genetic codes necessary to create a new human being, with all its inherited features from hair and skin color to certain personality traits. If the cells divide to create two embryos, they will become identical twins. Or if two eggs get fertilized at the same time, they will grow as fraternal twins (siblings born at the same time, but not exactly alike).

The fertilized egg takes about six days to reach the uterus. There it attaches itself to the lining, a process called *implantation*, and the embryo's

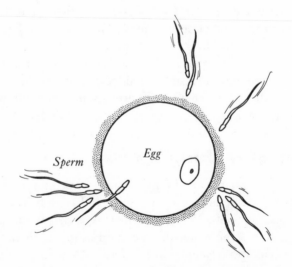

All it takes is one sperm to fertilize an egg and conceive a fetus.

life-support develops. The *placenta* (plah–SENT-ah) provides the embryo with nourishment and oxygen by borrowing from the mother's system. The embryo's blood supply is brought in through the *umbilical cord*, which connects the placenta to the embryo. By the end of the seventh week of pregnancy, the embryo develops into a *fetus*, and grows for another 33 weeks, a total of about nine months.

* One sperm is 2,000 times smaller than a woman's egg.

* A miscarriage occurs when a woman's body ends a pregnancy before the baby can survive on its own. Miscarriages usually happen during the first three months of pregnancy.

* Because the uterine lining is being used to house the fetus, it isn't shed. So during pregnancy, women don't get their periods.

* When a woman reaches the end of her fertile years, she stops producing eggs (ovulating) and stops getting her period. This stage, called *menopause*, usually begins when women hit their late forties or fifties, and like puberty, can take several years to complete.

Nine Months Till Baby

Full-term pregnancy is a nine-month process in which the fertilized egg develops into a baby able to survive outside the mother's womb (uterus). Pregnancy experts have broken down the nine-month period into three three-month periods called trimesters (sort of like the school year). Here's what happens to the fetus (unborn baby) during that time:

FIRST TRIMESTER (1–3 months): The first signs of pregnancy are a missed period, fatigue, breast tenderness, and possibly nausea. During this time a woman's body is building up to support a totally dependent fetus. The fetus develops a heart, digestive tract, circulatory system, arms, legs, bone, and the beginning of fingers and toes. At the end of this period, its weight is about a half ounce and length is three inches.

SECOND TRIMESTER (4–6 months): By the fourth month, the mother may already be "showing" her pregnancy because her belly begins to stick out. The fetus is sucking and swallowing, has fingers, toes, spine, brain, some hair growth, and can open its eyes. At this point, a doctor can run tests to determine whether the fetus is a boy or girl.

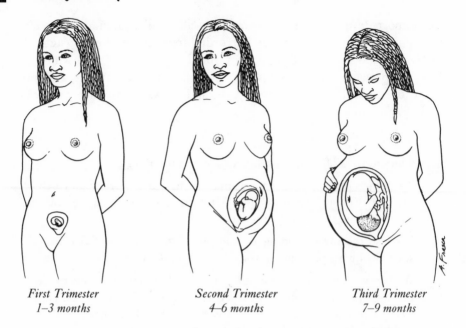

| *First Trimester* | *Second Trimester* | *Third Trimester* |
| *1–3 months* | *4–6 months* | *7–9 months* |

The nine-month pregnancy is divided into three-month intervals, called trimesters.

THIRD TRIMESTER (7–9 months): Some babies are born before they reach the full nine months in their mother's womb, which means they are premature. This trimester the fetus' brain, lungs, and body grow rapidly. It can also hear, see, taste, feel, suck its thumb, cry, and hiccup.

When the baby is about to be born, the mother will go into labor and her cervix will dilate (open) to allow the baby to pass out of the uterus, through the vaginal canal and out into the world, usually head first. If there are problems with getting the baby out through the birth canal, or if the baby is in distress, doctors may decide to perform a *cesarean section*. This is when a doctor makes an incision through the mother's lower abdomen and removes the baby from the uterus. The average baby weighs 7½ pounds and is 20 inches long.

What to Do If You're Pregnant

If you do become pregnant, before you decide to become a parent, ask yourself these questions provided by Carole Baker, executive director of the National Alliance for Optional Parenthood:

- What do I want out of life for myself? How would having a child interfere with my growth and development?

- Could I handle a child and a job at the same time? Going to school? Would having a child interfere with my educational or career goals?
- Am I ready to give up my freedom and social life and spend more time at home? Will I miss my free time and privacy?
- Can I afford to support a child? Do I know how much money it takes to raise a child?
- Do I want to raise a child in the neighborhood where I live now? Am I willing to move? Can I afford to move?
- Am I having a child to show how mature I am, to prove that I'm a "real" woman, or to make the father stay with me?
- Do I expect a child to make my life happy or be an ego-booster?
- Am I patient enough to deal with the noise and the confusion and the twenty-four-hour-a-day responsibility?
- Will I take things out on the child if I lose my temper?
- How will I take care of my child's health and safety?
- Does my partner want to have a child? What would happen if we separated after having a child?
- What if I have a child and find out I made the wrong decision?

If you find yourself pregnant, you have three options: getting an abortion, giving the baby up for adoption, or keeping the baby.

Abortion

Abortion is a medical procedure that ends a pregnancy. Almost half of all teen pregnancies are terminated by abortion, most of them with a parent's knowledge and support, according to an Alan Guttmacher Institute study. The same study cited the most common reasons that adolescent women want to obtain abortions are:

- Concern that having a baby would change their lives too much.
- Feeling too immature to take care of a baby.
- Lack of finances to support a child.

Though it's a relatively simple and safe operation, deciding whether to get an abortion is not always easy. Mixed feelings about readiness to have a child, fear of medical procedures, and pressure from conservative parents or groups that tell us abortion is an immoral choice, make the decision even tougher. Having correct information about abortion is key in determining whether it is the right choice for any of us.

What Is Abortion?

There are several different types of abortions that doctors can perform, depending on how far along you are in your pregnancy. Regardless of which one you get, there are several steps the medical practitioner will take before performing the abortion. First she will give you a pregnancy test just to make sure you are pregnant. She will also take a blood test for anemia and other possible problems, and then she will give you a pelvic exam. Once she has determined how many weeks pregnant you are, she will decide which method to perform. The two most common are the vacuum suction and the D&E.

Most vacuum suction abortions are done within the first three months of pregnancy. Under local or general anesthesia, the doctor inserts an instrument, called a speculum, into your vagina to keep it held open (the same instrument she uses to get a pap smear during a gynecological exam). She then dilates your cervix and places the suction tube (a clear plastic tube with a suction tip) into your uterus. As the doctor moves the tube around, the machine cleans out the uterus, including the placenta and excess lining. Finally she gently moves a utensil called a curette along the walls of your uterus to be sure there's no excess tissue. The entire procedure takes five to ten minutes.

Unfortunately many young women wait until after their first trimester of pregnancy to decide to get an abortion, at which stage a D&E is the method required. The reasons are absolutely understandable, such as fear of telling parents, underestimating the amount of planning it involves, not knowing the added complications of a second trimester abortion, and simply not having the money in time. However, waiting until the second trimester makes getting an abortion more physically and emotionally complicated.

A D&E (Dilation and Evacuation) is done within twelve to twenty-four weeks of pregnancy and can take place in a clinic, doctor's office, or (more commonly) the hospital. Though it's similar to the vacuum suction, D&E is more complicated because the fetus is larger and requires your cervix to open wider. To do this, a doctor will insert a laminaria stick into your vagina the day before the operation. The laminaria stick is a small piece of sterilized seaweed that gradually stretches the cervix open and is removed just before the abortion. The procedure is done under general anesthesia and takes up to twenty minutes. The doctor uses suction as with the vacuum method, but since the fetus is bigger, it takes longer.

After both procedures, you will go to a recovery room. Many young women feel fine afterwards, but still require assistance to get home, about an hour after recovery. Others begin experiencing cramping (like having your period), especially after a D&E. The doctor will prescribe antibiotics to prevent infection and a non-aspirin pain medication, and will send you home with specific instructions on how to take care of yourself. For about a week to ten days after the abortion most women bleed and continue to have cramps (which lessen daily).

Here are some rules to follow for abortion aftercare:

- Take your temperature every morning and night for five days after the abortion to see that it doesn't go higher than 100.5 degrees. If it does, call the doctor.
- Be aware of how much you're bleeding. It shouldn't be heavier than your normal period. However, it may stop and start or last for up to a week.
- Expect a normal period in four to six weeks.
- Any severe pain, long-term bleeding, heavy bleeding, or unusual or foul-smelling discharge should be reported to your doctor right away.
- Don't do any of the following for *two weeks* after an abortion: take a bath, swim, use tampons, have intercourse, or douche. Showering and normal washing are fine, but putting anything into your vagina could cause infection.
- Don't do anything strenuous for a few days or as long you feel necessary. Get plenty of rest and sleep, lay off the exercising and heavy lifting.
- Get a checkup two weeks after your abortion to make sure the procedure was successful (that you are not still pregnant and that you are in good health).
- Research and obtain information on birth control methods and begin to use them as soon as the doctor recommends that you're able to.

Where to Get It?

Most abortions are performed in a doctor's office, clinic, or hospital, usually by doctors or physician's assistants. However, it's best to pick a physician or medical professional who is licensed by the state and who can admit patients to a nearby hospital in case of emergency.

Women who are receiving financial aid from the government (such as Medicaid) may have to go to a hospital for an abortion, depending on state laws, but will not be required to pay. Most facilities expect full payment at the time of the procedure. When finding out how much an abortion costs at a facility, make sure it covers all lab work, medications, a follow-up exam, or any other charges necessary for the procedure. Some medical insurance companies cover abortion, but many do not. If you are strapped for cash, you may be able to get assistance from the facility. Generally costs for a clinic abortion are $300 for first trimester abortion, $525 for second trimester at sixteen weeks, and $1,000 for twenty weeks.

BEWARE: Some anti-abortion groups have set up phony abortion clinics to lure women into changing their minds. They are listed in the Yellow Pages under "abortion," but their goal is to scare us into keeping an unwanted child. New laws have also passed that prohibit right-wing anti-choice groups from harassing or blocking women from getting abortions. This is a serious offense and people have gone to jail for prohibiting women's right to exercise their choice. If you experience any problems in trying to obtain an abortion, call the National Abortion Federation free of charge at (800)772-9100 or (202)667-5881 to find a clinic near you or to get information on finding a safe facility.

What Are Your Rights?

Abortion is a legal procedure that every woman in this country has a right to. In 1973 the United States Supreme Court decision called *Roe v. Wade* legalized abortion based on the idea that a woman has the right to choose what's best for her body and her life. Since this landmark case, deaths caused by illegal abortions dropped by 90 percent, according to the National Abortion Federation. Having access to abortion has meant that millions of women each year don't have to go through the pain and emotional trauma of delivering a baby they cannot care for, do not want, or that would add stress to an overburdened family.

Unfortunately, since *Roe v. Wade*, there are anti-choice groups that want to take away all women's right to abortion by outlawing it. Though the majority of people in America support a woman's right of choice, the antics and strong financial backing of groups like Operation Rescue have put pressure on politicians to limit funding and access, as well as on health care providers who perform abortions. We all must respect that abortion is a difficult decision and that many women will not opt for it based on moral beliefs. However, imposing those views on others through violence or harassment is illegal.

In some states anti-abortion groups have forced government officials to pass laws that limit any woman under eighteen access to abortion. These limits include:

- Parental notification or consent of either one or two parents. In some cases minors can appeal to a judge, who then decides whether or not to allow an abortion.
- A waiting period of up to several days before obtaining an abortion, which requires two trips to the abortion clinic. This can be a huge obstacle to young women living in counties or states that don't have

abortion facilities and must travel several hours or stay overnight to reach one.

• Mandatory counseling, which is meant to discourage abortion.

In an ideal world we would all like to go to our parents for guidance during stressful times, especially when dealing with something as heavy as pregnancy and abortion. But we don't all have understanding parents, and even those of us who do don't feel comfortable sharing our deepest feelings at the time we're experiencing them. One young woman, Rebecca Bell from Indiana, died from an illegal abortion because of mandatory parental notice. Though she had a good relationship with her parents, she found it too difficult to tell them. Others of us are fearful of violence or other abusive consequences involved in telling our parents. According to the National Abortion and Reproductive Rights Action League, 30 percent of minors who didn't tell their parents about an abortion had experienced violence, feared violence, or felt they might be forced to leave home.

Because the laws vary from state to state, and because they often change, it's best to check with these agencies for information on your specific state:

National Abortion and Reproductive Rights Action League (NARAL),
1156 15th St. NW, Suite 700
Washington, D.C. 20005
(202) 973-3000

National Abortion Federation
1436 U St. NW, Suite 103
Washington, D.C. 20009
(800) 772-9100 or (202) 667-5881

Center for Reproductive Law and Policy
120 Wall St., New York, NY 10005
(212) 514-5534

• •

• Four in ten teen pregnancies end in abortion.
• The teenage abortion rate among women of color is much higher than among white women (75 per 1,000 women aged fifteen to nineteen, versus 36 per 1,000), because they have more unintended pregnancies.
• Sixty-one percent of minors have abortions with a parent's knowledge; 45 percent of parents are told by their daughter.

(Alan Guttmacher Institute)

• •

Adoption as an Option

Making a decision about whether to keep a baby is agonizing. You must ask yourself the same questions above provided by Carole Baker. But it will be harder to make the final decision. "When a young woman feels assured that the baby will be better cared for by someone else, she knows she's done the right thing by giving it up," states Ellen Pinderhughes, Ph.D., a psychology and human development professor at Vanderbilt University in Nashville who specializes in issues of adoption. However, just because the baby will be under someone else's care doesn't mean the biological mother won't ever see her or him again. As adoption has changed over the years, more birth mothers are opting for open adoptions rather than closed. Here's the difference:

CLOSED ADOPTION: The biological mother gives the child up and has no contact with her or him unless the mother agrees to be contacted when the child is eighteen or twenty-one (depending on the state laws). These are still the most common because they protect the privacy of the birth mother and give both mother and child the ability to make a fresh start.

OPEN ADOPTION: The biological mother gives the child up, but makes specific agreements with the adoptive family to be involved in the child's life. More birth mothers are choosing this because they want some level of contact with their child. Without contact, they find it difficult to go on not knowing how the child's life is progressing. The child is helped by knowing who her biological mother is and has access to any health information regarding that side of her family.

"Any mother deciding which kind of adoption she wants should consider how involved she wants to be in the baby's life," says Pinderhughes. "That includes asking whether she wants to know about the child's life and the child to know about hers." With any adoption agreement, the birth mother can insist on the kind of relationship she wants with the adoptive family and baby.

Once the baby has actually been placed with her new family, the birth mother will be left with intense feelings of loss and grief. "Sometimes these feelings are heightened with an open adoption," warns Pinderhughes, "because it interferes with the birth mother's ability to move on, though this isn't always the case." With any adoption the biological mother must come to terms with her feelings.

"Her immediate reaction will be sadness, anger, and hopelessness," says Pinderhughes. Many young women find it hard to carry on their day-to-day lives and even become depressed after an adoption. "Acceptance begins when she can make the adoption part of her life experience, but she may continue to feel sad." The sadness generally comes up around the baby's birthday, holidays, and for some women every day for the rest of their lives. "But women can also be comforted in knowing the baby is cared for by someone who can give her better care," Pinderhughes states.

"I gave my baby up for a reason—so I could get an education and do certain things I otherwise wouldn't be able to do. If I don't do those things, I've given him up for nothing."

ANGELIQUE, 18, ALBUQUERQUE, NEW MEXICO

I had just turned sixteen in September and I found out I was pregnant in December, the day after Christmas. I was a sophomore.

When I told my mom, she said, "Well, you're going to have an abortion." This was a shock because my family is very religious—like born-again Christians. My father is an elder in the church. At the time I didn't think abortion was morally right, so I told her, "No, I'll just have the baby and put it up for adoption." That was my decision and that's what I did.

I was able to make the decision so quickly because it had a lot to do with the birth father. I didn't want my child to be with him. He was so mentally abusive. I also didn't have unprotected sex with him; I think he punctured the condom intentionally. I didn't want to raise a child around this kind of person.

We found the adoptive parents in kind of a weird way. Once I told my parents, they got up and announced in front of the church that I was pregnant. It was humiliating for me, but my pastor ended up sending a letter to a network of pastors explaining that they had this girl in the church who was pregnant, and one pastor told him that he knew a family that's been waiting for a baby. They ended up writing me letters and sent a picture of them and one of their horses. And I just fell in love with them. They'd been through the adoption process three or four times, but the mother always changed her mind. I was willing to work with them.

After the baby was born, it was a hard, hard thing to distance myself emotionally from the child. I'm not even sure how I did it. I had him at home for ten days, and I breastfed him. It was real hard. That was a bonding time I shared with him that nobody could take away, nobody could change. Kelly gets to raise him for the rest of his life, but she didn't get to nurture him for the first ten days that he was alive. That was something I had to do. It made it easier for me to come to terms with the whole thing.

When I was breastfeeding him I just cried and cried. I couldn't believe I was going to do this. I cried for about four months nonstop. It wasn't just me, it was my whole family. This was the first grandchild out of six kids. I'm second to the youngest. Everybody was just attached to him, but they knew what had to be done. That was the atmosphere. Everybody was upset, but everyone was trying to hide it.

They named him Sam, and I named him Theodore. I've seen him twice since he's been born. My whole family took a vacation to see him in Washington, in Seattle. We drove out there, my mom, my dad, my brother and I—what's left of us at home—and spent a week out there. And at Christmastime '93 I went up there and stayed with them. Sam's not old enough to know I'm his birth mother, but someday he will.

It hurts to see him. But I don't know what else to do. It hurts for me to see somebody else do what I so much in my heart would love to do—raise him, and have him not want for anything.

This experience has definitely made me a stronger person, in the sense that I made a decision and followed through with it. I didn't graduate, I got my GED last month. That was a disappointment, but it was something I had to do. I'm one to make plans and never follow through, and that was something I did follow through on even though it was the most painful thing I'd ever done in my life. I know I can make difficult decisions now, and live through them.

I gave him up for a reason—so I could get an education and do certain things I otherwise wouldn't be able to do. If I don't do those things, I've given him up for nothing. Of course, he will have a better life, but I did it for me and him, and if I don't do something it will have been a waste.

If you're considering adoption, or have gone through one, Pinderhughes suggests the following:

- Don't consider adoption without getting counseling, preferably at a reputable adoption agency. They will help you understand all of your options and walk you through the process to help you decide what's best for you and the baby.
- Get counseling that's unbiased. Most agencies are good and will help you make the right decision, whatever it is. But you must be comfortable. If you feel pressured in any way, take it slow or find another agency.
- Understand you're not crazy or weak for having such intense sadness around the adoption. These feelings are typical and normal, though not any less painful.
- Seek counseling after the adoption. This is very important. A support group for birth mothers is the best option because other young

women going through the same experiences will help you feel understood. You can find one through a local adoption agency.

For more information on giving a baby up for adoption, contact: National Adoption Information Clearinghouse, 5640 Nicholson Lane, Suite 300, Rockville, MD 20852; (301) 231-6512. Or the National Adoption Hotline: (202) 328-8072.

Becoming a Teen Parent

Consider the demands of school, family, friends and activities. Now multiply that by at least one hundred, and that's what it's like to become a teen mother. It's difficult to comprehend how hard it is to care for a totally helpless human being with so many needs. Even young women who do know the difficulties involved in taking care of a baby may not be equipped to actually raise a child.

Ten Reasons Why Being a Teen Mom Is Rough

1. Girls who drop out of school before or after giving birth generally don't continue their education. Even mothers who do finish high school are less likely than older mothers to go to college.

2. Teen mothers are less likely than older mothers to be employed or work at a stable, full-time job. Teen moms who do work usually have low-paying jobs that make it hard to support a family.

3. Most teen mothers go on welfare and stay on for longer periods than older moms, especially if they begin welfare early in the child's life.

4. Teen mothers have a harder time than older mothers balancing child-care and work.

5. Adolescent moms tend to have more children closer in age than women who wait to have children. In fact, one-third of teen mothers will go on to have another child while they're still teenagers, says the Mayo Clinic Family Health Book.

6. Teenage mothers tend to suffer from depression during their child's first year.

7. Most teen couples having babies aren't in a stable enough relationship to raise a child. Says James Dobbins, Ph.D., assistant dean at Wright State University in Dayton, Ohio: "In a marriage, couples share mutual friends, incomes and common goals. They are legally bound and have an emotional bond that carries them through difficult times." Teen relationships usually don't have these binding qualities, and the stress of having a baby can end them.

8. Most teens—81 percent—who give birth for the first time aren't married. But even marriage is no guarantee either: according to the Alan Guttmacher Institute, the younger a couple is when they get married, the more likely it will end in divorce.

9. "Babies born to young mothers are more likely to have health problems during childhood and more likely to be hospitalized than are those born to older mothers," says the Guttmacher study "Sex and America's Teenagers." And studies show that as children of teen mothers grow, they fall farther behind their peers in school.

10. Teenagers who give birth are much more likely to come from poor families than are teenagers who have an abortion or teenagers in general. Being a teen mother makes it even harder to pull out of poverty. Plus, only one-third of mothers under thirty not living with the father receive child support.

Who Becomes a Teen Mother?

There's no poster child for teen motherhood. Teen moms come from all races and backgrounds, but they do differ in some key ways from those young women who don't become mothers. According to Jeanne Brooks-Gunn, Ph.D., a researcher who specializes in adolescent pregnancy at Columbia University in New York, here are some traits that teenaged mothers share. They tend to:

- Be early bloomers. Girls who mature early look older, are treated as being older and tend to hang with an older crowd, all of which can lead to early sexual activity.
- Be risk-takers. During the teen years, it may feel as though nothing bad can ever happen. This feeling can lead teens to take chances—such as having unprotected sex—without considering the consequences.
- Not like school. Young women who aren't into academics, aren't motivated or who have dropped out already, get pregnant at higher rates than young women who are doing well in school.
- Live in neighborhoods with lots of single mothers. Being an unmarried teen may not seem out of the ordinary if lots of other women are raising children alone.
- Have a hard time communicating well with parents. Teens who can't go to parents for advice, talk to them about problems, or get information (especially about sex education) from them have a harder time avoiding pregnancy.

- Rely on friends for sexual education. Most teenagers don't have very good information about sex. Their advice as well as their supposed experience (which may or may not be true) can lead their friends into trouble.
- Have other big problems. Teens who drink, smoke, take drugs, ditch school or get involved in criminal activities at an early age are at risk for becoming teen mothers.

Another expert in teen pregnancy, Karin Brewster, Ph.D., a Florida State University professor who specializes in teen pregnancy, believes many young women become parents because they think it's a way to grow up fast. According to Brewster, "In communities where opportunities for social and economic advancement are limited, teens of both sexes often experience considerable pressure to 'prove' their adulthood through sexual activity and parenthood." Brewster also says that young women who don't think that getting pregnant and having a baby in the teens is an obstacle to future goals will be more likely to have unprotected sex and not care about the consequences.

"I don't want to say that I don't want my kids, but I just wish I could have waited."

LAURA, 18, MINNEAPOLIS, MINNESOTA

I lived in Olympia, Washington, and I was going to school. I wasn't pregnant then, I wasn't even sexually active. When I looked at all the teen moms I was like, "That's not going to happen to me. It *ain't* going to happen to me cause I'm smarter than that." I had things I wanted to do. I was political, protesting and talking about Indian affairs and things like that. I had everything planned out then. I was going to help the Indian people, I was going to college, all these things. I had a whole bunch of dreams then.

I started going out with my first daughter's dad when we were both fifteen. The first time I had sex with him I got pregnant. He was a virgin, and I had only had sex once before that. We didn't use a condom the first time, but the second time we did.

At first, I thought I had the flu because I was throwing up in the bathroom. I had a teacher I was real close to, and she took me to get a pregnancy test. I found out that I was pregnant, and it felt like it wasn't real. I didn't know what was going to happen to me. I couldn't believe I had a real baby growing inside of me. I was scared about telling my mom, and I was sort of mad that I was that dumb, or that young.

I was also scared of what my boyfriend would think—that he would leave me. When I told him, he just looked at me. He was waiting to see if it was

OK before he even showed any emotion. He wanted to see if I was OK about it. After that he was just happy, saying, "We're going to have a baby." He had already made the decision that we were having the baby. I didn't know what I wanted. I was really confused. I didn't really want a baby. It wasn't even in the picture at all. I was too young. I had things I wanted to do. I was only in ninth grade.

I told my mom the same day I told my boyfriend. I had thought about every way of telling her—over the phone, having someone else tell her. But I ended up writing her a two-page letter. In the letter I told her I was scared, and I didn't know what I was going to do.

She came in my room crying, and she asked if I was OK, and she told me she wouldn't make me leave, and not to be scared. She gave me a hug and said she loved me. Then she got my boyfriend, and we sat down and talked about having a baby. She said she'd stand behind me whether I decided to keep the baby or have an abortion. She hugged my boyfriend and said, "Welcome to the family." She said she was happy for us if we were happy.

I didn't tell any of my friends because we always talked about going to the same college, seeing the world, and never talked about kids. I was embarrassed to bring it up. I didn't know what they would think about me. They would think it was cute for a while, but their parents would look at me like a slut and tell them not to hang around with me. I ended up dropping out of school, not wanting anybody to see me pregnant.

Soon after she was born, the relationship didn't last between the baby's father and me. Eventually, I moved back with my mother. The baby's now two years and five months. We're close. She's in her terrible twos, so she's acting up quite a bit.

I'm also a mom again. I have a six-month-old son. Now I really don't have time for myself. From the time they get up in the morning until I put them to bed, it's an all-day job, bathing them, feeding them, clothing them, watching them, keeping them out of trouble. When I take a shower it's with my daughter. I don't even have *that* time to myself. Or when I go to the bathroom she always has to come in there, too. I don't have a minute to myself.

I live in the projects now in a three-bedroom apartment. I pay $98 a month. My mom lives with me now. My son's dad lives with me, too. I've shortened up my goals a lot. I wanted my diploma, but I'll settle for a GED. I wanted to be a doctor, but I'll settle on being a nurse. I don't want my babies living on welfare. It's been a year now, but it's too hard. I wish I were making my own money and doing my own things and had my own things, like my own car, and could afford them all by myself. That's all I want is to be self-sufficient.

I guess I should have taken more responsibility, sexually. I know now I could have waited. It would have been a lot easier. I don't want to say that I don't want my kids, but I just wish I could have waited. I didn't need all this responsibility all at one time, but now it's there.

THE MENTOR MOTHERS PROGRAM OF
INDIANAPOLIS, INDIANA

First-time teen mothers need the special guidance and support of an experienced older mother, even if it's not their own. "When I had my first son, I didn't know anything. I had my mother, but she wasn't as open-minded as my mentor," says Shavon Dabney, nineteen, teen mother of two boys, and part of the Mentor Mothers, an offshoot of the Big Sisters of Indianapolis, Indiana.

Young mothers like Shavon are matched with an adult mentor who's been through parenthood. Over the course of a year with her mentor's help, Shavon has gotten the help she desperately needed to learn better parenting and increase her self-esteem.

Starice Easley, fifteen, was shell-shocked struggling to raise two-year-old Darius while trying to manage a personal life and continuing her education. "My grades were really bad, and I wasn't getting my homework done," says Starice. But Mentor Mothers has been a big help. She and her mentor, who is twenty-six and has two kids of her own, work together to target and achieve goals—for both of them. Says Starice: "My mentor and I made a pact to do better. She's in college and I'm in high school. She would pick me up and bring me to her house so we could do our homework together. It really worked. I brought my grades up from an F to a C."

As with Starice and her mentor, everyone in the program makes a commitment to see each other at least twice a month and go to a monthly group meeting. At the meetings the young mothers learn practical information that helps them manage their lives independently. They learn about parenting tips, infant immunizations, job training, family planning, dealing with stress, and self-image. The meetings also give them a place to talk. From Shavon's point of view, being with other young mothers means a lot.

"We had a Thanksgiving potluck for all the girls and mentors. I really enjoyed that because we got to be with all kinds of different people and ate different kinds of food. It brought together people in the same situation; we were all teen mothers."

For more information or to learn how to start a similar group, contact Denise Jones, Mentor Mothers, 615 N. Alabama Street, Suite 336, Indianapolis, IN 46204; (317) 634-6102, ext. 29.

Where to Turn

Recommended Reading

Abortion

The Abortion Controversy, Carol A. Emmens, Julian Messner, Simon & Schuster, 1991. This book gives a complete view of the abortion controversy, both its pros and cons, including the history of abortion's legalization in the historic *Roe v. Wade* decision.

Changing Bodies, Changing Lives, Ruth Bell, Random House, 1988.

A Woman's Book of Choices: Abortion, Menstrual Extraction, RU-486, Rebecca Chalker and Carol Downer, Four Walls Eight Windows, 1992.

Being a Teen Parent

Everything You Need to Know About Living With Your Baby and Your Parents Under One Roof, Carolyn Simpson, Rosen Publishing Group, 1995.

Surviving Teen Pregnancy: Your Choices, Dreams and Decisions, Shirley Arthur, Morning Glory Press, 1991.

Teen Pregnancy: The Challenges We Faced, the Choices We Made (Teens Talk to Teens: What It's Like to Have a Baby), Donna and Roger Ewy, Pruett, 1984.

What to Expect When You're Expecting, Arlene Eisenberg, Heidi Murkoff, and Sandee Hathaway, Workman Publishing, 1991. The longtime bestseller.

You and Your New Baby: A Book for Young Mothers. Ginny Brinkley and Sherry Sampson, Pink Inc! Publishing, 1991. Available in Spanish.

Young and Pregnant: A Book for You, Ginny Brinkley and Sherry Sampson, Pink Inc! Publishing, 1989.

Your Baby's First Year, Jeanne Warren Lindsay, Morning Glory Press, 1991.

Support Groups and Organizations

Abortion

Catholics for a Free Choice, 1436 U St. NW, Suite 301, Washington, DC 20009; (202) 986-6093. Provides a pro-choice Catholic voice.

Federation of Feminist Women's Health Centers, 633 East 11th Ave., Eugene, OR 97401; (503) 344-0966. The FFWHC offers professional abortion services, pregnancy testing and counseling, innovative well-woman gynecological care and birth control services. Phone counselors are available Monday through Saturday during business hours to answer a wide range of health questions and concerns, including birth control, and provide referrals for health services. Call for a clinic in your area.

National Abortion Federation, 1436 U Street NW, Suite 103, Washington, DC 20009; (202) 667-5881. NAF distributes educational materials about all aspects of abortion, including fact sheets, a guide to making a decision about an unwanted pregnancy, and a bilingual (English/Spanish) guide to recognizing a safe facility.

National Abortion and Reproductive Rights Action League (NARAL), 1156 15th Street NW, Suite 700, Washington, DC 20005; (202) 973-3000. The political arm of the grass roots pro-choice movement, NARAL also offers information about sex education, family planning, and freedom from coercive reproductive policies.

National Women's Health Network, 514 Tenth Street NW, Suite 400, Washington, DC 20004; (202) 347-1140. If you need financial help with an abortion, contact the National Women's Health Network for a list of groups in your area that provide support and assistance.

Planned Parenthood Federation of America, 810 Seventh Ave., New York, NY 10019; (212) 541-7800 or (800) 829-7732. Planned Parenthood provides a wide range of services including birth control, pregnancy tests, abortions, and counseling. Planned Parenthood can provide you with information about restrictive laws, if any, in your state, and what your alternatives are if you still want to have an abortion. Call (800) 230-PLAN to find a clinic in your area.

The Religious Coalition for Reproductive Choice, 1025 Vermont Avenue NW, Suite 1130, Washington, DC 20005; (202) 628-7700. The RCAR is a coalition of thirty-five national Protestant, Jewish and other denominations and faith groups unified in their commitment to preserve reproductive freedom as an intrinsic element of religious liberty. They are the only national pro-choice organization with an initiative targeted toward women of color. The Women of Color Partnership Program serves as a vehicle through which African American, Latin American, Asian/Pacific Islander American, and Native American women can become actively involved as decision makers in the reproductive rights movement. Write for more information.

Reproductive Health Technologies Project, 1818 N Street NW, Suite 450, Washington, DC 20036; (202) 328-2200. For information about abortion, RU-486, and other forms of reproductive health technology.

Being a Teen Parent

Birth to Three, 3875 Kincaid, #15, Eugene OR 97405; (503) 484-4401. Dedicated to strengthening families by offering programs for parents of infants and children and teenage parents, the organization also offers support and education groups, operates a "warmline," and publishes a newsletter.

Center for the Improvement of Child Caring, 11331 Ventura Blvd., Suite 103, Studio City, CA 91604; (818) 980-0903. Offers a wide variety of parenting workshops nationwide, including two ethnic programs, Effective Black Parenting and Los Niños Bien Educados.

Chicanos por la Causa, Inc., 1112 East Buckeye, Phoenix, AZ 85034; (602) 257-0700. CPLC offers counseling for adolescent parents and expectant mothers as well as single parents and displaced homemakers. Participants attend classes on child rearing skills, health, self-esteem, nutrition, basic education, pre-employment, and occupational skills.

Effective Parenting Information for Children, Buffalo State College, 1300 Elmwood Ave., 340 Cassety Hall, Buffalo, NY 14222; (716) 886-6396. EPIC provides parenting education to help young people develop self-esteem, and skills necessary for facing difficult decisions throughout their lives.

First Steps, Georgia Council on Child Abuse, 1375 Peachtree St. NE, Suite 200, Atlanta, GA 30309; (404) 870-6565. Trained volunteers offer emotional support, parenting education, referrals to community services, and follow-up contacts to expectant and new parents in Georgia and 15 other states. Program also includes a 24-hour helpline and home visits for high-risk families.

Institute for Women and Children, 4680 Lake Underhill Road, Orlando, FL 32807; (407) 381-0907. Provides information about programs and materials on adolescent pregnancy and parenting, including *Inside-Outside: A Guide to Positive Parenting,* a magazine for teens.

La Leche League International, 9616 Minneapolis Avenue, P.O. Box 1209, Franklin Park, IL 60131-8209; (708) 455-8317. Distributes a range of materials on maternal and child health topics focusing on breastfeeding. A publications list is available free from the agency.

March of Dimes, National Office, 1275 Mamaroneck Avenue, White Plains, NY 10605; (914) 428-7100. The March of Dimes can provide pregnant teens with information to ensure they get the special help required to assure healthy pregnancy. You can request a wide array of brochures and information sheets including "Be Good to Your Baby Before It Is Born," "How Your Baby Grows," "Eating for Two," and "Making the Right Choices."

MELD for Young Moms, 123 N. Third St., Suite 507, Minneapolis, MN 55401; (612) 332-7563. MELD offers information and support groups in locations around the country.

National Council for Adoption (NCFA), 1930 17th Street NW, Washington, DC 20009; (202) 328-1200. NCFA is a membership organization of private agencies and individuals who are involved in the field of adoption.

Sponsors the National Adoption Hotline, (800) 333-NCFA, which provides information about adoption and will refer an individual to the agency responsible for adoption in her state.

National Organization on Adolescent Pregnancy, Parenting and Prevention, 4421-A East-West Highway, Bethesda, MD 20814; (301) 913-0378. NOAPPP is a network of individuals and organizations working to prevent adolescent pregnancy and problems related to adolescent sexuality, pregnancy and parenting. Call for referral to an organization or program nearest you.

Hotlines

Abortion

National Abortion Federation Hotline: (800) 772-9100 (weekdays 9:30–5:30, EST); (202) 667-5881 (in Washington, DC). Will answer urgent questions about abortion, pregnancy, restrictive laws, and help women find the nearest medical facilities for the care they need.

National Youth Crisis Hotline: (800) 448-4663 (24 hours). Provides counseling and referrals to counseling services. Responds to youth dealing with pregnancy.

Safe Choice Hotline: (800) 878-2437.

Being a Teen Parent

Bright Beginnings: (800) 641-4546. For nonmedical, nonlegal child-rearing concerns and questions about children from babies to twelve years old.

Parents Anonymous:
(800) 421-0353. This hotline provides help for people who feel overwhelmed by parenting. Also offers local crisis intervention and services.

CHAPTER 8

ME, MYSELF, AND I

When adolescence hits, it seems like everything that made sense before suddenly doesn't. Teens are separating from families by trying on new selves, choosing values, setting personal limits, and finding talents. Sounds great on paper, but in reality stretching boundaries also means more self-doubt and questioning of things that used to be taken for granted. Welcome to self-discovery, where all the choices and possibilities—not to mention hyper hormones—can trigger a complex mix of depression, relief, happiness, and confusion.

For some young women of color, the cultural pressure to be "strong" and "independent" can add another layer of emotions. It can inspire some to become self-sufficient while others suffer alone. These feelings can be compounded by the "double whammy" of being both female and nonwhite, and can affect self-esteem. Some young women of color feel that if they don't succeed, they've failed their whole communities. And if they do succeed, there's more pressure to perform at top speed.

Regardless of ethnic background, everyone needs to learn to deal with moods and feelings. The better you understand yourself, the easier it becomes to face life's ups and downs. Through self-discovery you come to see that the way you view yourself affects feelings, beliefs, and actions.

Moods and Feelings

Sometimes it may feel like you're walking around in a haze, unaware of how you're feeling at the moment. Maybe you can't put your finger on it, or maybe you're too busy thinking about other things or maybe something bad has happened and you're trying to avoid thinking about it. But being "in touch" with your feelings and moods is an important part of knowing your-self—and it may take years of growth. During the teen years, because moods and feelings fluctuate so much, it's easy to lose sight of just how to keep moods and emotions in check. But, chill, there are ways to sort it out.

What Are Emotions?

According to Dr. Carol J. Eagle, head of Child/Adolescent Psychology at Montefiore Medical Center in New York City and co-author of *All That She Can Be* (Simon & Schuster, New York, 1993), every person is born with feelings and the ability to express them in words that we call emotions.

It's important to remember that everybody feels a range of feelings from good to bad. "Don't make the mistake of thinking you should always feel good," Dr. Eagle cautions. "But without some of the bad feelings—anxiety, sadness, depression, nervousness—you wouldn't know the good ones." She believes it's crucial to acknowledge the down times, as bad as they can be, as just a part of life.

Though we hear about it all the time, almost to the point of overkill, hor-mones are a huge part of the strong emotions young women and men feel during adolescence. As Dr. Eagle states, "From the ages of twelve to four-teen expect to feel very weepy, like you're riding an emotional rollercoaster until about sixteen or eighteen years old." Even adults have emotional cycles that last about twelve hours, meaning that someone can feel great the first half of the day and terrible the second half. For teens these cycles can be exaggerated and can change from minute to minute. To keep from feeling too crazed, remember that's the way life goes.

How Do Emotions Affect How We Feel About Ourselves?

During the teen years, while boys generally get broader, taller, and more muscular, girls tend to grow out—developing more fat and more curves. "As a result many girls get anxious because they don't know what their bodies will look like from one day to the next," says Dr. Eagle. This in turn adds to insecurities about appearance, acceptance, and becoming a woman, and can affect social lives, school work, and family relations.

When puberty occurs it can also contribute to how you feel about your-self. Dr. Eagle breaks down three maturation types: early, on-target, and late bloomers. With each, she believes, there are pros and cons.

EARLY BLOOMER: Physically matures around ten or eleven years old.
PROS: envied by peers, looks older, gets tons of attention from boys.
CONS: everyone treats her as much older and expects more out of her at too young an age, is pressured to be more mature, at greater risk for depression, gets tons of attention from boys.

ON-TARGET BLOOMER: Physically matures around twelve or thirteen.
PROS: feels normal in comparison to some other peers.
CONS: can feel envious of early bloomers and better than late bloomers.

LATE BLOOMER: Physically matures around fourteen to sixteen.
PROS: no demands placed on by others thinking she's older, has longer time to deal with transition into womanhood, with support feels more confident and self-assured than earlies or on-targets.
CONS: feels majorly left out, ashamed to be seen naked because not showing any female curves yet, feels like a little girl still.

How to Keep on Track

To help keep control over your emotional life, Dr. Eagle suggests these tips:

- Take responsibility for your emotions. This means recognizing how you feel, and may also include 'fessing up and admitting it to others, especially if you've hurt them or they've hurt you. Denying that feelings exist is the worst way to build relationships and self-confidence, while being honest about how you feel keeps you connected with others—and yourself.

- Watch your calendar. The body is closely tied to emotions, so pay attention to changes, such as getting your period. You'll be able to cope a lot better with problems by noticing patterns and marking them down, especially three to five days before your period.

- Talk, talk, talk. Though it may be embarrassing to talk about body changes and feeling emotionally out of control, think of the alternative—feeling isolated and alone. Find someone older with more experience to talk to about your feelings. Though friends can be a good support, a mature woman can usually give a different perspective because she's been there and made it through. Ask her "did you ever feel like this" and nine out of ten times she'll say "yes."

- Start a girl group. Rap sessions of up to ten people are an excellent way to put feelings and changes in check. Try to organize a weekly meeting where members can talk freely, and bring in an occasional expert speaker to give good info on burning issues. Cool schools might let you earn credit for a semester's class if you organize it.

- Remember that feeling bad doesn't last forever. The biggest (and most embarrassing) mistake some of us make is being overly dramatic about everyday things. Ending a relationship may feel like the end of the world, and no doubt it hurts. But realistically, is life over because of one bad romance? On the other hand, problems such as abuse, death of a loved one, or parents divorcing can cause deeply painful feelings. If under any circumstances you feel bad consistently for more than a week or two, or you're thinking seriously that life isn't worth living, GET HELP IMMEDIATELY. Talk to a parent, school counselor, teacher—anybody who will listen.

"The most beneficial thing about the group is realizing that you're not the only one."

TRACY, 16, TOLEDO, OHIO

One day I started crying in gym class, and my teacher took me down to see the counselor. The following year he got me into a group. I thought it was a neat idea because I figured maybe someone else has the same problem I do, and I could learn different ways to cope with it.

The group helped me understand what was going on in the first place with my family. Basically, my whole family is nothing but alcoholics or recovering alcoholics. It helped me understand why sometimes my mom would come home and be really happy and sometimes she'd come home and be really mad. I knew she was drinking, but I didn't know about alcoholism in terms of a disease. And I didn't know how serious it could get. It helped me learn more about it so that I could learn different ways to cope with it. The most beneficial thing about the group is realizing that you're not the only one.

My group is specifically dealing with drugs and alcohol within the family and how it's affecting us. There are about fourteen people in my group now, and we meet once a week for an hour. Everything that we talk about in the group is confidential.

In the group, I've learned that my biggest problem was that I kept trying to take everything on my own shoulders, and that I tried to change everybody. I was trying to be the parent figure, I guess. I'd be like "No Mom, you're not having another drink because you're driving." Or my mother and stepfather would get in a fight and I'd put her in one room and him in another. When my mom and I would go out together, she would introduce me as her boss.

My mom and I don't really have that many problems now. She's always been good. She's kept us fed, and clothed, and put a roof over our heads. She's paid the bills. My mom's not drinking that much anymore; she's been doing real good lately. I'm proud of her.

This group helps me relax. Talking helps me get my feelings out, so they're not all bottled up. If you keep your feelings bottled up, it creates more stress. Now there's not really anything I don't feel comfortable talking about. I used to hate to admit that my parents were alcoholics. I used to hate to admit that my parents got into fights. I hated talking about it because I wanted to have the perfect family, and I never wanted anybody to be afraid to come over.

If I didn't have group, I'd probably be in an insane asylum right now. Seriously, I probably would have tried committing suicide several times. I also probably wouldn't have that many friends. I have more friends now because I'm a much more easygoing person. I like to have fun. Before, I was afraid to have fun. I was hanging around the wrong people—they were drinking and trying to get me to drink. With my friends now, we watch movies, go to the mall, drive around, hang out. Sometimes we play pool. We have fun just hanging out, talking and joking.

I've also become a PAL: peer assistance leader. If students have a problem, they can come and talk to us, and we're supposed to just let them talk and get it off their chests. I have my heart set on being a psychologist. I love dealing with people, evaluating them, and trying to help. I love it.

Self-Esteem

Self-esteem is a measure of how valuable a person feels. In other words, if you have high self-esteem you think, "I like who I am, I count, I'm lovable, I'm as good as anyone, and I have something to offer." You can have different levels of self-esteem in various areas of your life, such as with friends, academic abilities, or athletic skills. And don't forget: even young women who have the highest self-esteem sometimes feel insecure, and that is completely normal.

What Affects Self-Esteem?

Within a person's lifetime levels of self-esteem can change. In a study conducted by the American Association of University Women, 60 percent of girls aged eight and nine said "I'm happy the way I am." By the time girls reached high school, though, only 29 percent said they were happy the way they were. Many young women felt they weren't good at "doing things," and lacked self-confidence in their abilities and talents. Though boys had the same concerns, their levels of self-confidence remained much higher than girls.

One area that young women focused on in the study most was appearance. In American society, girls are taught to value popularity, looks, and clothes above their abilities in leadership, sports, or having a good sense of humor. "When girls hit puberty, they are praised less for their school performance than for being thin or pretty," states Dr. Harriet Lefley, Ph.D., professor of psychiatry and behavioral sciences at the University of Miami School of Medicine. "After puberty, the rules change for girls and it sets up an internal conflict, because what used to be important to parents, teachers, and peers has changed." This leaves many confused, doubting themselves, depressed, or moody.

The media, especially TV, can affect young women's self-esteem. According to *Recasting TV: Girls' Views*, a study conducted by Girls, Inc., children's TV shows have the smallest percentage of female characters. (People of color are also invisible—they make up only 13 percent of prime-time casts and 5 percent of characters in kids' programs.) Girl characters on TV are also often limited; most are interested in only two things—boys and clothes. Says Marissa Jones of Girls, Inc. of Pittsfield, Massachusetts: "Television is really getting out of hand with women. It makes us look like the only important quality about women is our body, or that we have no mind or strength." Because young people watch so many hours of TV, over time, these kinds of images affect the way boys feel about girls, and young women feel about themselves.

Race, Culture, and Self-Esteem

Many experts believe self-esteem drops during the teens, because, as their bodies change, young women become more aware of what it means to be a woman—and in this country, being a woman isn't as highly valued as being a man. For every culture, being a woman means something different. In some communities women are highly valued and young women have a strong sense of themselves throughout their adolescence. However, in other cultures women are considered less important than men, and girls growing up find it hard to feel good about themselves.

Researchers have discovered, for example, that young African American women may have the highest self-esteem of all young women. Dr. Janie Victoria Ward, Ph.D., associate professor at Simmons College in Boston, believes that's due to strong female role models. "In healthy black families there is a very high premium placed on individual and personal self-worth," explains Dr. Ward. "Girls are given very strong messages about independence and assertiveness from their mothers, and in the culture there's a lot of support for feistiness and being your own woman."

Girls from some other ethnic cultures also tend to be secure about themselves. Dr. Lefley studied Native American children and discovered that young women from the group with more traditional values had higher self-esteem than the more mainstream group. "In the more traditional group, women's work and roles (like sewing and cooking) were highly valued, and the daughters got a strong sense of themselves from within the Indian culture," says Dr. Lefley. Girls from the other group were more aware of how they didn't fit into the larger American society and felt less important.

Unfortunately many girls come from communities that don't reward women's contributions. Dr. Reiko Homma True, Ph.D., a psychologist who specializes in Asian American cultures, acknowledges that among many Asian groups, girls aren't as highly valued as boys. "Many girls have generational differences with their parents, like all American kids. But some parents, often immigrants, tend to be more old fashioned. They give their daughters less freedom to date, pursue their careers, and sometimes expect them to sacrifice for their brother's achievements." Dr. True explains that young women from Korean, Japanese, and Chinese backgrounds are generally taught to be subservient to men. On the other hand, she points out, a new generation of Asian women recognize the need for girls to assert their identities and are paving new roads.

As in the Asian culture, traditional Latino culture tends to encourage girls and women to put everyone else's needs before their own. Dr. Lefley states that often women are praised for their attractiveness and ability to mother. But, where women are the primary caretakers of children *and* seen as valuable contributors to the community, for example among Puerto Ricans, young women have more of a sense of their worth.

In general, Dr. Lefley's studies show that what affects self-esteem most is having strong women role models that let young women know that anybody can achieve whatever they set their mind to. The most important lesson that African American mothers teach their daughters is to decide for themselves what their goals are and not let anyone stand in the way of them. And that's a lesson everyone can learn from.

Raising Self-esteem

Though different cultures can greatly influence self-esteem, ultimately how you feel about yourself comes from within. That means that in order to think highly of yourself, you must believe in your heart that you are capable and valuable, regardless of what friends and family—and society—may have told you. Getting to this point takes a lot of effort and will require you to actively work on knowing who you are and what talents you have.

In their book *Make an Appointment with Yourself*, Maida and Alena J. Berenblatt give suggestions that can help you gain a more positive self-image:

• Make a list of the most important people in your life. You should be included on the list—right at the top. If you aren't, think about why. It doesn't make you conceited to consider yourself the most important person in your life. With high self-esteem comes ambition, goals, good friends, and good relationships. You deserve all of this and more.

• Don't hold onto negative images of yourself. It's fine to be honest about your personal limitations ("sometimes I'm too impatient" or "I need to study more to do well in English"). But thinking you're "bad" or "not good at anything," either because someone told you or you're comparing yourself to someone else, is destructive. Instead, think of what skills you do have: good listener, great artist, effective organizer. The more you know about yourself and can make your talents work for you, the easier it will be to set goals for yourself.

• If there are things about yourself you'd like to change, there are steps to follow:

1. Ask yourself what areas of your life you would like to be different. Look through your journal and see what troubles you most in your life: trying to please other people, overeating, dealing with teachers or other authority figures, not saying how you really feel, getting high, procrastinating, or feeling angry all the time. It's scary to make changes, but scarier to do nothing and be unhappy.

2. Find ways to meet your needs. This is the most important step to change. If you discover that you don't like the friends you hang around because they're always gossiping, try to meet some people that are into what you like. If photography's your thing, sign up for a class and make some friends. If you feel you're too stressed out, take yoga classes or rent a workout video. Start trying to find solutions to what's missing in your life.

3. Pat yourself on the back for taking the steps to change. Rewarding yourself through praise is one of the best feelings in the world. Giving that gift to yourself is even more important, because nobody can take it away. Besides, no one can appreciate your achievements more than you. So take a bow, you deserve it.

4. Tell a friend what a great thing you've done. Sharing your most proud moments with people you care about will give you an extra boost. If your friend was helpful and supportive, let her know how much you appreciate it.

• Spend time alone. As the Berenblatts claim, "Higher levels of independent thought and activity trigger higher levels of self-esteem." When you can be alone with yourself, you'll be able to listen to the deepest part of you. It's there that you can learn to trust your feelings and judgment and feel the most secure. Have the courage to look inside and know what's best for you.

• •

According to the American Association of University Women:

- Males get more feedback, praise, and attention from teachers than females, all of which affects self-esteem.
- Feeling important within the family, and having academic confidence, are more important to teen girls than being accepted by peers.
- Girls who like math and science like themselves more, feel good about their school performance, and are more confident about their appearance than girls who don't. These girls also have more confidence than adolescent boys!

• •

Sexism And Racism

When someone makes a judgment based only on race or gender, that's called racism or sexism—and that judgment can be very painful for the person on the receiving end. Both racism and sexism are damaging because they make people feel bad about who they are, when in fact those doing the judging are the ones who really have the problem. Racism and sexism can also impact negatively on a person's life when those doing the discriminating have power in society, and their prejudices can affect important concerns such as getting hired for a job. Not everyone does harm intentionally, but when they do it's important to speak up—whether you're the person being directly affected or you've just seen or heard a racist or sexist incident.

Sexism

What Is Sexism?

When someone treats another person negatively just because she's a female, it's called sexism or gender discrimination. Generally we think of men as those who discriminate most because they have more "juice" or status in our society than women. They make almost twice as much money as women do, have the most powerful jobs, are mostly responsible for writing laws, decide on most of the movies, books, and TV shows that get seen, and get greater recognition for their accomplishments. That also means they're in charge of decisions that can influence your life. So if a man in a position of power has any negative feelings about the abilities of women—whether consciously or not—that could affect your grades, job, home life, and college admission.

Unfortunately that can leave you with less control over your own life and can be damaging, not to mention frightening.

But men aren't the only ones who have different expectations for females. Because feelings about women's abilities are so ingrained (and sometimes so subtle), women and girls, too, can have lowered expectations for themselves and for other females. Anybody that has even thought that a man would be better suited for a job when put next to a woman, without knowing either person's abilities, is guilty of sexism.

- In a study by the Center for the Learning and Teaching of Literature, the top ten books taught in public, private, and Catholic schools included only one woman writer and no people of color.
- A study of popular American history textbooks shows that women were discussed only 1 percent of the time, says *Education Digest*.
- Thirty-seven percent of girls drop out of high school because of family obligations (not including pregnancy), compared with 5 percent of boys, according to *Teachers College Record*.
- When girls in a Michigan Department of Education report were asked "How would your life be different if you were a boy," most said they would get into sports more. Unfortunately in 70 percent of the schools in the study, boys had better athletic opportunities than girls.

"Now I've learned that it really is cool to be an intelligent young woman."
KIM, 17, SHAKER HEIGHTS, OHIO

I've been at my all-girls since the sixth grade. Before that I was in a coed school. One of the reasons I came here was that my parents felt I wasn't getting what I needed, and that at the school I went to I was just kind of glanced over and lost in the shuffle.

Before this school I was really bored at school. What happened was in the area where I lived there weren't enough kids in the school system, so all the fifth and sixth graders went into one school. I was doing OK, but I wasn't doing all that well because I didn't care, and I wasn't excited about going to school anymore. It was really hard. But one day I remember my parents said, "All right, you're getting tested at [an all-girls school]" and I said OK. I was totally excited, I couldn't wait.

It didn't really faze me, going to an all-girls school. I mean, sure, my friends in public school were like, "I can't believe you have to go to a school with all girls." But personally I love it. I wouldn't want to go to another school. When I first got here I noticed how close everyone is, because it's a very small school, and everyone's very close and cares about everyone else. It's really a family-like atmosphere. I noticed this right away with the teachers and with the students. There are different dynamics in an all-girls school, as opposed to a coed. Boys in the fourth and fifth grade are a little rambunctious and most times dominate the whole classroom, and how they act is how the discussions and the lessons go. I remember the teachers spending most of their time trying to correct a problem child or a guy that was throwing airplanes or something like that. Or else the guys would always be the ones with their hands raised. They were the ones that always had the answer and always seemed ahead of everyone else. They were definitely getting more attention in the classroom than the girls. And the teachers went to them for answering questions more.

Plus, when I was in my regular classes the girls never wanted to be too smart, because if you were smart you were not well liked by the guys. Guys didn't like the girls that would always raise their hands. They liked the kind that sit there at their desks, write notes to each other, not really pay attention. If you were smart, you weren't really cool in the eyes of the guys. We all kind of wanted to impress at that age. Now I've learned that it really is cool to be an intelligent young woman, but at that age you don't really think about stuff like that. You just want the guys to like you.

At my school—it sounds so trite—but I've learned I can do anything. I'm doing the senior speech this coming Wednesday, and I'm writing about how we can all instill a passion for learning in ourselves, and I think that's something that this school really has given me. I have an intense love of learning and of knowledge. I've learned here never to feel ashamed of any opinion I have, or never to feel afraid of like crashing and burning in class, because we all go through it. Everybody's ideas get sacked out at some point, and I've been taught never to be afraid of that, and that fear is part of the learning process. I've learned you should always be there raising your hand and sitting in front. You're definitely more free to be who you are. Everyone has these grand plans for themselves; one of my best friends wants to be the president of her own company. It's great. I feel so prepared to go to college, and I plan to go to a coed college. I could pack my bags today. I feel so prepared to go out into the "real world" now. I can't wait to be in a class with guys actually. It's going to be a learning experience for me, because I want to see if these scientific studies showing that girls are less assertive when they're in class with guys are really true. For me I know I'm going to get to college and sit right up there and raise my hand and not really care.

What to Do About Sexism?

Dealing with sexism will be a lifelong struggle for us as long as women are treated unfairly. Alison Amoroso, co-founder and executive director of

Women Express Inc. and publisher of *Teen Voices Magazine* in Boston has some excellent advice:

- Always ask what you want and need before taking care of others. As a woman, you've probably been conditioned to look out for others first, and in the process you may have begun to sacrifice your own wishes. The more this happens the more you stop listening to your inner voice. But when you pay a little more attention to yourself and your needs, deep down, you'll be able to figure out what's best for you and how to get it.

- If your parents make you do things that you think are based on their own sexism, try to write down some examples in your journal and then sit down and calmly discuss with them what changes you want. If they tell you you have no choice as long as you're in their house, understand that when you get out on your own, you'll be able to do things differently.

- If your school is discriminating against you, or against girls in general, organize some students and go before the school board or principal. Many female students are demanding their schools spend as much on girls' sports teams as boys', offer all-girl math and science classes, or include more women authors in class reading material. If you and your group make a list of reasonable demands and back them up with a solid argument, you'll probably win the support of a lot of other students and make some changes.

- Form a women's issues or women's history group in your town or school. Learning about women's accomplishments, and discussing how being female affects your life, can be amazingly enlightening if you get some thoughtful people together. If you work with a supportive teacher or counselor, you may be able to get credit for the group.

- Get a girls' column in the school newspaper. This is a great way to spark discussion, give information on women's events, or just be heard. If doing it by yourself is too much, try rotating the column and get a variety of perspectives.

- Go to a women's bookstore. Most school libraries don't have much of a women's studies section, especially for teens. But go into a women's bookstore (or the women's studies section of your local bookstore), and it'll open your eyes. Not only are there a lot of women from all over the world out there with something to say, but there are many topics that relate to us that never get discussed. Look in the yellow pages for a store near you, or join a women's mail order book club if it's too much of a trek.

• Refuse to see movies that feature women as helpless victims or "crazy bitches." Slasher movies are particularly disturbing as far as portraying women, because they mix sexiness with violence. The message becomes that violence is sexy and that sex is violent, and it's OK to hurt women. On the other hand, movies that show women as devilish, scheming murderers distort the reality that women almost never commit murder except in self-defense. While some of us can do some awfully strange or outlandish things, the overwhelming majority of women are stable, productive citizens struggling to succeed and usually to support our families.

• Buy the *Women's Yellow Pages* at your nearest bookstore. This is a yellow pages like the one the telephone company gives out, but all the businesses are either owned by women or provide support specifically for women's needs. It's another way to see how many successful women there are in your community, and a good resource if you're job-hunting. (Fact: Women are the fastest growing business owners and are more successful at keeping their businesses going than are men.)

• Take action by joining a women's group. If you feel like you want to do something—anything—to promote the equal treatment of women, there are groups around. The National Organization for Women is a great place to start. It also has a young feminist group with sister chapters in high schools and colleges across the country that hold demonstrations, workshops, and meetings. Also the Women's Action Coalition (WAC) is a group of fired-up young women who take to the streets on a variety of issues. If neither of these groups satisfies your needs or isn't available to you, start your own group beginning with one issue that you want to see changed.

• Get involved in politics even if you can't vote yet. Too many of us take politics for granted, thinking we can't make a difference. But history has proven that when women decide to vote or run for office, we can be highly successful. If there's a candidate that shares your views, volunteer a few hours a week during her campaign to stuff envelopes, make phone calls, or pass out flyers. The best way to learn how the political system works is from an insider's experience.

THE TEEN VOICES ADVISORY BOARD IN BOSTON, MASSACHUSETTS

What's the hardest thing about explaining sexism to teen girls? Convincing them that it exists, says Marie Celestin, nineteen, chairperson of the Teen Advisory Board (TAB), a group of six Boston teens that give presentations at area high schools and advise the editors of *Teen Voices* magazine.

"The girls in the audience can't believe it. First they believe sexism doesn't affect them. And then they see, through discussion, that sexism is all around them. Most of us are so used to it, we're waiting for something to come out and bite us when it's already right there."

Marie joined TAB as a way to learn leadership. "Girls that want to get involved in our group must have an interest in the magazine and in making positive changes in the community, such as fighting racism and sexism," says Marie.

She and other TAB members are taught how to conduct workshops, use computers and speak in public. When they're invited to speak, they must research statistics on a certain issue and then practice their presentation. Melinda Huang, twenty, a TAB member who's responsible for marketing and outreach, recalls, "Training for the workshops was fun. We had arguments about gender discrimination in different traditions, because it's very hard to draw the line sometimes."

The school workshops are open to everyone, but the topics are directed specifically to teen women. "When we go to the schools we brainstorm with the audience," says Marie, "then we finally break it down to one main issue. Then people talk about their own experiences." They ask questions like: Who are you more afraid of, your mother or your father?; what kind of job does your mother have?; how much does it pay compared to your father?; whose job is more interesting?; who does the housework at home?

After the discussions, TAB members pass out copies of *Teen Voices* and participants are encouraged to contribute or come into the office to work with the group. Marie thinks she's showing other young women by example not to be passive about things that they find unfair. "Instead of sitting there worrying about the way things are, [they can] take action, do something. There is always something you can do about it." For more information, contact Teen Voices, 316 Huntington Avenue, Boston, MA 02115; (617) 262-2434.

Racism

What Is Racism?

Many of us mistakenly assume that the only racists are people like the Ku Klux Klan, Nazis, or skinheads. Unfortunately, racists rarely wear a badge and often don't even realize their attitudes are racist. "Racism is behavior or thoughts and feelings of superiority toward another person based on racial identity," says Jessica Henderson Daniel, Ph.D., associate director of the adolescent health training program at Children's Hospital in Boston.

Racism can be very subtle. Daniel gives a common example of how a white teacher treats kids of color versus white kids. "The teacher calls on the white student, and even if she gives the wrong answer, will help her until she gets the answer right. But then the teacher calls on a black or Latina student and if the answer is wrong, she'll get passed over without any extra help." The message the Latina and black kids get is that they can't do it. The teacher expects the brown-skinned kids to fail because of her own racist attitudes and doesn't give them a fair shot.

When someone says or does something racist, it's devastating to the victim. "It's like getting chipped away at your heart," describes Daniel. The person on the receiving end may start to believe that what others think and say is true. Those insecure, negative feelings can lead to anger, sadness, discouragement, or even overcompensating—trying desperately to prove that the racist is wrong. Either way the wound is real. "We feel assaulted when we come to realize others only see us as a negative stereotype and not as an individual," says Daniel.

Racism has such a powerful effect in our society that those who fear being targets sometimes try harder to fit in. Some people work to lose accents, wear "the right" clothes, deny liking certain kinds of music, put in colored contact lenses, or change their hair to be accepted. Many buy into the assumption that light skin is prettier than dark, that straight hair is better than curly, and that blond is sexier than brunette. We get these impressions by the media and society telling us that the blond, skinny, white woman is the ideal.

Young women who don't look like the so-called ideal sometimes try to look more "All-American" by trying methods of change, such as bleaching the skin or changing the shape of the eyes with plastic surgery. Even within cultures, people may develop hierarchies—such as lighter skin being superior to darker skin among blacks, less slanted eyes being better than more slanted among Asians, or blondes with blue eyes being more highly prized than dark hair and dark eyes among whites.

But, thankfully, many people aren't having it. The recent movement towards Afrocentric appreciation among black people is a good example of not buying into society's standards and raising racial pride. Instead of measuring yourself against a standard that is genetically impossible, you can let your unique beauty, body type, and skin color shine through.

How to Handle Racism and Racist Situations

Daniel's first bit of advice is to pick your battles. "It's impossible to respond to everything all the time," she states, "because you only have so much energy. If you become consumed in fighting every racist fight, you'll just end up constantly frustrated and angry." In some instances it's appropriate to speak up, if you feel you have the strength. But she believes there are other effective ways to deal with racism that focus on making yourself more informed and stronger:

- Know your history. Nothing can take the place of putting things in perspective. There are several books, such as *Everything You Need to Know about Latino History* by Himilce Movas (Plume Books, 1994) or *Don't Believe the Hype* by Farai Chideya (Plume Books, 1995), that can give you insight into what your community has gone through to survive, why certain traditions were preserved, and in what ways history keeps repeating itself. This is especially good information for when you do decide to confront someone's bigoted remarks.

- Learn from your elders. Many of us come from cultures that cherish our ancestors and older family members because they have lived through a lot and carry a great deal of wisdom. Hearing their stories can help you see your family's accomplishments and successes and help you to be proud of what they've gone through.

- Have cultural heroines. So much of the time we turn to TV and movies for our heroines, and all too often they look nothing like us, nor do they have the same life experiences we do. Look around the community at some women that you admire for their daily acts of courage or for their commitment to something you feel is important. Magazines like *Ms.*, *Hispanic*, *YSB*, *Essence*, and *A* all feature people of color doing average and extraordinary things. Reading them will help you see that there are people who look like you that can make it.

- Find a mentor. Older people have been through what you're going through and they can be a great comfort when you feel down. Having someone outside your family to lend support is a good way to feel honored within your culture. Many schools, churches, girls' organizations have mentoring programs.

- Spend time with your own people. Especially for those of us who are in minority situations at school or in the neighborhood, being around friends of the same race can be a relief. It allows us to share experiences and not always feel like we're in the Sesame Street jingle "which of these things is not like the other." Cultural and community groups are a good choice, but they don't have to be with people your own age. Consider volunteering for younger kids or seniors too.

- Understand that not all whites are racist. Some people who are noticeably Latina, Asian, American Indian, or black think the only thing people—especially white people—notice is their race. Though it may be true sometimes, that's not always the case.

- Stand up against racism. If you're the target of a racist remark, you don't necessarily have to say anything, but if you feel up to it, respond, so that the other person's ignorance doesn't erode your self-worth. Try saying:

  "I don't believe you just said that."
  "What you just said was offensive and disrespectful."
  "You owe me an apology for what you just said."

If you aren't the target, you can still respond with any of the above, but you might want to add:

  "I think you're full of it."
  "I think you owe my friend an apology."

And at any point after a racist remark or joke has been made, you can always walk away.

Talk it out. One of the best ways to handle racism is to talk about your feelings. You may feel most comfortable doing this among people who've been through the same thing, otherwise you'll find yourself teaching rather than sharing. Some high schools and college campuses have cultural groups that address issues of racism.

CAN WE BE DOWN WITH *LA RAZA*, OUR HOMIES, OUR CULTURES, AND STILL BE A STRONG WOMAN?

Is it possible to want to uplift the race and still be down for women's rights? Definitely! A lot of young women of color are afraid to speak their minds in front of their homeboys because they're afraid of seeming like

traitors to their culture. On one hand they don't want to seem like male-bashers, but on the other hand, it's rough to put up with the sexist bull that guys can dish out. What's a culturally minded feminist supposed to do?

First let's put things in perspective. Women have been told to "stand by your man" much more than encouraged to stand up for themselves. Although young women can have loving relationships with guys, these must be based on equality and respect. Many young women fear that being too assertive alienates guys. But look at the alternative: saying nothing to men who call women "hos" and "bitches" doesn't make you feel any stronger. And who wants to go out with a guy who doesn't honor and value women? No guy is worth giving up your personal dignity over. Period.

One more thought: Racism and sexism are both wrong, so why should anybody be forced to call one worse than the other? Let's work on getting rid of both!

When It's Too Much

Sometimes life just sucks. It isn't enough having to deal with the normal pangs of growing up, like your body feeling all out of whack and teachers on your last nerve. But on top of that, the future, SAT scores, family, and relationship all figure into the mix. When the stuff hits the fan and everything feels out of control, the mind and body react by either hyping up or shutting down. Have no fear, though, there are ways to deal with the ups and downs of life.

All Stressed Out

Believe it or not, stress can actually be good. A little bit helps add "spice" to life, like the rush of going on a first date. Without it, life might be pretty boring. But a ton of stress feels overwhelming and will even negatively affect health if we don't learn how to deal with it.

Generally, stress is a bodily reaction to a situation that is challenging, threatening, or harmful. The brain fires off chemicals that raise the heart rate and blood pressure and cause muscles to tighten. According to Bruce Compas, Ph.D., a professor of psychology and a specialist in stress and adolescents at the University of Vermont, stress falls into two categories: acute (or one traumatic incident, such as the death of a loved one), or chronic (which means ongoing, like constantly fighting with a parent). "Many people can handle one or two problems," says Dr. Compas, "but when there are three or more at once, it can lead to depression."

It's important to address stress head on, and Dr. Compas emphasizes that there's no one way to deal with it. Here are his suggestions:

- Problem solve. The best way to tackle stress is to actively work on a plan that helps you gain control over the situation. Make lists of what you want to accomplish, but start small so that you don't feel overwhelmed.

- Don't run away. Avoiding, doing nothing or, worse, trying to escape through food, drugs or alcohol, only compounds the problem. So, if someone says not to think about it, *don't* take their advice. "Trying not to think about something only makes us think about it more and never solves the problem," says Dr. Compas. In fact, if you don't actively work to alleviate stress, it affects the immune system and can cause you to get sick.

- Relax or meditate. Both are good ways to soothe a racing mind and help you become a better problem solver. Other activities, for example running, walking, or playing sports, can shake some of the tension and help you think more clearly. Also, when you're under stress try to take care of yourself by exercising, eating right, and getting a lot of rest.

- Accept what can't be changed. Some problems can never be solved, for instance the death of a parent. "Part of coping with events beyond our control is coming to terms with the situation," says Dr. Compas. This means trying to learn from the event or find something positive out of it. "When a tragedy happens, it may be an opportunity for the family to come closer together," Dr. Compas believes. Often the best road towards acceptance is to find support.

- Understand that stress is a part of life. "Though the kinds of things that stress us will change over time," explains Dr. Compas, "we can't assume that one day we'll be stress-free." Stress itself isn't always the problem, it's how we deal with it when it hits.

WHAT STRESSES TEENS MOST?

Family: death or illness of family member, divorce, sharing a room, fights with family members, experiencing or witnessing abuse.

Peers: rejection from friends, getting dumped, starting a relationship, becoming sexually active, experiencing or witnessing violence.

School: failing a test, taking a big exam, keeping up grades, dealing with difficult classes or teachers.

Too Depressed for Words

A lot of us say "I'm so depressed" when really we just have a case of the blues. Feeling down usually comes and goes with the everyday drama of living. But real depression, called clinical depression, is a serious health problem that affects the overall mood, body, and thoughts of those who have it. According to the National Institutes of Mental Health, 17.6 million Americans are affected by depression each year, and up to 5 percent of those are teens.

There are many reasons that depression hits, says Dr. Adrian Angold, MRCPsych., an adolescent psychiatrist and professor at Duke University in Durham, North Carolina. According to Dr. Angold, depression tends to run in families and can be due to chemical imbalances in the brain, a stressful life event, difficulties within the family, an eating disorder or chronic strains that make life difficult. However, in some people there is no one trigger that sets off a depressive episode.

Dr. Angold explains that young women are more prone to depression during and after puberty than are young men. "Boys may be more prone to depression as kids than girls, but after age thirteen it changes," says Dr. Angold. Researchers aren't sure why, but puberty seems to sensitize girls to stress, which can lead to depression. "By adulthood, depression is twice as common in women as in men."

Symptoms of depression generally fall into these categories:

- Mood changes: feeling sad, empty, hopeless, guilty, worthless;
- Thought changes: unable to make decisions, can't concentrate, unable to enjoy things that used to be fun;
- Physical changes: unable to sleep or sleeping all the time, tired or restless, unable to eat or overeating, headaches, stomach aches, or backaches;
- Behavior changes: moodiness, withdrawing, skipping school, drinking or taking drugs.

More serious symptoms include: talking about suicide, making plans for suicide, giving away belongings, purchasing or carrying a gun or other weapon, or pills, attempting suicide. If you or anyone you know has expressed any of these thoughts, GET HELP NOW. *Most people who have committed suicide told someone at least a week before.* So, don't think you're betraying your friend by letting someone else know that she is in serious danger. You'll be a true friend for saving her life.

Luckily, depression is treatable. Many people require either psychological therapy, medication, or both. Dr. Angold believes the most effective therapy treatments include parents, and many people are helped within a short period of time. Talk to a parent, school counselor, teacher, or contact a help line or hospital.

. . . . **ARE YOU FEELING BUMMED?** . . . .

If you're going through a case of the blues (*not* clinical depression), there are a few things you can do to lift your spirits:

- Chat it up. Call a friend and talk about how you feel.
- Get busy. Rather than zombie-ing out in front of the TV, go to a movie, coffee house, or a long in-line skating adventure.
- Sing-a-long. Put on your favorite uplifting song and play it a few times.
- Get a grip. Try to put your situation in perspective. Writing in a journal can show us that even the most embarrassing situations can be funny, if not trivial a few weeks later.

SUICIDE: IT DOESN'T MAKE SENSE

Teen girls are four to five times more likely to attempt suicide than boys, says the American Association of University Women. Generally when someone has committed suicide, she has tried it eight to twenty-five times before, according to the National Institute of Mental Health (NIMH). When someone has reached the point of attempting suicide, she is in deep pain and crying out for help.

But would you know when someone has attempted suicide or is even thinking about it? Most often when someone is considering suicide, she'll let you know with small clues. (*Newsweek* magazine reports that 90 percent of suicide victims leave clear warning signs.) First, understand that not everyone who attempts or commits suicide is mentally ill or even depressed, though these can put her at risk. The most common risk factors for teens are depression; alcohol or drug use; aggressive or destructive behavior (such as fighting, carrying or using a weapon, breaking the law or getting arrested); family history of mental illness, drug abuse, violence or suicide. However, clear warning signs of someone contemplating suicide include:

- talking about suicide or threatening it;
- previous suicide attempts;
- talking about death and dying or wanting to die;

- putting affairs in order or giving belongings away;
- personality changes or strange behavior, like moodiness, apathy, crying, anxiety, lack of appetite, or inability to sleep;
- feeling worthless, hopeless, or helpless;
- withdrawing or isolating, losing interest in otherwise fun activities;
- sudden switch from feeling down to feeling at peace or happy.

When a friend is suffering from any of these symptoms, there are many steps that can help. Rita Robinson writes in her book *Survivors of Suicide* that the best way to tell if someone is contemplating suicide is that she talks about it. So, the most effective response is to talk to her about it. Here are some dos and don'ts.

DO:
Ask why she's thinking of killing herself.
Ask how serious she is about carrying through with her plans.
Assure her of your support as a friend and remind her there are alternatives.
Encourage her to get professional help.
Give her a hug or tell her how much you love her.
Immediately get in touch with her family *and* a professional who can handle the situation.

DON'T:
Blow off her talk of suicide thinking she's only "trying to get attention."
Tell her she's crazy, stupid, or throwing her life away.
Think that she wouldn't really do it or isn't the type.
Encourage her to drink or get high to "forget about her problems."
Think you have the ability to talk her out of committing suicide and therefore don't get professional help.

Places to get help are:
- suicide hotlines or crisis helplines, such as the Boys Town National (24-hour) Hotline at (800) 448-3000;
- hospitals;
- health care providers;
- family members;
- teachers or school counselors;
- clergy.

Sometimes our best efforts fail to keep a friend or loved one alive. We may wonder why she did it or what could have stopped her. Unlike some other kinds of death, suicide carries the burden of guilt for those left behind, who wonder how they could have helped or if there were warning signs they missed. Some of us even begin to contemplate suicide ourselves because the loss is so great.

However, Robinson warns us not to feel we are to blame. When grieving the loss of a suicide victim, we must accept that we may never know why she killed herself. To come to terms with the catastrophe we may adopt imaging techniques as do the Native Americans or Japanese, who communicate with their ancestors and talk to them about how the suicide has affected their lives. Others of us may need the help of a professional or suicide survivors' support group to work through the grieving process.

For a survivor group in your area, contact the American Association of Suicidology at 2459 S. Ash St., Denver, CO 80222; (303) 692-0985.

SUICIDE FACTS

- Suicide is the third leading cause of death for young people age fifteen to twenty-four, says the National Institute of Mental Health (NIMH).
- NIMH also reports that suicide by guns is the most common method of suicide by men and women, making up 60 percent of all suicides.
- Handgun control laws in Washington, D.C. helped decrease the rate of suicide in that city, reports a study in the *New England Journal of Medicine*.
- The availability of guns, especially loaded handguns, poses a risk of suicide even for kids not suffering from a psychiatric condition, note several articles.
- Nearly one-third of all teen suicides involve someone struggling with lesbian/gay/bisexual issues.

Where to Turn

Recommended Reading

After a Suicide: Young People Speak Out, Susan Kuklin, G. P. Putnam's Sons, 1994.

Becoming Myself: True Stories About Learning from Life, Cassandra Walker Simmons, Free Spirit Publishing, 1994.

A Circle of Women: Stories of the Sisterhood, Patra McSharry Sevastiades, editor, Rosen Publishing Group, 1994. A teen collection of fiction and nonfiction that explores the connections shared by women.

CityKids Speak on Prejudice, Citykids, Random House, 1994. In this book city kids speak up through quotes, surveys, interviews, photographs, drawings, and honest talk about what prejudice is.

Don't Be S. A. D.: A Teenage Guide to Handling Stress, Anxiety, and Depression, Susan Newman, J. Messner, Fireside Books, 1991. In candid interviews teens speak about stress, anxiety, and depression and how they found a way to cope. This book will help you avoid clinical anxiety and depression, build your self-esteem and make better choices in your life.

Everything You Need to Know About Bias Incidents, Kevin Osborn, Rosen Publishing Group, 1994.

Everything You Need to Know About Self-Confidence, Matthew Ignoffo, Ph.D., Rosen Publishing Group, 1995.

Getting Up When You're Feeling Down: A Woman's Guide to Overcoming and Preventing Depression, Harriet Braiker, Pocket Books, 1990.

Growing Up Feeling Good, Ellen Rosenberg, Puffin Books, 1989.

Heart Smarts: Teenage Guide for the Puzzle of Life, Doc L. Childre, Borgo Press, 1992. A hands-on manual to provide you with short cuts to relieve stress, build self-esteem, and manage your mental and emotional energies.

I Can't Take It Anymore: How to Get Up When You're Really Low, Joyce L. Vedral, Ph.D., Ballantine, 1987.

Kids with Courage: True Stories About Young People Making a Difference, Barbara Lewis, Free Spirit Publishing, 1992.

Making the Most of Today: Daily Readings for Young People on Self-Awareness, Creativity, and Self-Esteem, Pamela Espeland and Rosemary Wallner, Free Spirit Publishing, 1991.

New Moon: The Magazine for Girls and Their Dreams. A bimonthly publication to inspire and empower girls in the face of discrimination. For more information, write or call: New Moon Publishers, P.O. Box 3587, Duluth, MN 55803; (218) 728-5507.

Perfectionism: What's Bad About Being Too Good. Miriam Adderholdt-Elliott, Ph.D., Free Spirit Publishing, 1987. This book explores the differences between healthy ambition and unhealthy perfectionism.

The Power to Prevent Suicide: A Guide For Teens Helping Teens, Richard E. Nelson, Ph.D., and Judith C. Galas, Free Spirit Publishing, 1994.

Recovery of Your Self-Esteem: A Guide for Women, Carolynn Hillman, Fireside, 1992.

Respecting Our Differences: A Guide to Getting Along in a Changing World, Lynn Duvall, Free Spirit Publishing, 1994.

Speaking Out: Teenagers Take On Race, Sex, and Identity, Susan Kuklin, ed., G.P. Putnam's Sons, 1993.

Survivors of Suicide, Rita Robinson, Newcastle Publishing, 1989.

Waking Up Alive: The Descent, the Suicide Attempt, and the Return to Life, Richard Heckler, Ph.D., Grosset/Putnam, 1994.

When a Friend Dies: A Book For Teens About Grieving and Healing, Marilyn Gootman, Ed.D., Free Spirit Publishing, 1994. Understanding, gentle advice, and practical suggestions for any teen who is grieving the death of a friend for any reason, including suicide.

Writing Down the Days: 365 Creative Journaling Ideas for Young People, Lorraine Dahlstrom, Free Spirit Publishing, 1990. A year's worth of fresh, innovative creative writing assignments, designed to encourage creativity and self-discovery.

Support Groups and Organizations

Self-Esteem, Sexism, and Racism

Be Your Own Best Friend Program (BYBF)/Organizacion Nacional de la Salud de la Mujer Latina/National Latina Health Organization, P.O. Box 7567, Oakland, CA 94601; (510) 534-1362. BYBF conducts support groups for young adolescent Latinas to help develop and promote self-esteem; learn positive cultural identity; address the pressures of becoming sexually active, involved in gang activity and dropping out of school; to counteract the negative image portrayal of Latinas in the media; and to develop an understanding of inherent racism and sexism.

Big Brothers/Big Sisters of America, 230 N. Thirteenth Street, Philadelphia, PA 19107; (215) 567-7000. A Big Sister is someone who takes a personal interest in your life, someone you can share your problems and feelings with, whose example can help to guide and inspire you. If you're interested in having a Big Sister, call Big Sisters of America at the above number.

The Cherokee Challenge Program, P.O. Box 507, Cherokee, NC 28719; (704) 497-7291. A program that helps prevent drug and alcohol abuse and crime by encouraging such outdoor activities as camping, hiking, and rafting. Most participants are Native American.

Comunidad y Cultura/La Nueva Vida, 1409 Second Street, Santa Fe, NM 87501; (505) 983-9521. Comunidad y Cultura helps teens overcome fear and insecurity by creating experiences that enhance self-esteem and develop self-respect and respect for others. Special sessions focus on substance abuse prevention, sexual responsibility, personal goal planning, and positive life planning.

The Citykids Foundation, 57 Leonard Street, New York, NY 10013; (212) 925-3320. Citykids is a multicultural foundation dedicated to the "survival of today's youth." Citykids sponsors discussion groups and provides a repertory of music and dramatic material that carries Citykids' positive message.

"Girls Can!" Community Coalitions Project, American Association of University Women Educational Foundation, 1111 Sixteenth Street NW, Washington DC 20036; (202) 785-7713. Girls Can! is a national community-based program to eliminate gender bias in public schools. If you feel your school falls short in providing programs that promote gender equity, write to the Association for information about what you can do about it.

Girl Scouts of the U.S.A., 420 Fifth Avenue, New York, NY 10018; (212) 852-6548. Girl Scouting gives girls a chance to develop their potential, make friends, and become a vital part of their community. The Contemporary Issues series tries to recognize and cope with many of the problems confronting teen women, including substance abuse, teen pregnancy, and family crises.

National Youth Leadership Council, 1910 West Country Road B, St. Paul, MN 55113-1337; (612) 631-3672. NYLC advocates for and supports youth service through environmental action groups, international service projects, multicultural projects, and those addressing racism and sexism.

Self-Enhancement Inc., 1730 North Flint, Portland, OR 97227; (503) 249-1721. Self-Enhancement offers programs that emphasize self-esteem, academic enhancement, career development, cultural development, and athletic development.

Take Our Daughters to Work, Ms. Foundation for Women, 120 Wall Street, New York, NY 10005; (212) 742-2300. Held the fourth Thursday in April every year, Take Our Daughters to Work Day allows girls to be "adopted" by businesses.

Today's Girls, Tomorrow's Women, 1437 N. Prospect Avenue, Milwaukee, WI 53202; (414) 272-0725. Helps girls and young women develop into responsible adults and maximize career potential. Offers information and referrals.

United National Indian Tribal Youth, Inc. (UNITY), P.O. Box 25042, Oklahoma City, OK 73125; (405) 424-3010. UNITY promotes spiritual, mental, and physical development among Native Americans in over 100 youth councils nationwide.

Mental Health and Suicide

American Academy of Child and Adolescent Psychiatry, 3615 Wisconsin Avenue NW, Washington, DC 20016; (202) 966-7300. The academy represents over 6,000 child and adolescent psychiatrists and provides nationwide referrals. "Facts for Families" are information sheets on issues such as teen suicide, manic-depressive illness in teens, teenagers with eating disorders, when children have children.

American Association of Suicidology, 4201 Connecticut Avenue NW, Suite 310, Washington, DC 20008; (202) 237-2280. The AAS produces a number of suicide prevention pamphlets, including a guide for students called "Suicide in Youth and What You Can Do About It" and "Directory of Suicide Prevention and Crisis Intervention Agencies in the U.S." You can also request publications and activities for and about those who have lost someone to suicide.

American Psychiatric Association, DPA Dept.,1400 K Street NW, Washington, DC 20005; (202) 682-6220. The Association makes nationwide referrals to psychiatrists who specialize in treating adolescents and offers a wide variety of pamphlets on topics such as teen suicide.

American Psychological Association, 750 First Street NE, Washington, DC 20002; (202) 336-5700. APA provides brochures on a variety of topics including "What You Should Know About Women and Depression," "Answers to Questions About Panic Disorder," "Sexual Harassment: Myths and Realities" and can put you in touch with a licensed mental health provider in your community.

American Society for Adolescent Psychiatry, 4330 East West Highway, Suite 1117, Bethesda, MD 20814; (301) 718-6502. A national association of psychiatrists that can provide names of professionals in your area who specialize in treating adolescents.

The Association Of Black Psychologists, P.O. Box 55999, Washington, DC 20040. Write for a referral in your area.

Emotions Anonymous, P.O. Box 4245, St. Paul, MN 55104; (612) 647-9712. Chapters nationwide offer Youth Emotions Anonymous groups.

First Step, Youth and Family Services, 8303 Liberty Road, Baltimore, MD 21244; (410) 521-4141. First Step offers counseling to seven to eighteen year olds and their families in three ways: individual, family, and group. They also provide crisis intervention for runaway and homeless youth, employment training, drug and alcohol abuse counseling, parenting education, suicide prevention, as well as community education about issues that affect adolescents and families.

National Association of Social Workers, 750 First Street NE, Suite 700, Washington DC 20002; (202) 408-8600. Ask for the Clinical Register Office for a list of registered clinical social workers in your area.

The National Self-Help Clearinghouse, 25 W. 43rd Street, Room 620, New York, NY 10036; (212) 354-8525. Facilitates access to self-help groups and maintains a database and "switchboard" to provide information and referrals to self-help groups and regional self-help clearinghouses.

Suicide Prevention and Crisis Service, P.O. Box 312, Ithaca, NY 14851; (607) 272-1616 (A 24-hour crisis line that provides counseling and referral information.) SPCS is a not-for-profit corporation whose Postvention Program provides an After Suicide Support Group to respond to the needs of traumatized friends and families of individuals who have killed themselves. They also have pamphlets for young people about how to recognize signs of crisis and suicide and how to help oneself and others.

Hotlines

National Runaway Switchboard: (800) 621-4000. For kids in crisis who've left home.

Focus on Recovery: (800) 888-9383. An information referral line for people looking for self-help groups or someone to talk to.

Covenant House National Crisis Hotline: (800) 999-9999 (24 hours). For teens in crisis to talk about any issue.

Youth Crisis Hotline: (800) 448-4663 (24 hours). Provides counseling and referrals, especially for youth dealing with suicide.

CHAPTER 9

IT'S A FAMILY AFFAIR

People can be related by blood—parents, siblings, aunts, uncles, grandparents, cousins; marriage—stepfamilies; or choice—adoption or close friends who seem like family. Even though adolescence is the time in life when hating parents is supposed to be cool, deep down most teens know that they still need their love and support. Even when they're annoying.

We Are Family

A lot is said about "traditional" families, as if they're the only normal kind of family to have. In reality, very few people live with their biological mothers and fathers, 1.4 siblings, a dog, and three goldfish. Actually according to the latest U.S. Bureau of the Census, 50.8 percent of kids live with both parents of origin, while 24 percent live with one parent. That means that a great many young women and men aren't growing up like the Cleavers or the Cosbys—and there's nothing abnormal about that. "We need to be broad about how we define family," states Andres Nazario, Ph.D., co-director of the Gainesville Family Institute in Florida. "Families can be a variety of structures, like single parents, blended, gay or lesbian, or even nonblood related."

Plus many young women who don't live with immediate families have been taken in by extended family members. Historically many communities, especially communities of color, have relied on uncles, aunts, grandmothers, godparents, or cousins to provide either extra help when things get tight or take family members in when necessary. These informal "adoptions" can be great for building relationships with family members of different genders and generations.

"I've actually begun to call both Janet and my mom 'my mom.' "

ERICA, 16, WESTON, MASSACHUSETTS

My parents got divorced when I was twelve. My mom started seeing Janet pretty much after that. I always suspected, but I don't know if I was old enough to put two and two together exactly. It wasn't really any one thing. I just felt there was something special between the two of them.

I actually asked my mom. My mother has a lot of gay friends who we knew were gay. We were talking, and Mom was like, "If I were gay, would that bother you?" And my brother and I were like, "No." She was like, "Do you have anything you want to ask me?" "No." I didn't know how to talk about it. And then later that night I asked her, "Are you?" She was like, "Yeah." And I was like, "Janet?" And she was like, "Yeah." And I was like, "Oh." And that was the extent of our conversation. You would think you would be stressed out by it, but I was actually relieved. My suspicions were confirmed, and it felt like a weight was lifted off my chest.

Still, a whole bunch of stuff was going through my head. It was like, "Yeah, I was right." And at the same time it was like, "Oh my god, what are my friends going to say?" At the same time it was like, "I'm glad it's Janet and not somebody I haven't met." There was a lot of confusion. I wasn't sure I was happy about it, but I also wasn't sure if I should be upset either. I was just trying to figure things out. I don't have any friends who have gay parents, but I had heard about a few things—whether I read it or saw it on television—about how you're supposed to feel: "Oh, it was so awful, it was such a hardship." I didn't really feel that way.

For a long time I didn't tell anybody. I kept it very quiet, because it was at the height of when gay jokes were popular in school—stupid little cracks about famous stars who had just come out. It was supposed to be really funny, and the immature kids in my class would just crack up, mainly because they were embarrassed to talk about it and couldn't deal with it. I didn't want to do anything that would jeopardize my relationship with my friends. But I decided if they were really my friends they would accept me *and* my mother's lifestyle, so that's when I started telling people.

So far all of my friends have accepted it, and we're none the worse for it. But none of my friends have actually asked, "Is your mom gay?" I actually discussed it with two of my friends. I asked them, "Did you guys know my mother was gay?" And they're like, "After we've been over to your house we sort of figured it out." The closest I've ever come to discussing it with anybody else was like, "Well who's Janet?" "My mom's friend." "Does she live with you?" "Yeah." "Well where does she sleep?" "In my mom's room." "So there's two beds in there?" "No . . . " "Oh . . ." And that was the extent of the conversation.

The worst thing that's happened to me is one of my best friends' mother—my friend happens to be a guy—is, as he quoted, "very old fashioned," and doesn't want him to spend time with me. She doesn't think what my mom and Janet are doing is right. It's not like gay-bashing or anything, but it hurts.

Janet moved in about two years ago. The four of us at home have a good time together. I've actually begun to call both Janet and my mom "my mom"—not consciously. It's kind of scary, but at the same time it's kind of cool. I'll talk to myself and I'll be like, "Oh yeah my mom—I mean, my mom and Janet." We're at that stage where we're all really close and I consider them both my mom.

Having gay parents and being around gay people has made me more aware of gay people in my community, whether they're out or not. That's been a cool experience. I hope people can learn to accept it.

Despite what some folks might say, one type of family isn't better than any other. There are many young women growing up in two-parent homes who have lots of problems and others who are raised by single moms or grandmoms who are happy, high-achieving and stable. What's most important is having a network of caring, loving people to share our lives with.

Why Are Families So Important to Us?

According to Dr. Nazario, what's important within a family isn't how many members there are, but whether the people who are there provide nurturing, solid role modeling, warmth, and a sense of direction. These are the building blocks that are necessary to move out into the world securely during the progression into adulthood.

"The essence of adolescence is moving from family into the broader culture, which is very difficult," says Mary Pipher, Ph.D., author of the book *Reviving Ophelia: Saving the Selves of Adolescent Girls* and a therapist in Lincoln, Nebraska. Girls, in particular, have a harder time going through this period because there are so many mixed emotions. On the one hand you may want and need your parents' guidance and support, but on the other hand, society tells you that you're immature or weird for trying to stay close to the family. Many turn to friends for those times when they should be relying on family. This can be risky, because no matter how behind the times parents can be, they generally have more experience and stability than peers.

As Dr. Pipher believes, "In American culture, many life decisions come at about seventh grade." Sexuality starts budding and goals like education and careers start to come into focus. "The amount of trauma that girls face today is enormous, like death of peers, sexual harassment, and drugs and alcohol, and comes at a time when they aren't ready to handle it."

Moving away from the family can also be problematic for many young women from communities that value loyalty to parents. Dr. Pipher believes many communities of color expect that children will remain close with their families. Therefore, girls get caught in the middle, between mainstream society, which expects them to break away, and their own culture, which expects them to stay connected.

What's Up with Mom and Dad These Days?

It's become painfully obvious to many of us that once we hit the double digits our parents don't know what to make of us. Those of us who used to pal around with Mom after school now would rather be dropped off at the mall, preferably blocks away where no one can see. And Dad seems to move further into the background, even more clueless than Mom about "kids today." What happened to the good ol' days?

Maybe it's you who's changed, and the parents don't know how to deal with the new you. Think of it from their perspective. One of the hallmarks of teendom is Mom-bashing. According to Dr. Pipher, one of the ways young women show their independence is by separating and devaluing their mothers. Yet, moms are still expected to be there to wipe up the tears.

Dad's another story. The majority of fathers have a hard time knowing what to do when their "little princess" starts growing breasts and curvy hips. Suddenly there's a woman standing in front of them, and they don't know how to react. Unfortunately instead of being able to talk about the changes, most fathers withdraw or act awkwardly.

Relationships with parents often don't bounce back to normal until adulthood.

But give them credit. Your parents know you better and tolerate more of your snideness than anyone else on the planet and still hang in there. Still it would be nice if the 'rents gave you an ego boost once in awhile by acknowledging you're becoming your own woman.

· · · · · · · · · · · · **WHAT FAMILIES ARE MADE OF** · · · · · · · · · · · · · ·

According to *Parenting* Magazine:

- Twenty-three percent of all American kids live just with their mothers.
- More than 2 million kids lived with just their fathers in 1993.
- In 1993, more than 1 million children were raised by their grandparents.

- There are more than 14 million children of gay and lesbian parents in America.
- There are 1.4 million adoptive families in the U.S.

GROWING UP WITHOUT DAD

Being raised in a single-parent family isn't uncommon. (And let's get real and stop calling them single parents since they're doing the work of two parents. How 'bout double parents?) In fact, in some communities it's more common to live with one parent than two. Among black families, for example, 58.4 percent are headed by single mothers; among Latinos, 30.1 percent of families are headed by women. No big deal, right? Then why are some people still harping on the issue?

First, many people have decided to blame the ills of troubled teens on their mothers. They claim that if these women were better mothers or if they were married, their teenaged kids wouldn't be such problems. However many of these people overlook three important points:

1. Thanks to dedicated moms, the teens are being cared for.

2. Women earn less money than men and are often poor, which means that most teens living with Mom are impoverished.

3. The overwhelming majority of teens being raised by their mothers go on to lead healthy, constructive lives.

Though some narrow-minded people will try to stigmatize others (like using backward terms such as "illegitimate") rather than offer a helping hand, being raised by Mom alone isn't anything to be ashamed of.

Yet, while there's nothing wrong with coming from a female-headed household, many young women have strong feelings about our fathers' not being around everyday. Some have good relationships with Pops and talk to him or visit with him all the time. Though he may not live with the family, he's available and there when he's needed.

Others have less involved dads who usually only turn up on holidays or perhaps send an occasional check. These dads can leave young women hoping for a stronger bond and often disappoint when they don't provide the emotional support.

Then there are those people who have no real relationship with their fathers, either because they don't stay in touch or they were never a big part of the family. Some people are OK with this arrangement, feeling that you can't miss what you never had. But others have "father hunger" and feel abandoned by Dad's absence and wonder what happened to drive him away. That longing can cause an empty feeling, and some people, without knowing it, try to fill up the void in other ways (dating older men, sleeping with dates to get affection and attention, looking for male role models).

Even when Father's not part of the daily picture, don't forget that he's not the last man on Earth. Brothers, uncles, stepfathers, godfathers, male teachers, friends' fathers can all be sources of male support if you feel it's missing. What's important is that you have examples of different kinds of men and can form attachments to those who are committed to seeing you thrive.

Family Feuds

Is there such a thing as families that don't fight? Probably not. Though all families don't scream and yell during the heat of an argument, all have their way of working out conflict.

Why All the Fighting?

Everyone knows relationships are at their best when there's trust, communication, and recognition that each person is a unique individual. Ironically, this is exactly the reason that many relationships between young women and parents get into trouble during the teen years. As Dr. Pipher states, "Girls want to be out in the world and experience what their friends are experiencing, while parents want their daughters to be safe." So touchy topics like dating, friends, curfew, and alcohol all revolve around the push-pull relationship with parents.

While some young women are lucky enough to have good relationships with parents, others can't get along for a second. The main difference between the two is trust, says Ann F. Caron, Ed.D., adolescent psychologist and author of *Don't Stop Loving Me: A Reassuring Guide for Mothers of Adolescent Daughters* (HarperCollins, 1991). "When a daughter interprets questions [about parties, friends, homework, etc.] as an interest in what she is doing, an atmosphere of sharing and trust prevails," says Caron.

Trust involves dedication to another area of conflict: communication. While adolescence is a time for letting go and gaining independence, many young women forget that parents start to feel really left out of their daughters' lives. "Girls tend to protect their parents because they fear they'll be too upset about the things that they do," states Caron, "but that only builds up a wall." Instead of sharing your feelings with your parents, you might instead call up a friend and rag about them. Parents don't know what they've done wrong, and the conflicts don't get resolved.

Caron feels that parents should be given a chance, if not for them then for you. "Begin communicating by asking parents how they felt when they were young and going through the same things. Taking the initiative will flatter them because they probably think their daughters don't want anything to do with them."

Not everybody goes completely berserk during the teens, but most young women do begin to defy and reject some of their parents' values and replace them with their own, which they have developed when faced with new experiences. "For some families this happens slowly [and parents respect the choices their kids make] as long as their goals and expectations are similar," explains Caron. Discussing common goals and what direction you want to go in your life helps a family stay close. The more you keep your parents involved in what you're up to, the easier it is to keep the peace at home.

"Talking to my parents, I get a better sense of where they're coming from. I know that all they want is the best for me."

GENNA, 18, MIAMI, FLORIDA

The problems between my mom and me were about dating. She never really liked anyone I went out with. She never thought that the other person was right for me or good enough.

My mom doesn't like the guy I'm dating now, for example. It's not really him that she doesn't like, but she thinks it's still the fifties and the guy should do everything for the girl. But it's different now. Girls are more in control in relationships. But my mom thinks, "Oh, the guy has to call you, don't call him! He'll think that you're easy." She doesn't want me to do anything. She wants him to bring all the flowers.

My mom wants the best, but it's very hard to find that someone special. I told her that I'm going to need to experiment with different people until I find the right person. She agrees, but she says that along the way I shouldn't get hurt by anyone because I don't deserve to get hurt. I agree with that.

When I wasn't communicating well with my mother, I felt very lonely. I don't have any brothers or sisters, and I had no one else to talk to. I usually tell my mom everything. Sometimes it was hard not to talk to her. But at times she wouldn't listen to me because she didn't agree with me. I told her that she had to realize that I'm growing up. I explained that I'd still love her no matter what, but I'd really like it more if she started listening to how I feel. My mom would never really get angry with me. She'd get more upset than angry.

Eventually I learned how to get her attention and communicate with her in the right way. I learned how to do that through my favorite teacher, and he was like a second father to me. I'd tell him, "Look, my mom and I are having problems." He would listen, and he would tell me how to communicate with her.

He told me I had to sit her down and tell her that it was serious—nothing bad or anything, but serious. I needed to say that lately I hadn't been communicating with her, because I felt that she was being hurt by my actions or my boyfriend—but that I loved her and that my family came first. I knew a little bit of this, but he helped me a lot.

My teacher helped me calm myself down, because I used to get angry. Before, I would actually go to my parents and start yelling, but he taught me how to make it a calm situation rather than aggressive. When I used to yell, my parents would say, "You shouldn't yell at us, young lady." They would yell, too, and nothing would get settled. I'd feel angry, because nothing got accomplished in the conversation. Nothing that I wanted to say from my heart came out; everything just came out from my mouth. The first time I tried to do it differently was a little more than two months ago. I sat my mom down and told her how I felt. Rather than just saying, "I really don't appreciate what you're doing to me. You never listen to me anymore," I said, "I need to talk to you seriously and this is my first time really expressing my feelings in the right way. I hope I can handle it and I hope you can, too. And this is the situation . . . "

I told her how I felt—that nobody was going to come between us, and that the mother and father relationship should stay the same because I would love them always, but that I didn't appreciate her not listening to me and how I felt. I told her that I really needed to talk to her about my dating situation and that this was the person that I was with now and this was his name. I explained that he would not do anything to hurt me and that I would not choose a person that would hurt me. She was good about listening. Sometimes she'd interrupt me and I'd say, "Can you stop interrupting and let me talk for a bit and then I can hear what you have to say?" It took a little sadness and crying, which usually happens when we talk to each other.

Talking to my parents, I get a better sense of where they're coming from. I know that all they want is the best for me, and that they want me to know that. They want me to be happy most of all. If I'm happy, they're happy. And if I'm hurt, they're hurt. Most kids hardly ever talk to their parents and others don't even have parents to talk to. I guess I'm lucky.

How to Avoid Family Feuds

When you can't stand the sound of your parents' voices or the sight of their faces, obviously it's time to change the way you're dealing with them. If you take the initiative to turn over a new leaf in the relationship, not only will you pleasantly surprise your parents, but you may really astonish yourself by how much easier it is to deal with them. Drs. Pipher and Caron both have some insightful advice about how to accomplish what seems like the impossible:

- Don't lose control. The one sure way to have your parents say "you're acting like a child" is to throw a temper tantrum. By using as much restraint as you can muster, stay calm and respectful, listen without interrupting, and acknowledge your parents' point of view by saying that you hear them.

- Make a deal. If you want the rules changed, the best way to appeal to your folks is to first explain why you want them changed and then suggest a reasonable alternative.

> Don't say: "I think coming home at 9 o'clock is really stupid, and I'm adult enough to come in at 2 o'clock." (Even if it's true, it won't get you very far.)
>
> Do say: "It's hard for me to get home by 9 because all my friends can stay out later, and I can't get a ride home. Do you think we could change my curfew to 10 on weekdays and 12 on weekends?"

- Make agreements and stick with them. If you do make a deal with your parents, don't blow it for yourself, for example by showing up two hours after your curfew without calling. Keeping your word gives you more ammo for future rule changes and shows you're a woman of character.

- Keep in touch daily. If parents know what you're up to, they're less likely to snoop around, eavesdrop, or constantly question you. Plan a date, like dinner several times a week, or arrange to run errands together after school.

- Consider your parents allies rather than enemies. Generally parents have your best interests at heart and, like most people, have a hard time accepting change. Just like you want them to give you a break, you should do the same for them.

SIBS: CAN'T LIVE WITH THEM, CAN'T KILL THEM

If you have them, you may either love them, want to kill them, or borrow clothes from them. They're your siblings, and they're like no one else in your life. If you're lucky, you have good friendships with your brothers and sisters. But a lot of people would rather send their siblings right back where they came from.

In some ways nature pits brothers and sisters against each other in what's known as sibling rivalry. As Adele Faber and Elaine Mazlish explain in *Siblings Without Rivalry: How to Help Your Children Live Together so You*

Can Live Too, "The root of sibling jealousy is each child's deep desire for the *exclusive* love of his parents."

It helps to keep in mind, though, that with any sticky sib situation, there's a bright spot. Dr. Daniel Blake, Ph.D., a clinical psychologist who deals with siblings, stresses that brothers and sisters provide a unique opportunity. "They give us the opportunity to learn how to become social and how to problem solve, compromise, and work out issues in the heat of our emotions."

Still, if you find getting along with bro or sis impossible, Dr. Blake suggests a few things to try during your next sibling war:

- Keep calm. Even if you aren't feeling calm, don't do or say anything to fuel the fire.
- Be very clear about what made you angry. Talk about how you feel rather than who did what.
- Try to see the other side. By listening and being patient, hear them out. There's always two sides to every story, and even if you don't agree, you owe each other the respect of hearing each other's perspectives.
- Remember that getting along doesn't happen overnight. This is true especially if you've had a long history of fighting.
- Get parents involved if you can't work it out alone. Try this as a last resort to smoothing over a conflict. It's best to learn how to resolve matters together.
- Be good to each other. Show each other basic courtesy, like saying "good morning" or asking about each other's lives.
- Spend time really getting to know each other. You may want to do this away from the parents and away from home, on neutral ground. Try walking to school together or joining a sports team together.
- Show you care. The best way to show concern for each other is to be there when the other's in need. After all, your identities are built on similar experiences, so who better to know what you're each going through during stressful times?

WHY FAMILIES FIGHT

With the folks: privileges, curfew, chores, friends, dating, grades, wearing makeup or certain clothes, watching TV, volume of music, talking on the phone.

With the sibs: sharing a room, borrowing clothes or other belongings, invading another's space or privacy, hogging the phone, stealing friends or boyfriends, parents' attention.

When the Family Changes

Rarely will anything change our lives as profoundly as when our families change. Because we depend on our families for our identity, strength, and stability, when things get shaken up, we get extremely stressed, if not depressed. We can also learn some important parts of ourselves, mainly that we can survive and sometimes become strengthened through the pain of loss.

Going Through a Divorce

Watching a family split up can be one of the most painful experiences to go through. As common as divorce and separation are, everyone hopes it won't happen to their families. Because half of all marriages end in divorce, unfortunately many young women and men will inevitably have to face this serious life change.

Divorce is hard on everyone involved. In his book *Helping Children Cope with Divorce*, Edward Teyber explains that teens have different reactions to this distressing situation, all of which are normal. While feeling sad is inevitable, some teens also get angry at their parents. Others feel betrayed and let down that their parents couldn't keep the family together. Others feel depressed, some more than others because they face decisions about who to live with and other complicated matters that go along with a divorce. Another common reaction is fear of the future, questioning whether all relationships fail.

Teyber also points out three common questions that crop up during divorce:

- Will I lose my parents? "Since I can't live with both parents, will I still be close to the parent who lives away?" "Will the parent I live with (usually Mom) be too freaked out to take care of me?" These strong fears of separation and abandonment usually last a couple of years after the initial separation, while the new arrangements settle in.

- Did I cause my parents to break up? When parents separate, children and teens almost automatically go through events of the past to see if there wasn't something that could've been done to keep them together. Even as adults, some people hold on to the idea that it was because they were somehow "bad" and caused so much grief that their parents divorced. Getting these fantasies out in the open helps to see that they're just that—fantasies. No child has the power to cause her parents to break up.

• Will my parents get back together? Unless family life is truly unbearable, most young people don't want to see their parents apart. Any change to the family feels threatening to the only sense of security most teens have ever known. So, it's only normal to wish for those times when the family *was* happy—and together—in hopes that things will be as they were. Even though most teens know that Mom and Dad are probably better off without each other, it doesn't keep them from feeling loss over the family that used to be.

According to Teyber, adolescent girls tend to recover from divorce better than boys. "Studies show that two years after the divorce, girls in mother-headed families tend to be as well adjusted as girls in intact two-parent homes," he says. In her book *The Good Divorce*, Constance Ahrons, Ph.D., associate director of the marriage and family therapy program at the University of Southern California, states that almost half of all children from divorced families didn't suffer any long-term trauma. However, if troubles feel too tough to handle alone, it's always best to seek outside help.

Dealing with a Stepfamily

Getting acquainted with a new family can be just as traumatic as losing the old one. Just as you've adjusted to the new situation, one or both of your parents throws a curve. "I'm getting married," Mom or Dad says, and suddenly a stranger becomes an intimate part of your life.

Stepfamily specialist and co-founder of the Stepfamilies Association of America Emily Visher, Ph.D., states that 33 percent of all Americans are in some stepfamily situation, and over half of us will deal with a stepfamily in our lifetimes. So, the good news is that if you are in a stepfamily situation, you have plenty of company.

One of the first problems teens encounter when parents decide to remarry is that they feel alone. "During the divorce, kids and parents have an understanding because they're going through their feelings together," says Visher. When the parent announces a new marriage, they're excited while the kids are depressed. This is especially hard on kids, explains Visher, because "once again their whole lives are going to change and they have no control over it. Change is hard for people because it involves loss, in this case it's usually the loss of the exclusive attention of one parent."

Visher mentions several other feelings that teens go through initially when family becomes stepfamily:

• Letting go of the fantasy that parents will get back together.
• Not being in control of parent's choice of a new partner.

- Having a sense of identity and position in the family threatened as new siblings appear on the scene.
- Feeling that one family is lost and forced to enter another.
- Fearing a move, change of schools, or being forced to share a room.
- Feeling left out and angry at having to share the parent.

Visher believes that one key to getting over some of these doubts and fears is time. It takes a while to get to know someone, so if you're in the situation you have to allow space for this new person (or persons) to blend into your every day life. Not living with the newlyweds can be more difficult, because you won't have the benefit of daily experiences to get acquainted. It's hard enough getting back into the swing with Dad on the weekends, but having to deal with his new wife and her kids makes it feel impossible. Visher says to go easy and talk about the concerns. "Parents seem to gain from the remarriage right away, but it takes kids longer to recognize their gains. With teens, if they can share their feelings they'll come to see that the stepparents are going through the same thing."

Dealing with the new couple can turn into a competitive thing. "Girls get into competition with stepmothers for their father's attention," says Visher, "or with their mother for their stepfather's attention if they feel they've lost their father." Equally frustrating may be your feelings if you've been living with a single parent. "Before the daughter may have been the mother's main companion. Once her mother remarries, she loses her function and, to her, a special place in her mother's life."

Although parents should take the lead when coping with stepfamilies, Visher feels there are ways to deal with the new situation:

- Know your feelings are normal. Understand that this is a big change and everyone feels strange. Whatever feelings you have are natural, so don't feel ashamed if you aren't dealing with the changes "perfectly."
- Communicate your feelings. The best way to get through any problems you have with your parents is to communicate them, don't act them out. The only way you'll get heard is to talk about your feelings. If you're having a hard time getting the dialogue started, try going to a counselor together or pick up a book on stepfamilies and read it together.
- If your parents don't listen or you feel you can't talk to them, find someone outside of the immediate family to talk to so you don't feel isolated and alone. Good confidantes are grandparents, aunts or uncles, cousins, best friends, or trusted teachers.

- Give yourself time. It takes a while to get comfortable with a new family situation. If you can, look at the addition in a positive light. It's more people who care about you, who can offer you examples, and who can give you a sense of family (maybe some members you didn't have before, like grandparents or siblings, you have now).

- Spend time alone with your parent. Alone time will reestablish your relationship and help you to feel special again. It will also help ease the sense of loss.

- Spend time alone with your stepparent. This will allow you to get to know the new man or woman in your life. Without your parent, you're more likely to discover what you two have in common that could help you build a separate relationship.

- Form a stepfamily group at school or in your neighborhood. You won't feel lonely any more once you see how many people are going through the exact same thing.

· · · · · · · · · · · · · · · · · · · **WHAT ARE YOU GONNA DO ABOUT IT?**

BEECH ACRES' BOYS AND GIRLS GROUP
ABOUT DIVORCE IN CINCINNATI, OHIO

Hardly anything hurts more about divorce than feeling there's no one to turn to. After a divorce, families often fragment and everyone seems to go their separate ways. In the end teens can be left with confusion, hurt, and deep feelings of loss, but often no one to listen.

In a unique program developed by the Aring Institute, the Boys and Girls Group About Divorce allows students at Purcell Marion High School in Cincinnati, Ohio, to come in once a week for up to ten weeks to talk about any problems they have surrounding their parents' divorce. For forty-five minutes, a group of ten students and two faculty leaders talk about various topics like relationships, stepfamilies, and life outside the home.

Lisa Hunter, eighteen, is a senior at Purcell Marion and has been a group member. "My brother was in the group and I thought it would be a great thing to work out my frustrated feelings towards my dad. The group helped me release my anger towards him." Though she was only one year old when her parents separated, she still has intense feelings of abandonment by her father. "I never talked to him. I would ask myself why can't he be there?"

Amy Knorr, also a senior at Purcell Marion, knows what Lisa's going through. At age two her parents split up and she was raised by her mother and stepfather. Then during her sophomore year, they divorced. "It felt like everybody had left me," confides Amy. "I couldn't talk about it with anybody. I held a lot in—my hurt, my anger, my questions."

Amy and Lisa both needed some place to vent their disappointment. Being in the group has allowed Lisa to come to terms with how she really felt about her father. "Before the group, I totally ignored my dad," admits Lisa. "I would joke and say that he was dead." Hearing other teens talk honestly gave her the courage to express herself. "The group opened me up and let me talk about something I hadn't with anyone. I realized a lot of other people have the same problems and that other parents are like this."

Amy found the atmosphere safe and accepting. "I could cry and it was OK," she says. "No one would tease me." Coming every week has helped her tremendously. "I got a lot off my chest. Now I'm able to express my feelings. The group made me realize that that was my home life and I shouldn't let it affect my grades. It took me a year, but I got my life turned around." For more information, contact Jackie Perry-Drake, Beech Acres, 6881 Beechmont, Cincinnati, OH 45230; (513) 231-7205, ext. 72.

Death of a Family Member

Probably the most difficult crisis any of us will face in our lives is carrying on after someone we love dies. We must do something we often avoid in our teens, that is face the fact that we will all die some day. Accepting this concept is hard because it also means coming to terms with the enormous loss: the person we love so much is never coming back.

With any death or loss everyone goes through a period of intense emotional pain—grieving. There is no magic cure for grief, and as unpleasant as the experience can be, the only way to overcome the feelings are to go through them. In time, the very intense feelings pass.

Though not everyone grieves in the same way or to the same degree, most people go through a similar set of emotions when faced with the death of a loved one. In his book *Straight Talk About Death for Teenagers: How to Cope with Losing Someone You Love*, Earl A. Grollman describes these stages:

1. Dazed: this is a period when life seems unreal because of shock. It may feel like numbness until the finality of the death has sunk in.

2. Disbelief: during this stage it's still hard to accept what's happened, and it may be easy to forget the person is really gone.

3. Anger: most people experience this feeling as "Why me?" It may also feel like "Why did she leave me?" The pent-up emotion may cause physical symptoms of stress, emotional withdrawal, or inappropriate anger.

4. Envy: when someone dies, seeing others enjoy themselves sometimes leads to feeling of jealousy.

5. Panic: death of a family member means life will change in some way. Not only is the grieving process itself disruptive, but the uncertainty about the future can also lead to anxiety and loss of control.

6. Relief: some people feel relief when a loved one has suffered before dying. Or sometimes the person who died was abusive, so the death means the end of mistreatment.

7. Loneliness: feeling isolated is one of the most difficult parts of grief. Few people want to deal with intense sadness alone, but the nature of grief is that nobody can totally understand the feelings.

8. Going nuts: when someone dies it may trigger intense feelings and cause unusual behavior—forgetfulness, daydreaming, visions, and so on. This happens as the person left behind tries to adjust to the absence of the loved one.

9. Depression: in death it may feel like life has little meaning. This, together with the emotional exhaustion, can cause depression. Depression, or anger turned inward, can make you feel hopeless and powerless. It can sap all the life away unless the grief is dealt with.

10. Regrets: there are many feelings of guilt and regret when someone close dies. Some people suffer what's called survivor's guilt—guilty for living or enjoying life after the person is dead.

"After my mom died, I got really sad. It felt like part of me died."
JANNA, 19, PORTLAND, OREGON

My parents got divorced when I was four or five. When I found out my mom had cancer (the beginning of September, 1993) I was living at home with my father. I hadn't talked to my mom for a couple of years because we weren't getting along, and my dad didn't want me to see my mom.

I had heard from my sister that my mom had gone into the hospital, and in the back of my head I knew that she had cancer and was going to die. I didn't know what kind of cancer, but I just knew.

When my mom came to my grandmother's house on the day I was visiting, it was weird because I wasn't expecting her. My grandmother already knew, my sister already knew, and my brother had just been told. My mom couldn't walk very well, so with her walker she came over to where I was sitting and said, "Get up." I stood up, because I didn't know what else to do. She gave me a hug and told me she loved me, and I just started crying, because I knew.

Then she sat down and told me she had liver cancer and that they gave her three to six months to live. I felt kind of nauseous. I knew, but I just couldn't believe it, and I was crying so hard I felt like I was going to throw up. I was so overwhelmed. I never in my whole life dreamed it would happen.

My mom explained everything really well. She told me how my benefits were going to work, like my insurance, so that if anything happened to her before she had another chance to explain it to me I would already know what would be going on and could take care of it myself. She was so calm about it.

After that I called my mother every day or every other day. I'd ask how she was feeling, and she'd ask about school and what I was doing. It really brought us together in a way. So much was lost before, and there wasn't much time to repair anything, so we just tried to pick up where we should've been anyway.

Not too long after that my mom got worse. One of the tumors in her liver had gotten bigger than a baseball—or maybe it was a grapefruit, I don't remember. But it had gotten really big, but she made it through. After I found that out it was so real. I was really freaking out about it, because I was thinking that could have been it. I couldn't grasp the concept that my mom was really close to dying.

I skipped school a lot. I just couldn't concentrate. Most of my teachers knew what was going on, because I had to tell them that if it got really bad I would have to take some time off from school. They were telling me a week ahead of time what my assignments would be, in case I had to go and didn't have time to get things together.

I couldn't go out and have fun anymore, and my friends really didn't want to hang around me because I wasn't having a good time. They didn't understand and they didn't know what to say or what to do. I had this one really good friend who would come pick me up at the hospital. She would never go in, though. We'd go out for coffee and stuff, but we never really talked about it. It was kind of an uncomfortable subject for everybody. My sister was so far away, my brother was freaking out, and my dad was not very supportive. I didn't have anyone to talk to.

My mom died on December 2nd, my eighteenth birthday. A couple of days before that she had said to me, "I just can't do this anymore. It's so painful, I just can't." For the next two nights I read to her *The Joy Luck Club*, which she had bought. It was all about this daughter and her dying mother, and here I am reading it to her. I would read it out loud to her, partly to keep myself awake and partly to soothe her, so she had something else to focus on.

After that, she started to let go. She was breathing quickly and her eyes were open really wide as if she was suffocating. I sat down with her and held her hand. I knew she was going to die right then. I called in my stepdad and my uncle from the other room, and I said, "This is it."

After my mom died, I got really sad. It felt like part of me died. But also, with her death I learned how short life really is, and that you don't really appreciate something until you lose it. Life has a different meaning after you've seen someone die. Now I look at things for what they are instead of what I perceive them to be—like I see birds flying around and appreciate them, because they're alive, and I appreciate all things that are alive.

Froma Walsh, Ph.D., co-director of the Center for Family Health at the University of Chicago, says that the best way to deal with death is to really deal with it. Withdrawing by not talking or by taking drugs is a way "to protect one's self from deep pain and to avoid losing control," says Walsh. By not facing pain, though, the grieving process will take longer and lives will become more complicated.

If a relative or friend is dying or has died, keep in mind that whatever you do feel is normal and that you won't feel it for the rest of your life. If you're having trouble facing your pain, Grollman and Walsh offer ways to survive grief:

- If you know your family member is ill, prepare your good-byes. Tell the person you love them and how much they mean to you. Ask them how they want to be remembered or what hopes they have for you in the future.

- If the person has died suddenly, stay connected to your family. When people fragment, there's no one there to support and comfort you. Try not to build a wall around yourself by reaching out and allowing yourself to be close to your family.

- Get a keepsake. Whether it's jewelry, a photo, or clothing, have a token that will always remind you of that person so you can transform the relationship into memory.

- Prepare a memorial speech or poem. Relate a story or memory that sums up how you feel or what was special about the person who's gone and, if you feel up to it, read it at their funeral or memorial. Whether you're able to give the speech or not, writing it will help you to be actively involved in saying good-bye and begin your grieving.

- Spend holidays with the family by commemorating the person who died. These are the most difficult times, but can be made a little easier by telling stories that bring up good feelings of the past.

- Forgive yourself. Any guilt, anger, regret, depression, shame, or other emotions you have surrounding the death are completely normal. Understand that in life there are some unfair, awful events and that this is your reaction to one of them. Give yourself permission to live fully.

• Allow yourself to spend some time alone. You can use this time to reflect on your life and your future, and be alone with your thoughts of your loved one.

• Instead of thinking of regrets, try to think of what you did while the person was alive that brought you both joy. Know that pain and disappointment are part of relationships.

Walsh explains, "During the first few months of grief there are very strong feelings a lot of the time. You may even be surprised about the ebb and flow of your feelings. There's no one right way to experience death." As time passes, the pain eases. "After a year, the feelings begin to diminish," says Walsh. "You have more energy for life." However, family times like holidays will still be tough for many years. Walsh says to "let your tears flow." By allowing for grief, we can face our pain and let it go. Only then can we move on.

BEHIND BARS: WHEN MOM OR DAD IS IN PRISON

Any time a family gets split up it's difficult, but it's doubly hard being separated from a parent who's in prison. Susan Bergmann, Ph.D., a child psychologist in Oakland who works with kids whose mothers are in prison, says, "Losing a parent for any reason is difficult, but losing a parent to a socially unacceptable situation is really difficult."

An added dilemma for children left behind, Bergmann explains, is that when a parent goes to prison, the family is put at risk. "Though there's a stigma when a father goes away, loss of a mother to prison is more devastating. Children experience a sense of abandonment." Girls are especially affected because it's often left up to young women to take over where Mom left off and try to keep the family together. The stress that builds over time can lead to depression or trigger acting out through substance abuse or behavior problems (like stealing, fighting, or joining a gang).

Because there are so few women's prisons, many women are incarcerated far from home, sometimes in entirely different states. This makes it difficult for families to visit and therefore stay close. Bergmann believes the most important way for families to survive a prison term is for them to stay in contact through frequent visits, calls, or letters. "If Mother is still seen as an active member of her life," says Bergmann, "it's much better for her daughter. Both of them can gain support by finding caregivers for the children that support their relationship and try to help the family stay close."

If your parent is in prison, Bergmann has a couple of suggestions:

- Try to understand what your parent did. Most parents are too ashamed to discuss what landed them in prison. But it's important for your mother or father to come clean so that you can learn from their mistakes. Talk with her or him to get her honest feelings and try to make sense out of it in your own life so there isn't a repeated history.
- Find support. Through a prison support group, family member, or counselor, get the support you need and get your feelings off your chest.

For more information contact Aid to Children of Imprisoned Mothers Inc., 599 Mitchell Street SW, Atlanta, GA 30314; (404) 221-0092, or Aid to Incarcerated Mothers at 32 Rutland Street, Boston, MA 02118; (617) 536-0058.

Where to Turn

Recommended Reading

Between Sisters: Secret Rivals, Intimate Friends, Barbara Mathias, Delacorte, 1992.

Bringing Up Parents: The Teenager's Handbook, Alex J. Packer, Free Spirit Publishing, 1993. Straight talk and specific suggestions on how teens can take the initiative to resolve conflicts with parents, improve family relationships, earn trust, accept responsibility, and help to create a healthier, happier home environment.

Coping in a Single-Parent Home, Bill R. Wagonseller, Lynne C. Ruegamer and Marie C. Harrington, Rosen Publishing Group, 1992. Living in a single-parent home can present special problems. This book explains solutions to the difficulties these families may present and encourages teens to support their in-home parent.

Coping When a Parent Is in Jail, John La Valle, D.C.S.W., Rosen Publishing Group, 1994. In this book Mr. La Valle addresses the emotions, such as fear, worry, guilt, and shame, that teens feel when a parent is in jail. He explains why some people end up in jail, what happens in prison, the visiting process, and where teens can find support.

Coping with Sibling Rivalry, Shari Cohen, Ruth Rosen, eds., Rosen Publishing Group, 1989. Sibling relationships have a profound effect on our feelings of self. Perceptions of injustices can last a lifetime. In this book, the author analyzes the family and the rapport with siblings.

Death Is Hard to Live with: Teenagers and How They Cope with Loss, Compiled by Janet Bode, Delacorte Press, 1993. Through interviews with teenagers who have experienced the death of a friend or relative, the author explores ways of making peace with the shock, guilt, and tragedy of death. Other books by Janet Bode (all published by F. Watts) include: *Different Worlds: Interracial and Cross-cultural Dating*, 1989; *Beating the Odds: Stories of Unexpected Achievers*, 1991; *New Kids on the Block: Oral Histories of Immigrant Teens*, 1989.

How It Feels When Parents Divorce, Jill Krementz, Alfred A. Knopf, 1984. Nineteen girls and boys from diverse backgrounds, ages seven to sixteen, share their deepest feelings about parents' divorce to show you that shock, anger, confusion, pain, are normal and appropriate as well. The book will also give you constructive ways to get through this difficult time.

Making Peace with Your Parents, Harold Bloomfield, M.D., and Leonard Felder, Ph.D., Ballantine Books, 1984.

Motherless Daughters: The Legacy of Loss, Hope Edelman, Addison-Wesley, 1994. This book examines the profound effects of this loss on a woman's identity, personality, family, and life choices, both immediately and as her life goes on.

Stepkids: A Survival Guide for Teenagers in Stepfamilies . . . & for Stepfathers Doubtful of their Own Survival, Ann Getzoff and Carolyn McClenahan, Walker & Company, 1984. This book, packed with solid, realistic advice, including communication tips, can help even the most well-adjusted stepkids.

Straight Talk About Death for Teenagers: How to Cope with Losing Someone You Love, Earl A. Grollman, Boston Beacon Press, 1993. This book explains what to expect when you lose someone you love. It will help you to work through your grief and begin to live again. Includes a journal section where you can record your memories of the person who died, feelings about loss, and hopes for the future.

Straight Talk About Parents, Elizabeth A. Ryan, Facts on File, 1989. Provides concrete examples about how you can work things out with your parents when they embarrass you, invade your privacy, make you feel frustrated or angry, misunderstand you.

Teenagers Talk About Grief, June Kolf, Baker Book House, 1990. Using true life examples and a personal style this book offers solid, compassionate help to grieving teenagers. The special problems associated with suicide are also discussed.

When Grownups Drive You Crazy, Eda LeShan, Simon & Schuster, 1988.

Support Groups and Organizations

Adoptive Families of America, 3333 Highway 100 North, Minneapolis, MN 55422; (612) 535-4829. A free self-help network that provides support and information for people in adoptive families. Local groups offer a setting for discussion and advice.

ALMA Society (Adoptees' Liberty Movement Association), P.O. Box 727, Radio City Station, New York, NY 10101-0727; (212) 581-1568. ALMA's primary purpose is to faciliate reunions of adopted children with natural parents. Membership is open to those eighteen and over.

Big Brothers Big Sisters of America, 230 N. Thirteenth St., Philadelphia, PA 19107; (215) 567-7000. Provides a broad range of services for teenagers, including matching children from single-family homes with adult volunteers.

COLAGE, Children of Lesbians and Gays Everywhere, 2300 Market Street, San Francisco, CA 94114; (415) 861-5437. National organization run by and for daughters and sons of lesbian, gay, and bisexual parents. Support and advocate peers by making voices of members public through conferences, local peer groups, and publications.

The Compassionate Friends, Box 3696, Oak Brook, IL 60522-3696; (708) 990-0010. A self-help association for parents and siblings of a child who has died. In local groups nationwide members talk over their experiences as a way of resolving grief and regaining emotional and physical health. Their pamphlets include "Understanding Grief" and "When a Brother or Sister Dies."

The Dougy Center, P.O. Box 86852, Portland, OR 97286; (503) 775-5683. The Dougy Center provides support groups for children and teens grieving the death of a parent or sibling, and their adult caretakers or parents. They have a national directory of all grieving programs in the U.S. Contact them to learn about groups in your area.

Families Anonymous, P.O. Box 3475, Culver City, CA 90231-3475; (800) 736-9805. FA is a nonprofit self-help fellowship of relatives and friends of people whose drug problems are seriously affecting their lives and their ability to function normally. FA is dedicated to doing something constructive about how to approach someone else's drug habit problems. It holds free twelve-step weekly discussion meetings where members share suggestions and emotional support.

Family Resource Coalition, 200 South Michigan Avenue, 16th floor, Chicago, IL 60604; (312) 341-0900. A national network of community-based programs that develop family strengths. The Coalition offers guides on how to find family support programs that fit your needs in your community. Call or write for more information.

Parents Without Partners, 401 North Michigan Avenue, Chicago, IL 60611-4267; (800) 637-7974. An international support, educational, and advocacy organization to promote welfare and interests of single parents and their children. Single parents and children gather in community chapters to talk about lives, learn to improve family life, and to socialize and play. PWP offers many activities and services for teens. They also provide publications for and about single-parent families.

Stepfamily Association of America, Inc., 215 Centennial Mall South, Suite 212, Lincoln, NE 68508; (402) 477-STEP. SAA has local chapters which offer a variety of programs such as "mutual help groups" and young people's discussion groups. SAA also has a catalog on books and tapes about stepfamily living.

Stepfamily Foundation, Inc., 333 West End Ave., Apt. 11C, New York, NY 10023; (212) 877-3244. Not for profit; for separated, divorced, and remarried families. Deals with couples and children through counseling. Also provides professional seminars, lecture series, and a crisis hotline.

Hotlines

Grief Recovery Hotline: (800) 445-4808. Provides counseling services on coping with loss.

CHAPTER 10

GOTTA HAVE FRIENDS

Friends

They come in all shapes, sizes, colors, and sexes. A friend of any kind is someone to depend on in a pinch. They understand your innermost feelings—or at least try to—and may even be going through the same things at the same time. They stick close in good times as well as bad; they're supporters and self-esteem boosters—and sometimes feel like a sister or brother. It's also important to keep in mind that, like siblings, friends can sometimes get on that last nerve. But it's the best of pals that will weather the storm.

Why Are Friends So Important?

Everybody needs friends. And by the time you hit your teens, you're pretty much dying to hang out with people your own age, instead of tagging along with Mom or Dad. This is true for a couple of reasons.

For one, even if you have siblings around the same age as you, you still need peers outside the family. James Youniss, Ph.D., professor of psychology at Catholic University in Washington, D.C., explains a friendship as "a unique relationship where you get to experience yourself as an equal in defining reality and determining emotions and events that you can't do with parents." Friends are great to bounce ideas and feelings off of, because that feedback will help you grow and define who you are. "You can't do those things alone," says Dr. Youniss. "You need friends to compare with others, which you can't do alone or with just anyone—it's too embarrassing." And who better can keep a secret than a good friend?

According to Lee A. Peck, author of *Coping with Cliques*, friends also sometimes act as parental substitutes. "The teen years are when girls start becoming independent from their parents," she states. "It's helpful to have friends to share dreams and fears." This is especially true when you're looking to talk to someone about body changes, emotional problems, and what a pain the parents are being.

And as great as guys can be, nothing can take the place of a heart-to-heart with your best girlfriend. Let's face it, there are just some topics that guys can't relate to, like getting your period. And instead of tearing each other down with gossip, competition, and jealousy, it's critical for young women to do some female bonding, because it leads to healthy relationships that thrive on trust, dependability, and support.

What Makes Someone a Good Friend?

Good friends are hard to find, at least that's how the saying goes. And if you think of what actually makes a good friend, it's true. Dr. Youniss offers three qualities healthy friendships have:

- reciprocity: sharing with each other;
- negotiating: working out conflicts and compromises;
- common interests: enjoying similar activities.

If you meet someone and find that you click, it's a good start. But to keep the friendship going, she should be:

- a good listener;
- supportive;
- someone who makes you feel good about yourself;
- honest, but not judgmental;
- easy to talk to and listen to;
- someone who you accept for who she is and who does the same for you.

Making Friends

If you've noticed a big change in the type of friends you're hanging out with now compared to a few years ago, it's because the way you make friends has probably changed. In grade school, most friends are what Peck calls "a matter of coincidence." They're the kids that live down the street or walk the same route to school. But in middle school or junior high, things change: "Friends become more a matter of choice," states Peck.

This shift is good, because you and your friends probably have a lot more in common than friends of the past. But it can be confusing, too. "Girls may ask where do I belong now. They miss the security they had." Life suddenly gets a little more complicated because your best friend isn't your next door neighbor, and she might be wondering what happened. "A girl who is moving on to new friendships needs to talk to old friends about what's going on, especially if there are hard feelings," says Peck. Her advice is to be direct and honest by telling the truth. "Interests change as one gets older and so do friends."

That's how to handle the old friends, but what about making new ones? For some young women striking up a conversation with someone is as natural as waking up in the morning. However, for those who are somewhat shy, Dr. Darlene Powell-Hopson of the Hopson Center for Psychological and Educational Services, offers suggestions on how to get to know someone:

- When you see someone you would like to develop a friendship with, approach her or him with a big smile and a "hello." Whatever you do, don't hold back. Most people are flattered with the idea that someone wants to be a friend. So why not make the first move by introducing yourself?

- Watch your body language. It's important to make eye contact when talking to someone to show that you're interested.

- Once the ice has been broken, think of something you both have in common. For example, if the person is in your math class, ask her how she did on the last test. If you have similar tastes in music, you could start a conversation about that. The key is to talk about something you feel comfortable with and the conversation will take off on its own course.

- To meet new people, look into joining an organization that focuses on teen issues. Or if you're into the arts, join a dance, music or theater group; or sports, hook up with an athletic team. Right off the bat, you know you have something in common with a potential friend so that makes it easier to strike up a conversation.

CAN A GUY BE A GOOD FRIEND?

Sometimes guys seem so strange, like brothers from another planet. But according to Carol Weston, author of the book *Girl Talk: All the Stuff Your Sister Never Told You*, girls and guys should have friends of the opposite sex. "They can give each other a look into how the other person is feeling. After awhile, you're not even aware of the gender difference."

Guy friends are great for those times when you need the inside scoop on the male mentality, a safe date for a spur-of-the-moment occasion or a reminder that all guys aren't dogs. It's always good to know that there are members of the male species that are interested in young women for their personalities, intelligence, and sense of humor.

Things can get complicated though if the friendship turns to romance. There are two simple ways to handle this if you're the one to feel something more than friendship:

> CHOICE A: Drop subtle but effective hints about your growing feelings. Be tactful. Rather than say, "Don't you and I make a great couple?" try "Don't you think it's funny how everyone thinks we're going out because we spend so much time together?" Wait for his reaction either in words or body language. If that doesn't work, resort to Choice B.
>
> CHOICE B: Come right out and tell him how you feel. Weston advises to be prepared for rejection. "Obviously it's hard when you find out the person you have a crush on doesn't feel the same way, but in the end you have to realize that it's better knowing where you stand rather than spending a whole year pining after someone that isn't interested."

Sometimes romance that starts as just friendship makes for a great relationship. Other times former friends wish they had remained so instead of getting involved and ruining a perfectly good friendship. Before taking the step towards romance, think how it would feel to lose him as a friend. And remember that friends—real friends who you can talk to and trust—are hard to find.

Will Our Friendship Stand the Test of Time?

As two friends become closer, it may feel like the friendship will never end or change. But that's not always the case. Like other relationships, friendships change—you change and your friend changes. And there's nothing wrong with that.

But if you truly care about a friendship and want it to last through the long haul, Mary Beth Whiton, a clinical psychologist of the Northfield Mount Hermon School in Northfield, Massachusetts, suggests teens develop a certain level of tolerance. In other words, don't be so quick to write off friends the moment they do something you don't like. It's important to realize that no two people are going to get along with each other perfectly all day, every day, or agree on every subject. When tempers flare up—and they will—learn to step back and let things cool down a bit before reacting. During this period it's also important to leave the door open for discussion or even an apology from your friend.

Can't We Just Get Along?

No one is perfect, not even your best friend. From time to time two friends may disagree and even stop speaking to each other, but it shouldn't mean the end of the relationship. If you think your friend has totally dissed you, Dr. Whiton offers a few ways to get things back on track:

- Talk it out. Often we ignore the fact that something is wrong, hoping that it will mysteriously disappear. This does more damage than anything else. Don't smile in your friend's face and act like everything is OK when you're really fuming inside. Be very specific and let her know what's bothering you. It's a possibility that she doesn't even understand that she has upset you. It's also your responsibility to the friendship to tell her how you're feeling. If she rejects you, then you know it wasn't a strong bond to begin with, and it might be time to rethink the friendship.

- Apologize. An apology is very important when it comes to resolving a conflict, but it's often left unsaid. In order for things to start fresh between the two of you, you need to make a formal apology stating exactly why you are apologizing. This lets your friend know that you fully understand why she is upset. For example, if your feelings were hurt, tell her. If she's any kind of friend, the convo will go something like this:

    You: "I was really upset when I found out you blabbed my secret. I thought I could trust you."

    Her: "I feel really bad that I told your secret. I am so sorry. I didn't think Terry would tell anyone."

- Reassert the rule. By restating to your friend that you cannot tolerate her behavior, it opens the door for the friendship to either progress or fade away if the rule is broken again. You say, "OK, Maria, I really want to be friends with you but I can't have you telling people my business. Please don't do it again, OK?"

NEVER-NEVERS IN A FRIENDSHIP

Never lie. It will only come back to haunt you.

Never blab your friend's secrets. Once the trust has been broken it's very hard to get it back.

Never con a friend into doing something she's not comfortable doing. It's OK to encourage, but don't be a pest.

Never take advantage of your friend's weak spots. Often when you know someone well, you know how to hurt her. Remember the Golden Rule: Treat others like you want to be treated.

● ●

"LaTrell helped me realize I wasn't the only one suffering over my grandmother's death."

JASMINE, 16, ANCHORAGE, ALASKA

My cousin LaTrell is my best friend. We've always been best friends because we grew up together. She's twenty-one and I'm sixteen, but we're the exact same person, she's my better half. No one knows us as cousins; we call ourselves sisters. You never see us apart. If we're apart everyone always asks where the other half is. We have jokes between the two of us that no one gets but us. We support each other as far as problems that come up or when a decision needs to be made. We're there for each other.

Our friendship became closer after what we went through together when my grandmother died in November 1990. LaTrell was the one who broke the news to me; she told me that my grandmother passed. See I wasn't around at the time, I was at a friend's house. She called me into the house and told me. I remember I was sitting in the kitchen, and I could tell something was wrong. I kept on asking her what was wrong, and she finally broke down and told me.

I kind of had a feeling what she was about to tell me, because my grandmother had already been sick for a while and it was something that was always in the back of my mind. But I didn't want to accept it. I didn't want to just come out and ask that question because I would never want that to come out of my mouth. She wasn't supposed to tell me though, she was supposed to wait until my mother got there so she could tell me. But she couldn't hold onto it any longer.

By LaTrell telling me my grandmother passed, it kind of enhanced our friendship. Before I never looked at her as someone to rely on, only someone to have fun with, spend the weekend with. Prior to my grandmother's passing, we would just sit and talk about people or do each other's hair, but this was the real turning point in the relationship. When she told me about my grandmother, I started to see her as an all-around friend. My grandmother was my lifeline all while I was growing up. If I didn't have LaTrell at this time I don't know what I would have done. LaTrell helped me realize I wasn't the only one suffering over my grandmother's death. It was a real lonely time for me but at least I knew someone was there for me who could relate.

Going with the Crowd

If finding one good friend is good, then having lots of good friends is even better. As long as you're able to keep your individuality, the more the merrier. But when more is less, as in less time to be yourself, it may be best to reconsider whether keeping company with a crowd is really for you.

The Lowdown on Peer Pressure

Think of the phrase "peer pressure:" Does it automatically make you think of all the negative things your friends try to get you to do? For many young women it does. But what exactly is peer pressure? Peer pressure is the power that peers have to influence others to do or not do certain things.

Leslie S. Kaplan, Ed.D., author of *Coping with Peer Pressure*, says that peer pressure usually goes into full swing around age eleven, and sometimes younger. "Teens want to be near people like them because it makes them feel safer," Kaplan says. "They don't have the skills or confidence to be independent, so they need the support of their friends to make the transition until their late teens when they go to college or work." This is why teens find it more comfortable to be surrounded by friends rather than be a loner. And since having friends is so important, most people will do what it takes to keep them, including going along with the crowd.

With peer pressure, the urge to conform to the group is strong. You may know of people who've been swayed by peer pressure to carry guns, smoke, or ditch class. But not all peer pressure is bad. "It can be helpful when the peer group values the same things as parents or society," Kaplan believes. So, friends that influence you to achieve in sports, stay on the honor roll, or avoid drunk driving are actually supporting your best interests. The power of peers works both ways.

A Power Struggle: Inner Strength vs. Outer Pressure

How many times have you said to yourself, "If I knew then what I know now, things would have turned out differently?" At least a thousand times, right? At some point, you will be subjected to peer pressure. Someone's going to ask you to do something that either you're not comfortable with or you know you have no business doing. According to Dr. Whiton, teens fall under the spell of peer pressure more easily than adults. Although adults also have to deal with peer pressure—they are pressured daily through advertising as well as from their friends—most adults are able to handle it better. They've had more experience thinking for themselves and deciding what's right for them. That's more difficult for teenagers. So it's important to remember: The more secure you are with yourself, the less likely you are to fall under the spell of anyone trying to tell you what to think and what to do.

Knowing you'll face peer pressure will allow you to prepare yourself to be strong enough to resist it. If you ever find yourself in a situation where you're being pressured to do something, Darlene Hopson, Ph.D., suggests you ask yourself these questions before acting:

- Will this affect the goals I've set for myself?
- Will I feel good about myself if I give in?
- Will this action damage my self-esteem or self-respect?
- Why am I considering this action? Is it because everyone else is doing it?

Teens who have a strong sense of self are less likely to fall prey to negative peer pressure, says Kaplan. She also states that knowing how to recognize a bad situation and learning to say "no" are very important skills. "Even if you did something you didn't want to or know you shouldn't, you can reevaluate the situation for the next time," she says. Knowing you have choices of behavior and friends to hang out with will give you confidence to make the right decisions. When you have these bases covered, fighting off negative peer pressure should be easier.

Cliques: The Good, the Bad, and the Ugly

By high school, most teenagers have found their niche of friends who they spend most of their free time with. Because people hang out with others like them, it's tempting to generalize about the different types: jocks, nerds, computer geeks, stoners, hippies, goodie-goodies. Whatever group you hang out with, all cliques serve the same basic purpose: "A clique can be a kind of support group made up of people with similar interests," says Peck.

Peck also believes cliques are important for young women for another reason. "A clique can give a girl a feeling of not being alone—of having a place where she belongs." Belonging to a group makes you feel more secure. If that group is supportive, being in a clique can be part of a growth experience. "They can help girls learn about others and others' beliefs," says Peck. "A person who belongs to a clique usually has some kind of a social life." This is how cliques can be a positive part of a young woman's adolescence.

On the other hand, most of us know first-hand how tacky some cliques can be. "Sometimes young people in cliques can stop making decisions for themselves," Peck says. "They end up conforming to what the clique wants them to be. They're not doing things they really want to, and they lose their individuality." When this happens it's time to decide whether the clique is working for you or against you. If it's not happening, then it's probably time to make a switch.

Other reasons Peck gives for wanting out of a clique:

- If you don't have qualities the clique wants, like being really into clothes.
- If the clique is really snobby and excludes people that aren't "as good as them," for instance if you aren't a glamour gal or your family isn't rich.
- If you'd be happier with just a few friends or even being alone most of the time.
- If the clique puts too much pressure on you to conform by not talking to you or making fun of you if you don't go along with them.
- You're getting a bad reputation or getting into trouble by being in the clique.
- The clique is getting too judgmental of others or too close-minded for you to tolerate.
- You realize that being in a clique isn't as fun as you thought and you're just not into it.

If you decide the clique isn't for you, Peck offers this advice: "Girls should remember that not all friendships last, and that there's pain involved in change. They should take the memories and move on. A girl needs to have the strength and courage to get out." This is especially true of young women who have high self-esteem and don't need cliques to define themselves anyway.

POPULARITY: DON'T TRY SO HARD

Some people think high school is one big popularity contest. They spend all their time trying to be cool so that others will want to be friends with them. But in a recent study by Steven Asher, Ph.D., a professor of educational psychology at the University of Illinois at Champaign-Urbana, people who are truly popular don't have to try so hard.

"Many people confuse popularity with other traits," states Dr. Asher. "The myth is that the popular kid is cool, visible, a leader, or not very nice." But popular people are actually defined as people who everyone likes. So kids that may be trendy, leaders, or the cheerleader-type are just well known, but not necessarily well liked.

According to Dr. Asher's research, popular people have a few personality traits in common that draw people to them. They are:

- friendly;
- cooperative;
- kind;
- social.

They also are very "real" people, meaning they're not phony and don't spend all their time trying to please others to be liked. "Some kids strive to be popular," says Dr. Asher, "but popular kids don't focus on it." Trying to be popular is an empty goal. If you spend all your time trying to be liked, that means you're relying on other people to boost your ego. It's better to concentrate on gaining self-confidence in more constructive ways like getting good grades, volunteering in the community, or planning for the future. The more comfortable you are being yourself, the more people you'll attract and the more friends you'll make.

WHAT ARE YOU GONNA DO ABOUT IT?

STUDENT ENVIRONMENTAL ACTION COALITION

Great leaders get inspired by what they believe in. And what better way to become a leader and influence people than to fight for a cause. Nelson Mandela and Mahatma Gandhi did just that, got off their butts and did something about injustices they saw. Linda Isakson isn't exactly Mandela or Gandhi, but she also focused on a cause and took action. At age seventeen she's the regional high school representative for Student Environmental Action Coalition (SEAC, pronounced "seek") and helps other students start environmental clubs in their schools.

After reading a Greenpeace magazine, Linda became deeply disturbed about the tens of thousands of dolphins that die each year due to the fishing industry. "I cried then became a vegetarian and an environmentalist," she remembers. It was in this same magazine that she learned about SEAC and decided to attend one of the conferences. "At the conference they said they needed someone to do outreach to high schools, so I raised my hand and became one of the coordinators." Lucky for SEAC, Linda's no flake and has not only started an environmental club at her high school in San Diego, but advises other students about how to start their own.

Yeijin Kim was one of those students. She had to reactivate the environmental club at her school in Fullerton, California. "I had to find a faculty advisor, who was my geology teacher," recalls Yeijin , a fifteen year old sophomore. "Then I had to get twenty signatures from students saying they would join or would like to see this type of club at school. After that I got a copy of the club's constitution." All she needed was a plan of action. Through an article in *Seventeen* magazine, she got SEAC's toll-free number.

"Linda was really helpful and gave me a lot of ideas about activities we could do," says Yeijin . "Our group wrote to the World Bank telling them they shouldn't support the destruction of the rain forest and indigenous people in Guyana. We got a response back thanking us for our letter and saying that they had stopped."

The club also wanted to paint a mural of the world on a school wall. "We decided to get the art club to draw the design and we painted it," Yeijin says. The collaboration was a success and now a former white wall will encourage students to think globally.

Despite the tons of school work Yeijin has, she remains dedicated to the club and to the environmental movement. Each week she has to prepare for meetings, and she still manages to pack a carload of friends and hit conferences, like the recent one in Los Angeles on the Endangered Species Act. Linda is even more hardcore. "I plan on majoring in environmental studies and political science in college next year," she says with determination. Both she and Yeijin are living slogans: Don't just follow the crowd, lead it! For more information contact SEAC at P.O. Box 1168, Chapel Hill, NC 27514-1168; (800) 700-SEAC.

Friendship Friction

Have you heard that saying "you only hurt the one you love?" That's very true for friends: Friends can make friends feel bad. In some cases, a straight from the heart talk is all that's needed to clean up the situation. Other times it may be necessary to reevaluate the friendship to decide whether it's worth staying friends. Here are some examples of when it's time to take a serious look at a friendship:

UNDUE PRESSURE. If a friend pressures you into something and you do it against your better judgment, that person is probably not a real friend, and you need to ask yourself why you gave in. Being forced to go against your instinct means betraying yourself, and this doesn't make for a good friendship.

JEALOUSY. There's often a fine line between admiration and jealousy. If someone admires you, she looks at you with awe and may try to imitate you. If a friend is jealous of you, she'll cut you down and try to diminish your character. If you have a jealous friend, try to encourage her to find her own talents. Boost your friend up by pointing out her good qualities. If you find you're the jealous one, let your friend know you admire her, but try to concentrate on your own good qualities rather than hers. People who play up their own uniqueness are leaders and can attract others.

COMPETITION. Competition between friends is generally not a major problem. In most cases, people realize that they can't be wonderful at everything, and they accept it. However, if you have a friend who's always in a competitive mood, try to get to the source of it. Your friend could be suffering from insecurity, and all she may need is a little encouragement from you.

TWO-FACED FRIENDS. Being betrayed by a friend is very painful. If you discover that a friend is talking about you behind your back, go to the source. Often friends stop speaking to each other because of hearsay only to find out later that the whole thing was a misunderstanding. On the other hand if what you heard is true, you may be better off without her anyway. The important thing is to talk before making any drastic decisions.

MALES IN THE MIDDLE. There are two common scenarios where a guy can come between two friends. The first is when one friend has a boyfriend and the other friend feels left out in the cold. The new happy couple spends all their time together and acts as if the rest of the world doesn't exist. When this happens, you feel left out and hurt that your friend can't seem to peel herself off her loverboy to spend even one afternoon with you. In this case, it's best to tell your friend how hurt you are, how much you miss her, and try to make an agreement to spend some time alone together. In the meantime, understand that it's nothing personal. You also might want to find some other running buddies or interests instead of waiting for her to call. More than likely she'll be crying on your shoulder in a couple of weeks when Mr. Right turns into Mr. Wrong.

Another way that guys can get between two good friends is when romance is involved. For example if both friends are interested in the same guy, if he's seeing both at the same time, or if one went out with him before and now he likes her friend. This scenario can cause feelings of betrayal, jealousy, or competition between friends as well as lasting hurt. One way to easily avoid these problems is to make an agreement with your close friends not to go out with any of their "leftovers." Most loyal friends understand that their relationship is more lasting and important than a flighty romance, and refuse to let a guy come between them. Otherwise tell your friend how it makes you feel to see the guy you like—or used to like—with her. You may have to live with the reality of the new couple and accept your feelings of discomfort.

Before Giving Up

As hard as it may be, remember to give a friend one last chance before saying good-bye to the relationship. If you're not good at expressing yourself when you're angry, write a letter. Do whatever it takes to let your friend know how you feel.

Another option is to spend some time apart. Instead of spending time together every day or every weekend, make it every other weekend. The time away will allow both of you to take a close look at the friendship as well as yourselves, and it may save the friendship. It would be a shame to end a friendship over something that could have been resolved by talking or having a cool-out period.

What to Do When It's Over

Ending a friendship is painful, especially if the relationship spanned a long period of time. However, people change, and sometimes it's better for two people to go their separate ways.

Once it reaches a point where things don't seem to be getting any better, it may be time to say good-bye.

Unfortunately, many friendships end in anger. Friendships can also just die out on their own with neither person saying "it's over." Other times separation will be the excuse. Here are a few signs to look for that could mean the end of your friendship is near:

- You constantly avoid your friend.
- You feel angry when you're around her.
- You have low tolerance and patience toward your friend.
- You notice patterns developing in the friendship; for example she frequently breaks dates with you.
- You no longer care, your feelings are neutral; you don't even get upset when she blows you off for the millionth time.

"My friend and I don't speak to this day, but to be honest, it was really time for our friendship to be over."

KHANISHA, 14, NORLINA, NORTH CAROLINA

I was friends with this girl for a long time, and I finally had to cut her off. She was always acting like she was my friend but, she was really talking about me behind my back. Every time I would go up to her and ask her she'd be like, "No Khanisha, I didn't say that, you know me and you, we're real cool." I found out she was talking about me through our other friends. She didn't know that every time she talked about me, that our mutual friends would come back and tell me.

Before I found out about all this we were real tight, I could tell her anything. She was in a lot of my classes, and we hung out together a lot. But after a while I got tired of hearing the same old stories about her talking about me. She was saying things like, "Khanisha thinks she's all that," or "Khanisha thinks she's so cute." It seemed like she was jealous of me for some reason.

One day I was so sick of it that I decided to confront her. I didn't go to her right away, I waited a few days. We were at school in the hallway, and I told her I was sick and tired of everybody coming to me telling me that she'd been talking about me. I wanted to know why she was talking about me, and what she had against me. I wanted her to know that I knew this was going on so she could stop dragging my name in the dirt. She told me she wasn't talking about me; she denied everything.

I finally told her if she didn't have anything good to say about me don't come up in my face no more. She said she still wanted us to be friends, and then she apologized. I told her we'd just leave it at that. She apologized but I was still mad and I didn't even care anymore. I didn't care whether she meant it [the apology] or not, I just walked off and left her standing there. The funny thing is she never admitted she was talking about me even though she apologized. When I asked her why she was apologizing if she didn't do anything she told me she said sorry just to get me off her back.

I was mad and hurt because she was supposed to be my friend and I felt that if she was talking about me, it was no telling how many of my other friends were doing the same thing. After we stopped speaking altogether she would call me every now and then to see what I was doing, but I didn't want to be bothered. My friend and I don't speak to this day, but to be honest, it was really time for our friendship to be over.

When Parents Don't Like Your Friends

It's a real drag when your parents don't like your friends. They constantly nag about how they don't want you hanging around "those types," or they criticize your friends without even knowing them. Rather than sneaking around to be with your buddies, it's better to take an up-front approach, as the experts advise.

First, give your parents a bit of a break. "Parents need to realize that a girl's choice of friends is a first step in separating from them," says Peck. "And parents might have trouble with the fact that their children are growing up and looking for independence. It's hard for them to start letting go." Most teenagers' main complaint is that their parents worry too much about them, and they're right. As Dr. Youniss states, "Parents are usually fearful of sex, drugs, and bad grades. They may think that their kids' friends will lead them into trouble." As long as your parents are left in the dark about your friends, they'll continue to have negative opinions.

The obvious solutions, according to Peck and Youniss, are to:

- Communicate with your parents about why you value your friends. Let them know how you are good for each other as friends and why the relationships are important. If you have a trusting relationship with your folks, they'll come to the conclusion that you have the judgment to pick friends that are right for you (even if they aren't your parents' type).

• Introduce your friends to your parents so that they can feel secure. If possible, introduce your friends' parents to them as well. The better they know your friends and their families, the more it will ease their minds and the less hassle you'll get.

LIVING WITH YOUR ENEMIES

An enemy can ruin your whole day, sometimes even your life. She (or he) can make going to school or hanging in the neighborhood unbearable just by her very presence. While you don't have to become friends with people you don't like, you do have to learn to live with them.

To help you maintain your cool around people you're not too fond of, Kaplan and Peck advise the following:

• **Don't provoke or initiate contact.** Giving evil looks or spreading gossip only keeps the feud going. Instead, just stay out of the person's way and if you cross paths, keep cool. She'll look stupid when she's all worked up over nothing.

• **Get neutralized.** Try to get her to agree to sit down with a mediator (a mutual friend, neutral party, or even a counselor) so you can work out a truce. Who knows, after ironing out your problems you may find you actually like each other.

• **Ask yourself the real question:** Why are you investing so much energy into this negative relationship? Be honest about what you're getting out of keeping things heated. Does she have qualities that you secretly wish you had? Is she someone you're trying to get back at because she hurt you? Are you looking for some place to direct your anger about other things in your life and she's an easy target? Getting to the heart of the matter can help you see that she's probably not the problem at all. And if she is, she's someone you want to avoid.

• **The best revenge is being happy.** By ignoring her and going on with your own life, your old rival will hardly be a thought in your mind. If you're truly comfortable with yourself and have better things to do, you won't have time to waste on enemies.

• **Don't let the problem get out of control.** If your rivalry moves from mutual dislike to harassment, you need to tell someone in a position of authority. If you are threatened, immediately get help. In this case

ignoring the person isn't the solution. Harassment and threats aren't
acceptable and need to be dealt with before things get out of hand.

Where to Turn

Recommended Reading

*But Everyone Else Looks So Sure of Themselves: A Guide to Surviving the
Teen Years,* Denise V. Lang, Shoe Tree Press, 1991. This practical book
addresses the problems peculiar to being a teenager. It has a chapter on
friendship with all its ups and downs.

Coping with Cliques, Lee A. Peck, Rosen Publishing Group, 1992. In this
book the author provides suggestions on building self-esteem, dealing
with peer pressure, making new friends, getting out of a clique, and
more.

Coping with Peer Pressure, Leslie S. Kaplan, Ed.D., Rosen Publishing Group,
1993. This book discusses the positive and negative effects that members
of a peer group can have on each other. Understanding the process can
help you deal with the phenomenon.

Everything You Need to Know About Peer Pressure, Robyn M. Feller, Rosen
Publishing Group, 1993. Young adults are especially susceptible to the
pressure of "the group." This book will help you learn to stand on your
own and follow your own instincts.

Greetings from High School: Teenspeak About High School and Life, Marian
Salzman and Teresa Reisgies, Peterson's Guide, 1991. This book, shaped
by stories from interviews with hundreds of teens, talks about the many
aspects of being a teen, including a chapter on friendship and cliques.

*When Kids Drive Kids Crazy: How to Get Along with Your Friends and
Enemies,* Eda LeShan, Dial Books, 1990. This wise, compassionate book
gives straightforward information about how to deal with hurtful or
changing relationships, how to build confidence in them, and how to gain
long-lasting friendships.

Support Groups and Organizations

Best Friends Foundation, 2000 N Street NW, Suite 201, Washington DC
20036; (202) 822-9266. The Best Friends Foundation offers a program to help
girls gain self-respect, make positive decisions, and support each other. They
do so by providing monthly group discussions. If you're interested in starting
a "Best Friends Program" in your school, write to above address or call.

"Be Your Own Best Friend Program" (BYBF)/Organizacion Nacional
de la Salud de la Mujer/National Latina Health Organization, P.O. Box
7567, Oakland, CA 94601; (510) 534-1362. BYBF conducts support groups

for young adolescent Latinas to help develop and promote self-esteem, and positive communications and relationships with peers.

Black Student Leadership Council, 25 E Street NW, Washington, DC 20001; (202) 628-8787. This is a project of the Children's Defense Fund.

Citykids, 57 Leonard Street, New York, NY 10013; (212) 925-3320. Citykids is a multicultural foundation where teens get together once a week to discuss issues that are important to them. For teens in the New York area this is an excellent place to make friends with teens who know how to listen and respect each other's differences.

Girls Inc., 30 East 33rd Street, New York, NY 10016; (212) 689-3700. At nearly 750 sites across the country, Girls Incorporated affiliates provide over a quarter million young women ages six through eighteen with informal education and personal development activities after school, on the weekends, and during the summer.

Girl Scouts of the U.S.A., 420 Fifth Ave., New York, NY 10018; (212) 852-6548. Girl Scouting is a movement that gives girls from all segments of American life a chance to develop their potential, make friends, and become part of their community. If you're interested in your school being a part of this movement, write to the above address for the Girl Scout Council nearest you.

Latin American Youth Center, 3045 15th Street NW, Washington, DC 20009; (202) 483-1140. The Latin American Youth Center has a teen drop-in progam that provides recreational and educational activities, the Latino Youth Leadership Program provides an opportunity to develop an array of leadership skills.

United National Indian Tribal Youth Inc. (UNITY), P.O. Box 25042, Oklahoma City, OK 73125; (405) 424-3010. UNITY is a Native American youth leadership organization designed to help young people make a positive difference in areas such as heritage, environment and community service. UNITY offers a wide range of leadership programs such as national conferences, regional training sessions, and youth council development.

CHAPTER 11

LET'S GET TOGETHER

By the time the midteens roll around, the hormones are in full swing creating strong sexual attractions. Because the feelings are so new, it's not always clear what to do with them or how to draw the line when things get hot and heavy. During this period it's very important to remember that part of becoming an adult is learning how to take control over your body and feelings so that you can make the best choices for yourself.

It's a Love Thang

Sexual attraction is one of life's big surprises. While some girls think boys are creatures from another planet, most start getting serious crushes around the beginning of puberty at age eleven or twelve. There are other girls who never have and may never look at boys as more than friends because they're more attracted to girls. Others may feel attracted to people of both sexes, and this whole range of feelings is natural. Regardless of gender, the important thing is to find someone who respects you for who you are.

Not everything about love and sex is logical and can be explained, but here's what several experts on adolescent sexuality have to say about some questions:

> All my friends are hooked up with guys already. Why can't I find someone to go out with?
>
> Wanna Date

Wanna Date,

Before you go out with just anyone, you need to ask some questions. First, how do you feel about dating? Peggy Brick, president of SIECUS (Sexuality Information and Education Council of the United States), says that dating attitudes depend on your culture and community, but it ultimately comes down to you. "Only start dating when you want to," says Brick, "and not because others are doing it. There's a lot of pressure and many people begin dating before they really want to."

Another consideration: your parents. "Definitely talk to your parents," suggests Anthony Drakeford, program coordinator for Planned Parenthood's First Things First/Sex or Not in Roanoke, Virginia. "Some are stricter than others," he says, and adds that you should be ready to give reasons for being able to date. He admits that most parents have a double-standard with girls, because families tend to be more protective of girls than they are of boys.

Finally—and most important—ask yourself what you would do on a date. This is a question of both safety and maturity. If you're not willing to take the steps necessary to have a good time *and* be safe, maybe you're not ready to date yet. Both Brick and Drakeford strongly advise young women not to be isolated on a date.

Here are a few more of their suggestions:

- Get to know him first. Know who you're dealing with, especially if he's someone you don't see at school every day. Even if he is, it's a good idea to see what he's really like before committing to a whole evening with him. He could turn out to be a complete goofball.

- Go with a crew. Double- or triple-date, but don't go alone for the first few dates.

- Go to a public place. Brick says that some boys think that a girl willing to go to a lonely spot is giving him permission to have sex with her. Good choices are movies, the mall, or a museum.

- Meet his parents and have him meet yours. Drakeford warns us that "guys do lie and might not be who they say they are." This is a great way to check him out.

- Go dutch. Some guys get unbelievably stupid notions in their heads that if they treat you to a movie and dinner, or take you to the prom, you owe them something. Drakeford suggests you find out up front what his expectations for the evening are and bring your own money.

- Don't drink or take drugs. This is considered a major risk factor for young women on dates. With substance abuse, you're more likely to make poor decisions that you'll regret later or get into a situation you can't get out of. Stay away.

- Take a quarter and enough cab fare to get home. Always tell a friend or family member where you're going, with whom, and when you'll be back. Also, have a Plan B in case the guy is a total moron and you want to bail out. Check in during the date if things aren't going well and *definitely don't drive with him if he's been drinking*.

Help me, I'm falling in love. At least I think I am, but I'm not sure. How can I tell? What do I do?

Head Over Heels

Dear HOH,

This is one of the toughest questions to answer, because it's such an individual matter. Peggy Brick warns that some teens confuse love with other feelings. "Young women can think being turned on is love. Or they can have a romantic idea of a guy loving them meaning that he'll take care of them." Feeling good about someone isn't the same as love. Another common mistake: thinking infatuation is love. Anthony Drakeford says, "Just because you think about someone all the time or want to be with him doesn't necessarily mean you're in love."

But if these intense feelings aren't love, then what is? Well, Drakeford explains, "Love involves knowing, caring for, and accepting a person for what's on the inside." Not everyone who's "in love" feels exactly the same, but being in love should make you feel good, happy, and affectionate. Love shouldn't feel miserable, and if you do feel miserable then it probably isn't love. It's just feeling miserable.

"I knew I was in love because I had never felt anything like it. It was pretty amazing."

HANNAH, 17, BOXFORD, MASSACHUSETTS

It wasn't love at first sight with Rolland. I had a crush on his best friend, actually, but we went out for only a week. Nothing happened, and we broke up. Immediately afterwards, Rolland was there to comfort me and it kind of happened. We had always been very cuddly friends, so all the time we would lie in my bed together, hold hands, or he'd give me a piggy back or we'd run around together laughing. There wasn't actually one moment when the relationship changed. We talked about his past, about our childhoods, about music, about people at school, about ways of thinking, about ways of being—pretty much anything. He was very sweet.

I knew I was in love because I had never felt anything like it. It was pretty amazing. I didn't know I could actually love anyone outside my family, and then to love this person so devotedly and know that I would be willing to risk my life and do anything for him.

When I was in love, I felt heavenly, like I was walking on air. It was ecstasy. Whatever happened that was bad didn't matter, because I had him. If I was sad he would give me a hug, then suddenly everything would kind of fade. No matter what negative emotion I was feeling, he would smooth it all away. I remember looking at him sometimes and just smiling, and he'd smile back, and we'd look into each other's eyes, and I'd burst with happiness. It was elation—just so happy, so full. Like you're warm and fuzzy all over.

But those feelings lasted only on and off. As soon as our relationship got really serious we started fighting—not all the time, but enough to make it maybe not being worth it. We fought about jealousy—on both of our parts. We fought about just stupid stuff. He was a lot more devoted than I was, even though I thought I was devoted. He'd be like, "Well I came over to see you here. I'm making all the effort in this relationship." I just felt overwhelmed. I'd never had a real boyfriend before. I'd never had anyone I had to "commit" myself to, commit my life to. It was too much to deal with all the time. I got sick of him.

We broke up and got back together several times. The first time, he went into a depression, then got over it and was fine, then I flipped out. I ended up starving myself, and being overly dramatic and depressed. Really stupid, basically.

The second time we broke up I was fine and he flipped out. Then after three hours of flipping out he was back to normal and moving on to the next girlfriend, and I flipped out. For two months I was whacko, depressed, suicidal, just crazy—awful, awful, the worst time in my life. I felt like my life wasn't worth it without him being in it. If Rolland wasn't going to be there to love me, I didn't want to be alive, period.

We got together again after this—I don't know what was going through my head. Eventually, we broke up for good.

The minute it was really over, he went out with another girl and that started the chain of girlfriends for him. This was the first time we broke up that I really didn't care. I cried maybe twice, but that was it. I was over it basically. I knew I could have a good time without him.

I have figured out something important since the breakup: when we were together, Rolland was distracting me from exploring a whole new life. I missed out on a lot by devoting all of myself to him. I missed out on friends, I missed out on adventures, I missed out on myself, even.

I now know that I don't need anybody else to make me happy, and I don't need anybody else to make my life complete. No matter who's around me, who's going to love me, who's going to be there for me, it doesn't matter, because I'm always going to be me, and that's just fine.

I'm really into this guy but my friends say he's a dog. How do I know he's right for me?

Doubtful

Dear Doubtful,

Before making any hard and fast judgments about this guy, Anthony Drakeford says you should consider two things:

1. What is your definition of a dog?
2. Can you trust your friends' opinion?

"The only way to know someone is to spend time with him," says Drakeford. "Your friends might have had a bad experience, but it could be different for you."

If you're wondering if he's right for you, try this tip from Cheryl Manning, a family life and sex educator in New York City: "I have girls write out a list of all the qualities they like in a guy, then they write the qualities of the guys they actually go out with." If the two don't match up, Manning has the girls discuss what they need and how to get it. "If the girls are ending up hurt and crying all the time, it's time to look at reality."

Everyone deserves to be in a good relationship, even if it's not "the one." When choosing a guy to go out with, Peggy Brick advises looking for the qualities below. Does he:

- listen to you and other people?
- respect your opinion or choices?
- pay attention?
- do things with you and other people?
- respect limits you set or your family sets?

If he doesn't treat you right, dump him. Don't waste your time trying to "make him change." It won't happen; it's best to move on to someone who can live up to your expectations.

I've been friends with this guy for a long time, and we just started a romantic relationship. We've talked a lot about having sex, but haven't done it yet. Does it sound like we're ready yet?

Quietly Questioning

Dear Questioning,

Major dilemma, girlfriend! But, according to most teen sexperts, you're handling it very maturely. According to David Landry, research associate at the Alan Guttmacher Institute, not many young people make rational decisions when it comes to having sex, especially for the first time. "Most find themselves in the situation and don't think of the consequences." As long as you're basing your decision to have sex on what's best for you and your future, you're ahead of the game.

"We had sex and it was terrible. I remember thinking, 'Is this all I have to look forward to?'"

LAEL, 17, TUCSON, ARIZONA

I started dating this guy in seventh grade. We went out all my eighth grade year and into my freshman year. Then we started talking about having sex and stuff. He was the one who brought it up. He said, "What do you think about us having sex?" I was like, "I don't know, I guess it would be OK." I didn't have any problems emotionally about losing my virginity. He was a virgin, too. I was in love with him at the time, so it wasn't as if I was feeling unstable about it. I felt he was the right person.

We really didn't know what to do or how to do it or anything. We had had sex ed classes in school, and my mom always talked about it. But it was still a big mystery. The reality was a whole lot different. We had been fooling around a lot before, and finally it got to a point where we decided to go ahead and do it.

It was during the day. We ditched school and went over to his house. On the way there on the bus I was thinking, "Maybe I should just leave. Maybe I should just get off and run away." We weren't saying anything. We were holding hands, just sitting there really silently. We were on his couch in his living room. We took our own clothes off because it was really awkward to take off each other's. It was kind of silly.

I always pictured some big romantic thing, but it really wasn't. We tried and tried but just couldn't do it. We couldn't really get it in there, and it hurt on me. So we just quit. I felt kind of relieved because I didn't *really* want to do it. He kind of wanted to do it more than I did, I think. We didn't really say anything about it afterwards, we just started laughing, and that was it.

The next time we tried was about a week later. We were in his room—in this little guest house his family had outside. I think it was in the evening. He said, "Do you want to try again?" And I said, "Well, yeah, OK." We had sex and it was terrible. It lasted for about five minutes; I remember thinking, "Is this all I have to look forward to?"

I didn't even get what had happened to him when he came. He was like, "That was wonderful." Then I just laid there for a long time, and we didn't say anything. We kissed afterwards, and that was really nice. I remember I liked that—I liked just lying there afterwards with him.

We were pretty good friends, and it changed things a lot. It was as if a new secret we had between us. We were more affectionate after that. I felt revealed to him in a way—in a good way, but I thought it was kind of weird. I didn't exactly like him knowing. I felt like he could know anything about me then, and that made me a little bit uncomfortable, being that vulnerable.

It sounds kind of cynical, but I felt as if I had gotten some certificate or something—as if I had gained some secret knowledge that all these women had had over the years, or became a woman. I didn't tell any of my friends about it; I'm kind of a private person. But our friends caught on; they knew after a while.

I also felt as if the childish part of me was taken away after that. At 14, I went from being a kid to not quite an adult—something else, something different than that. I think that after you have sex you can't be a kid anymore. I was kind of depressed about that, too. I wanted to grow up, but at the same time I didn't. I don't know how to explain it. Looking back, though, I'm glad that my first time was with someone that I cared about, not just with some person.

Rather than getting caught up in the heat of the moment, make the right call based on whether you can handle the level of emotional involvement, the intimacy of the act, and the consequences. A SIECUS study of first time sexual experiences shows that in 74 percent of cases sex "just happened." As a consequence, most teen girls wished they had waited until they were older before having sex.

Some teens become sexually active for the wrong reasons. Anthony Drakeford lists a few WRONG reasons:

- To have a baby and get out of the house.
- Being pressured by partner.
- Hoping it will make you look more mature.
- Because friends are doing it.
- Curiosity.
- Thinking it's romantic.
- To try to hold onto a boyfriend.
- Too embarrassed to still be a virgin.

"What's the worst thing to happen to you if you don't have sex," asks Drakeford. "Most people say they're afraid to be laughed at. But what's that compared to getting pregnant or contracting a disease or AIDS?"

About changing your relationship from friends to something more serious: that's a tough one. On the one hand, getting romantically involved with a friend can be a great experience. Who would be more trusting, loving, caring, and know you better than a good friend? On the other hand, if things don't work out, you run the risk of losing a good bud.

Keep in mind that sex, especially an act as intimate as intercourse, changes relationships. "Rarely can you go backwards," states Diane Morrison, Ph.D., social psychologist at the University of Washington in Seattle, Washington.

Before taking the plunge, "Look at your own motivation for having sex," Morrison suggests. "Are you doing it only to please your partner? A lot of young women get talked into having sex. Or they want to keep him or get closer." Morrison says that these reasons will only wear down your self-respect. Talk to your friend and see if you two have the same expectations from the relationship.

And one last bit of advice: researchers at the Alan Guttmacher Institute who put together the study entitled "Sex and America's Teenagers" recommend that teens postpone sex until "they are sufficiently mature to treat their partner with respect and to assume responsibility for protecting themselves and their partner from the negative consequences of sex." So, unless you're going to use contraception, including a condom, correctly *every time you have sex* to protect yourself against pregnancy and sexually transmitted infections, WAIT. You can purchase condoms at the drug store and keep them in your backpack in case "it just happens." There's no reason to risk your life or your future by not doing that one simple thing. Otherwise, it's best to stay friends until both of you are really ready to handle all that's involved.

"I would say to a girl who's being pressured into having sex, 'Do it when you want to do it, when you feel ready.'"

HENRY, 17, NEW YORK CITY, NEW YORK

To get a girl to have sex, guys'll say, "I love you a lot. I think it's time for us to do it." Sometimes they pressure girls a lot, and they'll say, "I love you, and I want to be with you for a long, long time, so I think we should do it, so we can be one with each other," and all of this. "You're so nice, you're so sweet, I just want to make love to you." Sometimes guys don't take that, sometimes they're not too nice. They'll be like, "What's up? You're going to head me off? You going to give me some of *that*?" That's the way they talk sometimes.

Some guys make girls feel like the girl's the only one. Sometimes guys tell the truth, but sometimes they're just telling a lot of junk and showing off. Some guys will be like, "I'll give you the world. I'll do anything for you." They'll eat their brain, acting stupid until they hit it. Then they'll say things like, "I did this girl, I did that girl. I just told her this and she melted."

Some guys wine and dine a girl to get her to have sex, buying her everything, taking her to the movies every day, giving her little hints, like buying her lingerie, buying her little cards saying "I want to be with you forever and ever."

Another thing a guy might do to get a girl to have sex is to give her his telephone number and say, "Just call me and you can come over to my house and chill." She'll come over to his house, talk, have fun, and sometimes it just happens. That's what guys mostly do. One thing leads to another, and they just take it from there.

Lots of guys don't want to wear a condom, because they say it doesn't feel good, doesn't feel right, it's too tight, my weeny's too big. And that's not right: a condom could fit over a person's head. These guys will say something like "Oh, c'mon, baby, I'll use a condom, it won't hurt. It'll feel real good. It's between two people and it's supposed to feel good. It's not supposed to hurt, so don't be afraid of it."

If a girl's a virgin and she's like, "I'm not having sex until I'm married," some guys will just leave her straight out. Other guys would say, "You don't have to save yourself till you get married, because nobody's doing it. I want to be your first." They'd just be trying to eat their brain, so the lady would give in. Some guys do that a lot.

Some guys like older women cause they're more experienced, but some guys go for the younger girls because they're hard to get. They want to break them in, show them, give them experience. Some guys brag, "I got a virgin, I'm going to do her real good. I can't wait to break her." Sometimes I hear my friends say, "I want a virgin girl, cause they're tight."

I would say to a girl who's being pressured into having sex, "Do it when you want to do it. Don't take any guy's advice. When you feel ready to do it, you do it. If you want to do it, think about the consequences. Don't let the guys eat your brain."

YOU'VE GOT TO BE KIDDING: UNBELIEVABLE GUY TACTICS

As you might already know, some of the lines guys use to get girls to have sex with them are so lame. Though he hasn't heard them all, Anthony Drakeford has heard enough ways that guys try to talk the panties off young women. Here are a few corny lines:

- "If you don't have sex by a certain age, your insides won't fully develop."

- "If you love me you'll do it."
- "I'm going to die, and I want to have sex before I go."
- "I got in a car accident and I'm sterile, so we don't have to use any protection."

Other winners include: shedding a tear, sensitive talk, getting her to feel sorry for him, and going to junior high schools to find inexperienced girls.

Sad to say that these lines and tactics come from some seasoned pros who say they actually work. So, it's up to you to use your sixth sense—intuition—when it looks like you're about to get duped. "If it sounds even the least bit fishy," says Drakeford, "question it."

DON'T BELIEVE THE HYPE: DATING OLDER GUYS MAY NOT BE AS GREAT AS IT SEEMS

They're smooth, they drive a car, they have their own apartments, they work, they have money, and they don't have a curfew. They're older men—unlike you, out of their teens—and they want your seven digits. You may feel flattered, but should you go through with it? Although each situation is different, before saying "yes" automatically, there's a lot to consider.

After coming down from the initial high of having been approached by an older hunk, ask yourself why is he interested in someone so much younger. Two or three years isn't so bad, but a man in his mid-twenties or thirties who's pursuing a teenager? After studying the birth rates of high-school aged girls of all races and economic levels, Dr. Michael A. Males, a graduate student in social ecology at the University of California at Irvine, notes that teenagers who date older men (20 years and older) aren't necessarily benefiting:

- About 70 percent of all teenage girls get pregnant from partners who are twenty to fifty years old.
- Men over twenty father twice as many babies with high-school girls and four times more with junior-high girls than do high-school boys.
- Almost all teen girls who contract AIDS, get it from sexual contact with men over age twenty.
- Girls who have sex with men are much more likely to have a baby than girls who have sex with a teenage partner.
- Girls use contraception less with adult partners and engage in more high risk behavior.

- Teens involved with older men tend to have behavior problems, like substance abuse and dropping out of school.
- Many teenage mothers report that they were coerced or forced into having sex by older men, have been sexually abused in the past, and got pregnant by an older man.

Reading between the statistical lines, Males explains that "most of the girls who are mothers wouldn't be if their peers were the only guys available." Males believes that some young women have a harder time asserting themselves with older men—such as demanding that they use a condom—compared to teen boys. He also notes: "Studies show that many of these girls feel sorry for their older boyfriends, and they're trying to help them. Many of these guys are troubled, have criminal records or a substance abuse problem."

Legal issues also come into play in relationships between teen girls and older men. In most states, if an adult man has sex with a girl under age 16 or 18, he can be arrested for statutory rape. Males sums up the situation this way: "Even though many adult men are attracted to adolescent girls, they don't have to act on it. Girls have a right to expect a higher standard of behavior from men."

So, before you start getting all giddy over that older Prince Charming, ask these questions:

- Why would someone his age be interested in someone your age?
- What do you want out of this relationship?
- Is this a relationship of equals, or does he have the upper hand?
- Do you look to him as a father figure that might be missing in your life?
- Would it really be so bad to go out with someone your age or a couple of years older max?

Sexual Orientation

No one *really* understands why some people are attracted to members of the opposite sex, some to members of the same sex and some to both. There are three possible explanations. One is the nature theory: that everyone's born with a specific orientation. Just as our genes determine hair texture, maybe they also program sexual likes and dislikes. Another is the nurture theory: that through life experiences people gravitate towards the gender they're most comfortable with. The third theory: nature and nurture combine to determine sexual orientation.

Some experts believe that sexual feelings are more fluid than the rigid labels of straight versus gay or lesbians. For example, someone may call herself "straight" (or be attracted to opposite sex) but have had romantic feelings for or even sexual experiences with another female. Also, sexual feelings can change through our lifetime. And, of course, the strong pull of society's "values" also plays a role in sexuality. Because our society is geared toward heterosexuality—images in movies and on TV, our laws, parents saying "I can't wait for your wedding"—someone who's attracted to someone of the same sex may feel afraid, isolated, and confused, and may end up suppressing her feelings.

If you're undecided about how you feel, the best option is to relax and go with your instincts. Making an absolute choice isn't as important as finding out what feels natural to you.

What Does It Mean to Be a Lesbian?

Let's get one thing clear: lesbians are women who are primarily sexually attracted to women. Other than this one characteristic, lesbians are no different from anyone else.

Although this percentage has been debated in recent times, many experts say that about one out of every ten people is either gay or lesbian. This equals millions and millions of people. Despite these numbers, a lot of people treat gay women differently. This fear, ignorance, or hatred of lesbians and gays is called homophobia and is the cause of great pain. Homophobia can take many forms, such as discrimination, ostracism, and violence.

Unfortunately because of homophobia, many lesbians are forced to hide their true feelings for fear of being made fun of—or worse—denied housing or employment or being physically attacked by others. They may live double lives by keeping their sexuality "in the closet" while trying to fit in. To ease the pain and rejection, some drink or take drugs, attempt suicide, or run away from home.

People who cause this kind of pain by making jokes about "dykes and fags" are not only being insensitive, they're also wearing their insecurities about their own sexuality on their sleeves. Because these are the years when questions about sexual identity come up, some teens get uncomfortable with the idea that they might feel attracted to someone of the same gender. They try to distance themselves from the thought by putting lesbians down or making jokes about them, hoping that it will prove they aren't like "them." When someone is comfortable with her or his own sexuality, that person doesn't feel threatened by someone else's sexual identity and won't feel the need to use lesbians and gays as scapegoats. So the next time someone makes a homophobic comment, know it's a reflection of how that person feels on the inside.

According to the Hetrick-Martin Institute in New York City:

- From puberty to age twenty, 17 percent of girls have one or more homosexual experiences.
- Eighty percent of lesbian, gay, and bisexual young people report feeling severely isolated from peers, family, and places to turn to get help.
- Eighty-three percent of young lesbians have used alcohol, 56 percent have used drugs, and 11 percent have used crack cocaine within the last three months.
- Lesbian and gay youth are up to three times more likely to attempt suicide than their heterosexual peers. Lesbian and gays make up 30 percent of all teens who actually succeed in killing themselves.
- Twenty percent of lesbian teens experience verbal or physical assaults at school, and 28 percent of these teens are forced to drop out of school because of the harassment.

● ●

FIVE MYTHS ABOUT LESBIANS

Myth: Women become lesbians because they can't get a man.

Fact: If this were so, communities that have more available women than men would be swarming with lesbians. But there is no proven relationship between the availability of men and the number of lesbians. Besides, women are lesbians because they feel romantically and sexually more attracted to women than to men. While most lesbians are primarily involved in sexual relationships with women, a good number have dated, had sex with, or even been married to men.

Myth: All lesbians are "butch" and try to look like men.

Fact: How do you spot a lesbian in a crowd? You can't! There's no way to tell a person's sexual orientation just by looking at her appearance.

Myth: Lesbians are sick people who need help.

Fact: Psychiatrists used to consider homosexuality a disorder. But after decades of tests and studies, there was no evidence that lesbians and gays were poorly adjusted or in need of help simply because of their sexual orientation. In fact, doctors now believe that it's denying sexual orientation that causes problems.

Myth: Lesbians shouldn't be around kids because they'll recruit them into being gay.

Fact: According to the Hetrick-Martin Institute, a recent study shows that most people's sexual orientation is "established before adolescence, regardless of whether they had been sexually active at that time." Lesbian and gay people can't brainwash anyone into changing their sexual identity. As far as lesbians being a threat to children, research shows that the vast majority of survivors of sexual abuse were abused by heterosexual men.

Myth: Lesbians are fine as long as they keep it to themselves. When someone's an "out" lesbian, it's good to keep a distance, because if you're nice to them, they'll try to make a pass at you.

Fact: First of all, most sexual harassers are heterosexual men. Second, most lesbians are not on a mission to convert straight women. Straight women who constantly think lesbians are after them probably have an ego problem or are dealing with their own same-sex attraction. Third, if someone you know is a lesbian, it's OK to be friends with her, hug her and confide in her. Being a lesbian isn't a disease, so there's no need to treat her any different than anyone else.

"Coming out made me realize I was OK as a person and as a woman, and that I really wasn't having this huge identity crisis about wanting to be a man."

YOSHIMA, 18, SEATTLE, WASHINGTON

I always knew. I didn't say the words to myself until I was about thirteen, but I was always attracted to women. I had better relations with them; I had crushes on female teachers and classmates. I just knew, but I didn't know exactly what it meant until later.

I thought there was something wrong with me because I was a little tomboy. I never wore dresses and sometimes felt that I didn't really want to be a girl. I think that was my solution, my under-the-age-of-ten logic: since I'm attracted to women I must really want to be a boy. It wasn't until later that I realized that wasn't true. I didn't really want to be a boy, and I still don't.

It took me a while to get more clear about my sexuality. It didn't seem like there was a way for me to figure it out. There just wasn't e nough information. Part of it was that I didn't have a name for it. I didn't know exactly what it meant. I was still trying to deal with this attraction to women. I thought it was abnormal. That was the common opinion. It really took a while for me to say, "Well, yes, I am a lesbian, and I am attracted to women, and there's nothing wrong with being a lesbian." Instead it was like, "Well, I'm attracted to women and therefore I must want to be a boy." Which I don't think is very unusual, although people don't talk about it that way.

The first person I told I was a lesbian was a girl I had a crush on. She was an out lesbian and a couple of years older than I was—I met her when I was twelve—but I never talked about it with her until I was fourteen. She was reading a book, and I said, "That looks like a good book. Can I read it?" So she said, as a joke, "I don't give these books to my straight friends." And I said, "How do you know I'm straight?"

We just started spending more and more time together. There were a lot of gay people at the school, so it was pretty obvious to everyone else at school what was going on between us. I had been pining for this person for two years, so everyone else said, "Finally! Now we don't have to hear about this any more." I hadn't told anybody about it, but once everybody knew it was no big deal. I'm pretty lucky.

At the time I was living with my mom, and my dad was living with his girlfriend. My mom made me tell her. She said, "I think you should tell me why you are spending so much time with this one person." And I said, "Mom, you wouldn't understand—really, you wouldn't." And she said, "I think you should tell me now." I had hardly ever used the phone before seeing her, and I was on the phone constantly and my mom got so sick of me and the phone she bought me my own phone line. So I said, "Well, it's kind of because she's my girlfriend, that's why." She said, "Thank you for telling me. Your sisters and I got together a year ago and pretty much decided that." I said, "What? Why didn't you tell me? It would have been so much easier!" She had friends who were lesbians, so I think that made it easier for her. But it didn't just mean that she was perfectly fine about it. It was much different when it came to her daughter.

It was harder with my dad. My dad is Japanese, and my mom Caucasian. We never talked about anything that was even remotely related to sex. We have a very strange way of communicating. I remember when I was twelve I said, "Dad, what would you say if I told you I was pregnant." Just a theoretical question. He said, "Well, I'd ask who the father was." And that was the end of the conversation. He never talked about his relationships and I never talked about mine. It was a mutual silence. So, what finally happened was, I mentioned to him about a project I was working on. I said, "There's some people who want to make a documentary about gay and lesbian youth, and they want me to be in it, and they want us to do an interview together. Will you do it?" He said yes. And that was the end of the conversation.

So the next time was the first time we ever talked about my being a lesbian: when the camera people knocked on the door a couple of weeks later. They set up the camera and we were sitting at the kitchen table. The fun part was that I was just as in the dark as everyone else about what my father would say. He said that when I was six or seven years old, I had told him that I was a homosexual. I was shocked. I think my mouth fell to the floor. It was all on camera, me going, "No way! Did I? I did?" I couldn't believe that I had actually said that that young, because it seemed like it took me so long to figure it out again.

Coming out didn't have a huge impact for me socially, but it did personally. It was the first time in my life that I actually felt comfortable being a woman. Coming out made me realize I was OK as a person and as a woman, and that I really wasn't having this huge identity crisis about wanting to be a man. I think that it's a big misconception that lesbians want to be men, or that if you're attracted to women you have to therefore be a man. For me coming out was really liberating.

Where to Turn
Recommended Reading
Relationships, Sexuality, and Sexual Orientation

Bridges of Respect: Creating Support for Lesbian and Gay Youth, Katherine Whitlock, American Friends Service Committee (Philadelphia), 1989.

Changing Bodies, Changing Lives: A Book for Teens on Sex and Relationships, Ruth Bell, Random House, 1988.

Chicana Lesbian: The Girls Our Mothers Warned Us About, Carla Trujillo, Third Woman Press, 1991.

Coming Out to Parents: A Two Way Survival Guide for Lesbians and Gay Men and Their Parents, Mary Borhek, The United Church Press, 1993.

The Family Book About Sexuality, Mary Calderone and Eric W. Johnson, HarperCollins, 1989.

Hearing Us Out: Voices from the Gay and Lesbian Community, Roger Sutton, ed., Little, Brown & Co., 1994. Through personal stories from both teens and adults, this book explores issues confronting the gay community, from AIDS and the military to gay parenting. It tries to give the picture of a community united in history, culture, political goals, and perpetual disagreement.

Is It a Choice? Answers to 300 of the Most Frequently Asked Questions About Gays & Lesbians, Eric Marcus, HarperCollins, 1993. Topics include self-discovery, coming out, family and children, work, dating, and more.

Living the Spirit: A Gay American Indian Anthology, Will Roscoe, ed., St. Martin's Press, 1989. This book explores lesbian and gay Native Americans through historical articles, personal accounts, stories, and poetry to compare traditional roles among Native Americans with the lives of gay Native Americans today.

Losing It: The Virginity Myth, Louis M. Crosier, ed., Avocus Publishing Inc., 1994. Stories by young men and women about how they lost their virginity and what they learned from the experience.

Love and Sex in Plain Language, Eric Johnson, 4th edn., Bantam Books, 1988.

The New Teenage Body Book, Kathy McCoy and Charles Wibbelsman, Berkeley Publishing Group Books, 1992.

Sex and Sense, Gary Kelly, Barron's Educational Series, Inc., 1993. This book deals with the physical, emotional, and social aspects of human sexuality. It helps us to explore our feelings and beliefs about sex. Includes chapters on AIDS, pregnancy, sexual harassment and abuse, and homosexuality.

Two Teenagers in Twenty: Writings by Gay and Lesbian Youth, Ann Heron, ed., Alyson Publications, Inc., 1994. In this selection gay and lesbian young people tell stories about discovering their gay feelings, deciding whether or not to tell friends and family and coming to terms with being different.

When Someone You Know Is Gay, Susan and Daniel Cohen, M. Evans & Company, 1989.

Young, Gay and Proud!: A Resource Book for Gay and Lesbian Youth, Sasha Alyson, Alyson Publications, 1991. This is considered the best in helping young gay people understand what it means to be gay.

Support Groups and Organizations
Sexuality and Relationships

Association of Multiethnic Americans, P.O. Box 191726, San Francisco, CA 94119-1726; (510) 523-AMEA. The association acts as a clearinghouse for information on inter- and multiracial relationships of all kinds and sponsors a confederation of more than ninety interracial support groups across the country.

Blacks Educating Blacks About Sexual Health Issues (BEBASHI), 1233 Locust Street, Philadelphia, PA 19107; (215) 546-4140. BEBASHI conducts community outreach programs to educate the public about STDs, HIV/AIDS, and human sexuality. Their Human Sexuality Series is designed to help adolescents understand the connection between self-esteem, values, self-image, and life decisions.

Sexuality Information and Education Council of the U.S., 130 W. 42nd Street, Suite 350, New York, NY 10036; (212) 819-9770. A clearinghouse that provides information on every aspect of sexuality.

Sexuality or Not, Planned Parenthood, 2708 Liberty Road NW, Roanoke, VA 24012; (703) 362-3968. *Sex or Not* is a program designed to help reduce the myths and misinformation surrounding sexuality, develop an understanding that sexuality is holistic, teach responsible ways to express one's sexuality, and build effective communication skills.

Teen Council, Advocates for Youth, 1025 Vermont Ave. NW, Suite 200, Washington DC 20005; (202) 347-5700. Teen Council is a peer education program that provides teenagers from the Washington, D.C. area with the opportunity to create their own solutions to teen pregnancy and other sexually related concerns. Once trained, Teen Council members do workshops on teen health and sexuality throughout the Washington, D.C. area.

The Training Center for Adolescent Sexuality and Family Life Education, 350 East 88th Street, New York, NY 10128; (212) 876-9716. The Center offers the Family Life and Sex Education Program which is a fifteen-week formal program for teens and parents covering sexual anatomy, reproduction, contraception, STD and AIDS, and exploring such issues as gender roles, family roles, body images, and patterns of affection, love, and intimacy.

YWCA of the U.S.A., 726 Broadway, New York, NY 10003-9595; (212) 614-2700. The Youth Development Program supports the empowerment of adolescent females by creating opportunities for education and leadership. The program works to meet this goal by promoting sexuality education and health education.

Sexual Orientation

The Bridges Project, American Friends Service Committee, 1501 Cherry Street, Philadelphia, PA 19102-1479; (215) 241-7000. The Bridges Project is a nationwide network of programs and organizations supporting lesbian, gay, bisexual, and transgender (LGNT) youth. They can direct you to a support group or organization in your area.

Gay and Lesbian Anti-Violence Project, 647 Hudson St., New York, NY 10014; (212) 807-0197. AVP services include a 24-hour hotline for crisis intervention, information and referrals, long and short-term professional counseling, support groups, pursuing complaints against the police and other authorities, getting court orders to help protect you from an abusive partner or neighbor. All their literature is in English and Spanish.

Hetrick-Martin Institute for Lesbian and Gay Youth, 2 Astor Place, 3rd Floor, New York, NY 10003; (212) 674-2400. An agency for bisexual, gay, and lesbian young people ages twelve to twenty-one. Offers free confidential counseling about sexuality issues. For *You Are Not Alone*, a state by state directory of organizations serving gay youth, send five dollars to above address.

Indianapolis Youth Group, P.O. Box 20716, Indianapolis, IN 46220; (317) 541-8726. IYG was created in 1987 in response to the needs of self-identified gay, lesbian, bisexual, and questioning youth. The IYG services include counseling, a drop-in center open seven evenings a week, health care, outreach to provide youth with education and interventions to reduce high-risk behaviors, a pen-pal network, and a national toll-free hotline ((800) 347-TEEN) where trained IYG youth respond to several hundred callers each month. They have a free brochure entitled "If You Think You're Alone . . . "

Parents, Families, and Friends of Lesbians and Gays (PFLAG), 1101 14th Street NW, Suite 1030, Washington, DC 20005; (202) 638-4200. PFLAG provides an opportunity for dialogue about sexual orientation and offers booklets and information packets, including "Coming Out to Parents" and "Be Yourself," a booklet designed for lesbian, gay, and bisexual youth and people who interact with them. They also have a state by state directory of PFLAG affiliates.

Sexual Minority Youth Assistance League (SMYAL), 333½ Pennsylvania Avenue SE, 3rd Floor, Washington, DC 20003; (202) 546-5940/5911. An organization for fourteen to twenty-one year olds dealing with all aspects of sexual identity including lesbian, gay, bisexual, transsexual, and transvestite teens. Provides structured weekly support groups with a rap-discussion format as well as a drop-in program which offers a safe space for socializing and recreation with peers.

Youth on Common Ground, American Friends Service Committee, 814 NE 40th Street, Seattle, WA 98105; (206) 632-0500. YOCG is a diverse group of young adults, aged thirteen to nineteen, committed to educating their communities on issues affecting gay, lesbian, bisexual, and transgender youth. YOCG provides a safe space for youth to learn and work together, help develop leadership skills and create public speaking opportunities for its participants. YOCG chapters have been started in local schools and their communities.

Hotlines

The Gay and Lesbian Anti-Violence Project: (212) 807-0197 (24-hour hotline). Call if you've been the victim of a crime, including bias crime, domestic violence, sexual assault, HIV-related violence, police abuse, or any other kind of crime.

Gay and Lesbian Youth Hotline: (800) 347-TEEN (Thursday-Sunday 7–11:45 p.m.). Offers crisis counseling and referrals to young people dealing with aspects of sexual identity. They will also refer you to groups in your specific area.

National Runaway Switchboard: (800) 621-4000 (24 hours).

Youth Development International: (800) HIT-HOME. Counseling and referrals for pregnancy, substance abuse, sexual abuse, homelessness, HIV and AIDS.

CHAPTER 12

IT'S ROUGH
OUT THERE

Violence here, violence there, violence everywhere. It seems that our society has become obsessed with violence. Deadly video games, shoot 'em up/blow 'em up movies, and songwriters who brag about killing their neighbors are all part of our national landscape. While this is all entertainment, there's nothing fun about real-life violence that keeps people afraid to walk home alone, go to school, or accept a date. That's why it's important to understand that there are alternatives to violence and ways to avoid violent situations.

Violence among Us

Though most violence happens in the home, a good deal also occurs out in the streets and at school. It's hard to believe but in some circles being violent is a sign of being cool and "respected," but what kind of respect is it when you hold a gun to someone's head? Most teenagers, even those caught up in violent situations, admit that violence takes its toll and that there are better ways of solving problems.

- Homicide is the second leading cause of death for all young women aged fifteen to twenty-four, and the single leading cause of death for African American young women aged fifteen to twenty-four. (Centers for Disease Control)

- Five percent of U.S. households had at least one member age twelve or older who had been the victim of a violent crime. (National Victim Center)

- Seven percent of girls surveyed in a Cleveland suburb in 1994 said they had seen a knife attack and 6 percent had witnessed shootings.

- Nationwide, 4.4 percent of students missed at least one day of school because they felt unsafe at school or traveling to or from school. (Youth Risk Behavior Surveillance System, 1993)

Why All the Violence?

These days a lot of parents say to their kids, "When I was your age, we left our doors unlocked and felt safe walking down the street at night." They also admit that they were living in a different time than teenagers today. And they're right. Violence, which is when someone physically (or emotionally) injures another, has become a big problem.

Fernando Soriano, Ph.D., of the University of Missouri in Kansas City, believes that violence affects communities differently. "People are exposed to violence at different levels depending on their communities and cultures," he states. However, he believes that with all the attention paid to violence now, pretty much everyone is nervous about being a victim. "There's a sense of vulnerability to being a victim because there's a heightened awareness of violence in the media," says Dr. Soriano. This in turn feeds our behavior as a society, where we learn to be a fearful victim or a physical aggressor.

According to Deborah Prothrow-Stith, Ph.D., a professor at the Harvard School of Public Health and author of *Deadly Consequences* (HarperCollins, 1991), youth violence has now become widespread since the mid-eighties. "We learn from cartoons that violence is funny," explains Dr. Prothrow-Stith. "Movies teach us that violence is glamorous and solves problems." Unlike real life, people in movies (including innocent bystanders) can die without anyone even feeling for them.

In the past boys have been more affected by the images of violence because the heroes—and most of the villains—were males. But Dr. Prothrow-Stith points out that girls are getting a piece of the action now too. "Violence is increasing with girls too because of the female images, like the Power Rangers and other female superheroes. Being mean and tough is a standard that girls are aspiring to too."

Eva Feindler, Ph.D., an associate professor of psychology at Long Island University C.W. Post Campus in New York, agrees that girls are more violent now because violence is seen as normal. "Physical aggression is a part of our culture that we have adopted as a problem-solving strategy." She gives the example of the strong negative peer pressure that can push a normally easygoing young woman to violence. "Even if it's not her nature, a girl may be pushed by her peers and feel stuck. She can't back down because everyone expects her to fight."

Researchers have learned that most people are violent because they have learned it from their families, society, the media, and their environment. Dr.

Prothrow-Stith says that most violent juvenile delinquents have been the victims of devastating and severe child abuse. Though not everyone who is violent has been abused, most have and are taking their anger out in the way they were taught.

Overall Dr. Soriano believes that so much violence, or even the threat of it, in young women's lives today adds to the confusion of adolescence. "For many kids there's a sense that nobody has any control, nobody's in charge," he says. "The feeling of unpredictability makes kids fearful of each other." This fear, combined with the fact that many of us move around so much we don't know our own neighbors, means that we don't have strong communities like those our parents might have had. All of these feelings lead to anxiety and stress, and little problems can turn into big fights. This snowball effect is how the tension that leads to violence starts, and with so many guns on the street, violence can be deadly. The trick is learning other ways to deal with the little problems when they start.

According to the American Psychological Association:

- There are five to six violent acts per hour on primetime TV, and twenty to twenty-five on Saturday morning kids' programs.
- By the time an average child leaves elementary school, she has seen 8,000 murders and over 100,000 other violent acts on TV.
- Watching violence on TV contributes to violent behavior and sets up patterns for adult violent behavior.
- Viewing acts of violence repeatedly can make the viewer "comfortable" with the material, even if she was offended at first viewing.

Gangsta Girls Don't Have Much Fun

To some people, living the gangster life seems glamorous. There's always something exciting to do, you always have friends around, and you get instant respect. This is the same fantasy that draws thousands of young people into gangs every year from cities like Los Angeles, New York, Chicago, Denver, Des Moines, Kansas City, and Baton Rouge. (There are 42,000 gang members in Los Angeles alone.) But the longer you gangbang (are in a gang), the quicker the fantasy becomes a real-life nightmare. For young women, the consequences can last a lifetime.

Young women join gangs for many reasons:

- to feel that they belong to something, especially to a group of people that feels like a family and helps give them an identity;

- to make money by doing things like selling drugs, especially since it's hard for teens to find jobs;
- to get away from an abusive home life (the gang gives them a place to stay);
- because everyone else gangbangs, including boyfriends, friends, family members, and people in the neighborhood and at school;
- because they're bored or have no money for other constructive outlets (like after-school sports, computer clubs, or theater groups);
- for protection, otherwise they'll get beaten up walking home from school, for instance.

To get in a gang, most people have to go through an initiation. This is when the gang decides what you have to do to belong. Some things that female gang members have to do are:
- get beaten up by other gang members (including guys sometimes) for several minutes;
- get a tattoo or scar with the gang's name;
- drink and take drugs until they pass out or get sick;
- have sex with several male gang members (some who are even HIV positive!);
- survive getting shot.

At first joining the gang seems like a lot of fun to some people. There are lots of parties, everyone hangs out and ditches school, most people get high, there's always good gossip, and, if you sell drugs, there's a lot of money. But most girls learn that the gang isn't all they thought, and the longer they stay in, the worse it is. They constantly have to prove how tough they are and are forced into doing things they don't really want to. They beat up innocent people, steal purses, or shop-lift. Hard-core gangbangers participate in carjackings, burglaries, and shootings as a way to gain "respect" from their homies (other gang members). Other girls get known as "sluts" because their role is to have sex with their homeboys. In the end young women quickly see their choices the longer they gangbang: they'll end up pregnant, in jail, or dead.

Ex-gang member Jonelle knows from experience that gangbanging is far from glamorous. After seeing her father go to prison, her mother get addicted to crack, and too many friends die, she decided to call it quits. "Most homies will tell you in private they wish they could get out," says Jonelle, "and what they really want is to just be wanted, noticed and loved by their parents."

Getting out of a gang isn't always easy. Some gangs will only let you leave if you get beaten up or shot. Still others have oaths that say the only way to leave the gang is to die. The easiest way to get out is to leave the environment by going to another neighborhood or city or into foster care. The key to getting out and staying out is to have a plan for the future and some help getting there.

> "I noticed that my body felt like a bowl of jelly. I couldn't get up. I was shot."
>
> PATTY, 17, COMPTON, CALIFORNIA

> I was born in Los Angeles and moved to Compton around the age of nine. About the time I was thirteen I had got involved in the gangs. I liked the gang because most of the time we were ditching out of school. We would hang out in the park, laugh and joke around.
>
> By the time I was fifteen, I had a boyfriend—my baby's dad. He told me not to gangbang, so I decided to quit. I went back to school, was getting everything together, and was finally apart from the gangs. Then one night me and the baby's dad were walking back from Blockbuster's through the neighborhood I used to live in. All of the sudden we heard shots, and got caught in the crossfire; at the time I was four months pregnant.
>
> I remember looking over at my baby's dad and he was just throwing up this blood. I'm like, "Oh God, no," and I'm screaming and shaking him. Then I noticed that my body felt like a bowl of jelly. I couldn't get up. I was shot, but I thought I'd broke my leg or something cause I fell. I noticed that when he got up after he was conscious again he said, "C'mon, get up." I'm like, "I can't, I can't, I can't move!" Then he opened my jacket and saw the blood on me. I got shot in my back and in my right lung. The bullet in my back went through my liver.
>
> It was weird, because after that I was real sleepy, and was having this flashback about my dad when he was showing me how to ride a bike. All I remember is telling my dad, "Let me go, let me go! I can do it, I can do it, let me go!" Then I just remember the cops putting a flashlight in my eyes. I was more worried about the baby's dad, cause I didn't really know what had happened to me. They didn't want to tell me I was shot, because I was pregnant and they thought I was going to lose the baby. I didn't feel any pain till they put me on the gurney. As soon as the cops picked me up and moved me, I felt real cold.
>
> The next day when I woke up the baby's dad was next to me and then my mom came in. I got real scared when I saw my mom, because I had tattoos on my body that she had never seen in her life. My big fear was that she was going to see the tattoos and she was going to know I was pregnant. The only thing I could move was my arms, and I kept pulling the sheets over my neck. I was more scared about what my parents were going to do to me than about my own health.

My mom was crying. I'm like, "Mom, don't cry." After that they gave me a pain shot and I went to sleep. I was just waking up, going to sleep, waking up, going to sleep.

I got operated on the night I got shot. The first thing I did when I was conscious was ask them about my baby. And they said, "Don't worry about the baby, what we're worried about is you. You're still young and you can have more babies later in your life." Luckily, the baby made it.

It was funny that no one told me I wasn't going to be able to walk. They told me I wasn't going to walk when I got to rehab. It was weird because I still felt my legs, and I could move one of my toes on my right foot. They said when the bullet hit my spinal cord it swelled my spine up and gave me spinal shock.

The baby's dad was in the hospital about a week. He came to see me a couple of times—about four times—and then he disappeared. My mom told me the pressure of me being in a wheelchair was what made him leave.

Eventually I was able to walk, and then he tried to come back and told me he missed me and all that. I simply told him what I'd been saying to myself all along. "If you really loved me you would have stuck by me when I needed you the most." If the tables had been turned, I would have been there day and night, no matter what. So I just had to let him go as much as it hurt me, and it still hurts me, but I wanted to go on with my life.

My family has really stuck by me, my mom especially. We ended up getting really close when I got shot. I needed her. When I was shot she was there day and night for me. When she wasn't at the hospital, I couldn't sleep. I was calling. "Mom, come, I'm scared, I want you here." And she would come, and I would sleep as soon as she got there. Like I had to have her there.

I've learned a lot through all of this. I learned how to survive and all that. And for me gangs are bad. Because of them, I feel like I'm marked. I'm marked for life with tattoos; I'm trying to take them off right now with laser. When I'm alone, I have to watch my back now. Most people don't think about that. They don't think about the future. No one tries to change until someone in their family gets shot—or it happens to them. Why wait for that to happen? Why not change now while you have a chance?

WHY GUNS AND PEOPLE DON'T MIX

Guns aren't cool or glamorous; here's the real deal:

- **Guns don't protect. Though you may think you'll be safer with a gun around, studies show that guns kept in the home are more likely to be stolen or to injure a family member or friend than to be used against an intruder. And in the case where there is a confrontation,** victims very often have been injured by their own guns (if they manage to find them at all) when the guns are used against them.

- Triggers don't work in reverse. In the heat of an argument, most people don't think, they act. And when you consider that drugs or alcohol are involved in most homicides, there isn't a lot of clear-headed thinking going on. Add a gun to the mix, and it's lethal. According to the Children's Defense Fund, one-third of all murders happen because of an argument. That's why having a gun around makes it too easy for someone to get injured or killed for no reason. And once the trigger is pulled, there are only regrets.

- Accidents do happen. A lot. Tragic and unnecessary accidents happen when kids find their parents' loaded gun and hurt themselves or their friends. By FBI reports, in 1990 over 500 children under twenty years old were killed in accidental shootings. Guns are the most deadly type of weapon, and an accident can mean death.

- On a daily basis, 100,000 students carry guns to school, 160,000 miss classes due to fear of physical harm, and 40 are injured or killed by firearms. (National Education Association)

- A survey of students at Illinois high schools revealed that one in twenty students had carried a gun to school in 1990. (Illinois Criminal Justice Information Authority)

- The presence of a gun in the home triples the risk of homicide in the home. (*New England Journal of Medicine* study, 1993)

- Gunshot wounds are the second leading cause of death for all people ages ten to thirty-four.

Surviving Violence

When someone is the victim of or witness to a violent act, she often goes through a range of emotions after the event. This is called trauma, which basically means that the event had a major impact on her life. Some people, though shaken up, are able to move on after some time and get on with their lives. Other people are more stressed out by their experiences and find that they're having a harder time coping, even if they don't realize why.

According to Dr. Rochelle Hanson, assistant professor at Medical University of South Carolina in Charleston, when a person survives a violent crisis, there may be a reaction that lasts for years that makes it hard to function normally. This person has what's called post-traumatic stress disorder (PTSD), and it's a normal way to deal with distressing events like:

- witnessing threat or harm to someone in your family or a friend;
- the destruction of your community;

* witnessing another person who is being physically abused or has been seriously injured or killed.

With PTSD, you find it hard to shake the event and wind up reliving it over and over in several ways:

* nightmares;
* disturbing images when thinking back on the event;
* feeling that the event is happening again;
* scary feelings associated with the event, like on the anniversary of the event.

You also try really hard to put the whole trauma out of your mind by:

* avoiding thoughts, feelings, activities, or situations related to the event;
* not being able to remember what happened during the event;
* losing interest in things you used to like to do;
* distancing yourself or feeling isolated from others;
* feeling like you don't have a future, or you don't expect to live long.

You also may feel like something's going on inside of you that you can't control that makes you anxious. Because of this you might:

* have trouble falling or staying asleep;
* have outbursts of anger;
* have trouble concentrating;
* feel jumpy or easily startled, especially when something reminds you of the event (loud noises, places, smells, for instance).

"I'm never dealing with anybody associated with gangs, killings, robbings, beating up on people. It cost my boyfriend's life and it almost cost me mine."

SANDRA, 17, WASHINGTON, D.C.

In my neighborhood there weren't any gangs, there were just groups of guys from different streets. That's all I'd call it: groups of guys who didn't like each other because of little stupid stuff like, "Oh this person had a car, and this person didn't." Or it would be drug or money related. They had guns and everything. They fight over nothing when it all comes down. The night it happened, it was summer. I called my boyfriend and stayed up at his house until about 8 or 9 o'clock. We argued about taking a cab to my house, because my grandma said to take one if it was getting late. He said, "No, we can walk." So we were walking, and from nowhere this guy shows up walking towards us. You know how you move over so the somebody coming the other way can get by? I was moving out of his way, and he just pulled out his gun and started firing. He didn't ask for money, he didn't say "freeze," "stop." He didn't say, "I know you," or even some little gang expression. He just started shooting. I got hit first. I got shot in my finger and my wrist.

My boyfriend pushed me into this little wooded area and he got shot in the chest and in the privates. Then the guy stood over me and shot me in my back. I was scared. I felt a lot of burning, like I was on fire. I thought I was going to die. I was in and out of consciousness. I was thinking about my boyfriend, but I couldn't think too much. Everything was kind of blurry.

After we got shot, a boy we knew saw us from his car and came and told us he would be right back. He got these three guys we knew and they got us in a car and took us to the hospital. I had an exploratory done, and my finger and wrist were put in a cast. The first days in the hospital I was under sedation. When I came out from sedation, I couldn't walk. My left side of my body was temporarily paralyzed from my arm to my leg because the nerves were so damaged. But other than that I was up, watching TV. I didn't eat.

On about the third day when I came completely out of sedation, my grandmother came and they were telling me my boyfriend was fine. As long as I thought he was doing fine I wasn't worried. I knew that if I worried about him I was going to stress myself out.

Five days after we were shot, my boyfriend died. I was thinking that it couldn't have happened, that they were lying. When they told me he died it seemed like everything we had done together flashed before my eyes and was gone. It just flashed as if I wasn't going to remember it anymore.

I stayed in the hospital about two weeks. They let me out the day before his funeral. I still couldn't believe it. When I went I had no feeling. He had just gotten out of jail; he was turning his whole life around. He was going to get a job. There was a lot of stuff we were going to do, and it seemed like somebody robbed me. They waited until he wanted to do something with his life, and then they just took it from him.

And I learned now that I'm never dealing with anybody associated with gangs, killings, robbings, beating up on people. It cost my boyfriend's life and it almost cost me mine.

I was seven months pregnant when I got shot. When I first had her, I didn't want her. I was in a maximum state of depression, I was beyond depressed. I just wanted to be by myself. I just lost my first love, and that's hard to do. She looked just like her father, and that made me push her away even more—to have to look in her face and see her father and know he's not there. It was too painful.

That feeling has gone away and my grief is milder. I know that my child is made of both our blood, so she is a part of both of us. And the part of him that's in her I want to have for the rest of my life. In fact, my accident and my baby motivated me to finish school. I realized I was never going to get any justice, I was never going to see the person that assaulted me get caught. So I plan on being a lawyer and a judge—and change things when I get there.

Coping after a traumatic event can be pretty hard. Even though you may not want to get help, it's definitely better than trying to suffer alone. "Counseling is important because it gives you the chance to grieve," says Dr. Hanson. "Many times your family may say, 'Oh, you should just get on with your life, move on,' but a therapist would never say that. They give you the opportunity to grieve at your pace."

Another important part of surviving after violence is to talk about it. Don't avoid the subject. Find someone you can talk to in an environment that is safe and supportive. Clinical studies and research show that people who talk about their traumatic experience recover faster than those who try to put their feelings out of their mind.

Choices: Violence Isn't the Only Way

Everyone wants to know how to stop the violence. It's obvious that we need to end poverty, have things for teenagers to do after school, and keep schools safe. But those solutions take time to work. Dr. Prothrow-Stith has suggestions for things you can do right now. She has put together a method for young people to help them solve their problems by working together. It's called nonviolent conflict resolution, and it's a way to settle disputes without anyone getting emotionally or physically hurt. That doesn't mean that the whole world becomes one big lovefest. "Most of the time people are working at not fighting," says Dr. Prothrow-Stith, "and they can be successful. But kids have to remember that it takes skill and work for conflict resolution. You're not always going to be successful, but you do get better with practice."

The key to conflict resolution is to work on the *solution* part in resolution. Here are the steps:

1. Try to ignore any comments, teasing, or taunting to get you to fight or stoop to the other person's level.

2. If you can't ignore it, or decide you don't want to, pick a time and place that you and the other person can meet. Don't do it around any friends or a crowd, and don't do it when you're angry.

3. Beforehand, think about what you're going to say. There should be two points to cover:

- why you're angry;
- what you want the other person to do.

HINT: Wait until you're calm and rational before you work on this. Don't think in terms of accusations ("You always get on my nerves"). Instead think of how you *feel*, like "I felt really dissed when you tried to embarrass me." Then focus on what you want, as in "I want an apology and for you to stop with the comments."

4. When you meet, remember that the goal is to work towards a solution. That means that you have to negotiate and compromise. And you have to stay committed to nonviolent means of working out your problems. If this seems too hard, try getting a neutral friend, a peer mediator, or counselor to intervene. You'll feel much better knowing you can put at least one problem behind you.

WHAT ARE YOU GONNA DO ABOUT IT?

PEER MEDIATION PROGRAM AT NORTH MIAMI BEACH HIGH SCHOOL IN FLORIDA

When most people get into fights at school, they're dragged into the principal's office and suspended. The students have a bad mark against them and an enemy to avoid when they return to school, not to mention very pissed-off parents. But the students of North Miami Beach High have a different solution for warring students.

When a fight breaks out, students are given a choice of a ten-day suspension or go into mediation. "Mediation allows everyone to be heard and gives control to the students to decide what's the best solution," says Denise Grandison, a former senior and peer mediator. Originally from Montego Bay, Jamaica, Denise believes that having alternatives to violence is a must at North Miami Beach High. "Students here come from all over the world, so it's important that we learn how to get along."

Interested or chosen students go through Dr. Michael Kesselman's training program to become peer counselor/mediators. They have to learn listening skills and how to guide two hotheads toward a solution. When a problem comes up, mediators are called on to intervene. First the mediator drafts a contract that states the five rules of mediation: no interrupting, no name-calling, respect for each other's feelings, be honest, and take responsibility for your actions. Then each person explains the conflict from her own perspective and both come to a mutual agreement on how to resolve their differences, which usually includes apologies and the promise to treat each other with respect in the future.

On one occasion Denise put her mediation talents to work when a fellow student called her a "stupid immigrant" because Denise was unknowingly blocking her view to the blackboard. "I told her this country is made of immigrants, including her relatives, and that I resented such a condescending remark," recalls Denise. Later the girl apologized to Denise and admitted she was having a bad day.

Sandra Jean-Louis, eighteen, who also went through the program, sees other lasting benefits of peer mediation: "We had 160 mediations solved in one year. All those people could have been suspended or gotten into fights." Things have really turned around for North Miami Beach High, because it used to be considered a little rough. Now Sandra says, "I don't see much violence in school. I've always felt safe."

Denise believes young people need to be taught how to resolve their conflicts peacefully. "Kids fight because they don't know another way," she explains. "They have to be taught how to communicate their feelings. Once students agree to the terms of the contract, they keep their word." She admits that it's not uncommon to see students who used to fight become friends after a mediation.

When Sex Is Violent

Sex is supposed to be a pleasurable act for both partners. Though it may not always be wonderful or satisfying, it should never be forced or humiliating. Sad to say, some young women have had painful sexual experiences that have affected them deeply. If you've been sexually harassed, raped, or been involved in an abusive relationship, there is hope. Part of picking up the pieces is realizing what you have gone through, admitting how much it hurts, and thinking about how to prevent it from happening again.

Sexual Harassment

"Oooh, baby!" "Honey, you sure fill that shirt out." "Girl, what's your name?" Hearing these comments from boys or men you don't know is probably the mildest form of sexual harassment—defined loosely as unwanted sexual attention. More and more women are beginning to tap into their feelings about hearing comments like these on the street: These aren't compliments, they are irritating.

Janet Waronker, M.A., director of the SHARE (Sexual Harassment Advising Resource and Education) program in Princeton, New Jersey, states, "Sexual harassment has four ingredients: it's sexual in nature, unwelcome, usually repeated, and someone else of your same gender would find it offensive." Since the publicity surrounding Professor Anita Hill accusing her former boss Supreme Court Justice Clarence Thomas of sexually harassing her, most people think that sexual harassment is when a boss makes advances or comments that threaten your job or getting a promotion. But sexual harassment can be verbal or physical and can happen at school, on the street, in a store, or basically anywhere.

Because we spend so much time there, young women are generally targets of sexual harassment at school. In a survey of students by the American Association of University Women (AAUW), about 70 percent of young women reported being sexually harassed at school. They reported having to deal with these problems from other students, teachers, or anyone else at school:

- Sexual comments, jokes, gestures, spreading of sexual rumors, comments about their sexual orientation, sexual messages or graffiti, sexual pictures, photographs, messages, or notes.
- Being spied on while showering or changing.
- Being flashed or mooned, touched, brushed up against, pinched, or grabbed in a sexual way.
- Being blocked or cornered in a sexual way, forced to kiss, or to do something sexual.

Waronker discusses another common problem: "Unwanted attention from a man is the biggest problem I know of. He'll continually call—or at worst follow her—after they've stopped dating. Sometimes he doesn't know he's harassing her, because she has had a hard time telling him no clearly." It's often the case that the harasser isn't intending to bug the other person. Actually, students in the AAUW report said they harassed others because:

- everyone else does it, and it's just a part of school life;
- they thought the person liked it;
- they wanted a date with the person;
- their friends talked them into it;
- they wanted something from that person;
- they wanted the person to think they had power over them.

Reading between the lines, many people harass to get something from the other person. "Harassers are hoping to get a reaction by embarrassing the person," says Waronker. "It gives the harasser a sense of power and that makes him feel better." Other guys simply think that young women are inferior and put them down as a way to bond with friends or just selfishly disregard their feelings.

Sexual harassment can also be a very direct abuse of power by an authority figure. Though most of us are harassed by peers, 25 percent of girls in the AAUW study said they were sexually harassed by adult employees at the school (including teachers). When adults or anyone who is in a position of authority make any kind of sexual advances, comments, or gestures towards us it's an abuse of their power and it's sexual harassment.

Sexual harassment can have a profound effect on the person targeted. "The impact of sexual harassment is usually that you feel powerless, degraded, and it can make you lose confidence," explains Waronker, "because someone's looking at your body and not your brains. When you're treated like a sex object, you question what's expected of you." She also says that during the teen years there's a lot of pressure on looks and blending in. Getting this kind of negative attention can make a young woman feel even more self-conscious about her body and push her to hide it with baggy clothes or extra weight or expose herself by acting sexy or wearing revealing clothes.

Because the pain of harassment is so great, the natural reaction is to try to avoid it. Most students reported that they didn't want to come to school after being sexually harassed, and some even cut school or class for that reason. Others found it hard to study, speak in class, pay attention, and sadly their grades were affected. In extreme cases young women began to doubt whether they had what it takes to graduate from high school.

For young women of color sexual harassment can be a matter of racial stereotyping. "Many minority women are seen as exotic and erotic and are considered more sexual [than white women]," says Waronker. Her advice is to head these comments off at the pass. "Even if you feel you have to fit in, it's better to stop these comments early or you'll indirectly reinforce them by putting up with them."

This is true of most cases of sexual harassment. The tough part is that people who sexually harass usually know their targets won't say anything either to them or to someone else. Still Waronker says the three best things to do are:

- Tell the harasser to stop. Firmly and clearly let him know that you aren't interested or don't want the kind of attention he's giving you and that if he continues, you'll report him.

- Write it down. Keep a journal of any incidents of sexual harassment with the date and behavior or comments. This way you can see a pattern and have something to show to someone who can help you later.

• Go tell someone else. It's a good idea to let someone else know what you're going through because sexual harassment can cause a lot of pain. You should also let someone in a position of authority in on the situation. The harasser is hoping you'll be too scared or embarrassed to tell, so by calling him out, you'll call his bluff.

· ## WHAT ARE YOU GONNA DO ABOUT IT?

NOW YOUNG FEMINIST TASK FORCE AT BERKELEY HIGH SCHOOL IN CALIFORNIA

All it takes is one young woman to make a big difference. In the case of Berkeley High School in Berkeley, California, that one woman was Heather Haxo-Phillips. As a senior, she took a women's literature class and started talking about women's issues among her friends. With the help of her women's studies teacher, she called the local chapter of NOW (the National Organization for Women) and started a task force to discuss feminist concerns. She put out fliers (including on the backs of bathroom stall doors) and a notice in the school bulletin, and fifty people showed up for the first meeting. Eventually, this high school chapter of NOW became the biggest club on campus.

At the time, the Clarence Thomas/Anita Hill hearings were going on. "Everyone was talking and thinking about sexual harassment," remembers Emily Hughes, nineteen. Now a freshman at Bryn Mawr College, she was a junior when the Berkeley High NOW started and co-chairperson of the sexual harassment committee. She and the other NOW task force women took a survey about sexual harassment at school. "We had the sense that something needed to be done about it," says Emily. "The first thing we needed to do was convince other people there was a problem."

They used the results to show students that sexual harassment had affected a lot of students and to get others involved in writing school policy about how to deal with it. "It was incredible to see how much it was happening," recalls Emily. "A great experience was to try to figure out what to do when people don't agree about what sexual harassment is." In the end, Emily says they agreed, "It's the whole concept of people defining their own boundaries and having other people respect them."

With the success of Berkeley High's NOW chapter, other schools asked for Heather's input in setting up new chapters. So she organized the Bay Area Teenage Feminist Coalition, which has over ten NOW chapters at various high schools, and is the chairperson. "The Coalition still exists today," says Heather, "and they meet monthly to talk about the school groups and plan Coalition events."

For more information on how to start a NOW chapter at your school or take a sexual harassment survey, contact East Bay NOW, P.O. Box 635, Berkeley, CA 94701; (510)287-8948.

Forced Sex

The image of rape is an assault in a dark alley by a stranger who uses a weapon. In reality, most women are raped by someone they know, trust, and maybe even dated. While rape is never the woman's fault, being educated about why it happens could help a woman recognize when there's danger.

What Is Rape?

According to Robin Warshaw, author of *I Never Called It Rape*, rape is a violent act in which "the aggressor makes a decision to force his victim to submit to what he wants." This can mean holding her down with his body weight or using a weapon, and may include penetration of her vagina, mouth, or rectum. Rape is not a sexual act, even though it involves sex. It is a form of violence that is meant to humiliate and make the victim feel powerless.

There are two kinds of rape that experts discuss:

STRANGER RAPE: perpetrated by someone the victim doesn't know.

ACQUAINTANCE RAPE: perpetrated by someone the victim knows, not including a relative (that's called incest; see Chapter 13). This includes friends, neighbors, boyfriends, teachers, or anyone the victim's had contact with before.

Why Do Some Men Rape?

Thankfully most men aren't rapists. That means that most men would not force a woman to do a sexual act she didn't want to. In the *Ms.* report on acquaintance rape (which is published in Warshaw's book) 8 percent of the men surveyed had either raped or attempted rape. The scary part is that the majority of these same men didn't see their behavior as rape. They believed that sex was something they had a right to "take" from a woman even if she didn't want it.

It's impossible to look at someone and tell if he's a rapist. But Warshaw has shown that many of the men who admitted to forcing sex on women are similar in key ways. Most of them drank often, came from abusive backgrounds, read pornographic magazines a lot, were sexually active at an early age (around fifteen) and believed myths about women "asking for" rape. In general these kinds of guys think of sex as something to "get" regardless of what their partners want, because it boosts their egos.

Aside from what these guys may have in common, Warshaw lays out some stay-away personality flaws that could spell trouble with a man you may already know:

- He wants to run the show, as in telling you what to wear, who to be friends with, where to go to dinner.
- He is emotionally abusive. He puts you down, criticizes you and your ideas, makes you feel unimportant.
- He puts women down and treats them as inferior.
- He gets jealous for no reason.
- He drinks or does drugs to get high or stoned or tries to get you to do the same.
- He puts pressure on you to have sex, or be alone together.
- He is physically violent, including grabbing or pushing or acting in a threatening manner. Or he doesn't respect your physical boundaries, by touching you when you don't want him to.
- He gets mad when he doesn't have his way, like if you don't want to have sex.
- He is into weapons or hurting animals. (This is a major clue of a disaster date waiting to happen.)

What's Different about Acquaintance Rape?

A woman who's been raped by someone she knows has a different set of emotions than if she'd been raped by a stranger. For one, many times with acquaintance rape, the victim can't really believe she's been raped. "Because you know the attacker," states Warshaw, "it's hard to put the word 'rape' on it. The victim feels she should have done something to stop it, and all along the way was doubting that what was happening was happening."

It may be easier for the victim to blame herself rather than believe someone she trusted forced her to have sex. She may feel like she "led him on" or that he had a right to do what he did because he's a guy and he "needs it." "The society's messages say that if something happens it's because the girl made it happen," says Warshaw. "In the world of TV girls are supposed to be sexual to get a boy, and boys just can't help themselves." Young people who get these messages believe women exist to please men and don't deserve the same respect that men get.

As teens, acquaintance rape is especially hard. According to the *Ms.* study, 38 percent of women were raped between the ages of fourteen and seventeen. In other studies on sexual assault and teens, almost all survivors knew the rapists because they were friends, boyfriends, or dates. Because most teens are new to the "dating game," they don't have much experience. This is part of what victimizers look for and also what can cause trauma in teen girls for years afterwards. "Many young acquaintance-rape victims are virgins at the time of their attack," Warshaw says. "For them, the incident may distort their perceptions about sexual intercourse and radically affect their future relationships with men. Because the teen years are a time for sexual exploration and identifications, the fallout from an acquaintance rape may last for years."

Teens are also vulnerable because sometimes the attitude is "I'll just let things 'happen.'" This is especially true when it comes to partying. Here's the usual scenario:

1. A young woman is at a party with lots of cute guys, good music, and tons of alcohol or drugs.

2. She wants to show everyone that she can party harder than anyone else by getting smashed or stoned.

3. After drinking and/or drugging, her judgment is messed up. So anything that happens she might not be able to control or even remember. This is exactly the time that many rapists strike.

It can be very difficult for a teen girl to tell somebody that it happened. Because teens are trying to gain independence from families, a young woman may be afraid that if her parents found out that she was raped, they'd limit her life even more as a way to protect her. Even if parents do react with more rules, telling them or another adult is always better than trying to handle it alone.

Warshaw believes that all young women should know their sexual rights. You have the right to:

• make your own decisions;
• walk away at any point;
• say no;
• be your own person without a guy.

"Young women need to be supportive of each other," says Warshaw. "They need to create an environment that's positive and safe."

* *

According to the National Victim Center,

> Over 12 million American women have been raped; 44 percent of these women have been raped more than once.
>
> Most rape victims are between eleven and seventeen years old.
>
> Nearly twice as many women are raped by someone they know (for instance, a boyfriend or an ex) as by strangers.
>
> In 70 percent of all rapes there were no injuries. But almost half of all victims report being afraid of serious injuries or death during the rape.

According to the *Ms.* survey on acquaintance rape:

- Eighty-four percent of men who raped didn't think what they did was rape.
- Seventy-five percent of men and 55 percent of women involved in acquaintance rape had been drinking or taking drugs before the attack.

* *

Surviving Rape

When rape happens, it's critical that the victim begins to take action to help her recover from the devastating effects. The most important step is to go to the hospital emergency room immediately. According to Kathy Simmelink, R.N. and therapist at the Minneapolis Sexual Assault Resource Services:

- Doctors can prevent pregnancies and sexually transmitted infections by prescribing medication within 72 hours.
- Police can get important evidence, such as sperm, which can prove that penetration took place, and ripped clothing, which shows force. So, it's important that the woman who was raped not shower or change clothes before going to the hospital.
- While at the hospital it's vital to report the rape to police to make it clear that this is a crime.
- A sexual assault victim advocate is generally available in the emergency room. Getting counseling as soon as possible is one of the most important ways to begin recovery.

The trauma of rape can bring on a set of physical and emotional symptoms called rape trauma syndrome. Though any reaction is normal after a sexual assault, Simmelink lists these feelings that victims may experience:

In the short term, physical symptoms can include muscle tension, headaches, nausea, neck and shoulder pain; emotional symptoms include feeling out of control, like she's going crazy, hard time concentrating, not sleeping, fear, humiliation, angry, fear of physical violence, reliving the rape over and over, crying, feeling damaged or destroyed, happy (especially for the woman who's survived a stranger rape).

In the long term some of the same symptoms are seen, but to a lesser degree. More common long term reactions include making changes (like switching schools), dreams, nightmares or other sleep problems, fears related to rape (for example, if rape happened at a bus stop, afraid to take the bus), taking precautions to lessen risks of it happening again.

Another reaction is for the victim to blame herself. "Girls tend to doubt their judgment and think of what they could have done to prevent the rape because it gives them a sense of control," explains Simmelink. She believes it's important to know the difference between blame and vulnerability. "No matter how drunk a young woman is or if she uses poor judgment, she's never to blame for a rape. But she does have the power to change her behavior to put her less at risk." Understanding choices and options is an important part of getting through the trauma of rape. "There's no amount of time that's considered normal for recovery," says Simmelink. "It depends on the individual's circumstances, support network, and home situation." She does assure that time will help ease the pain, but reminds that some victims may have strong reactions whenever the anniversary of the rape creeps up on the calendar.

The first step to recovery is to tell somebody. "Most teens are afraid to report a rape, especially if there was a threat involved," says Simmelink. This includes the rapist saying he'll kill the victim or hurt someone in her family. "I know of no case where a rapist has carried out his threat," she explains, "because he's afraid of getting caught."

Threat or no threat, it's crucial to say something to someone. Keeping the trauma inside hoping that it will "just go away," can trigger more problems later on. "Some women come to me ten or twenty years after a rape and haven't told anyone about it before," says Simmelink. "By waiting this long, they've started to substance abuse or have developed an eating disorder to hide the original pain. And all this time they've suffered alone with a big secret."

Telling another adult you trust besides parents is sometimes a good idea. Some good choices are:

- school counselor
- teacher
- clergy person
- relative

Abusive Relationships

Only certain kinds of young women get involved with abusive men, right? Nope, says Melinda Kaiser, education coordinator at My Sister's Place, a battered women's shelter and outreach center in Tuckahoe, New York. "Anyone from any background or culture can get involved in an abusive relationship," she says. That's why studies show that about 30 percent of teens report being involved in a violent relationship and 60 percent report being in an emotionally abusive relationship. These numbers are scary, but the reality of being in an abusive relationship is scarier.

What Happens in an Abusive Relationship?

There are many ways to abuse someone that don't involve fists or weapons. Here are different types of abuse according to the experts:

- Emotional/verbal: controlling, restricting behavior or time with friends or family, criticizing, interrogating, accusing, being extremely jealous, telling the woman she's ugly, worthless without him, unlovable, or trying to make her seem crazy.
- Physical: shoving, hitting, kicking, slapping, shaking, pulling hair, burning, choking, throwing things at her, using any weapon against her, punching holes in the wall, or acting in a way that makes her feel afraid of him.
- Sexual: forcing, intimidating, or manipulating her into having sex or doing sexual acts that are humiliating or she doesn't want to do.

How could any woman get involved with a man who hurts her? According to Barrie Levy, psychotherapist and author of *In Love and in Danger*, abusive men don't come into relationships swinging their fists. In fact, most of them seem like regular guys, until they show some warning signs. There are three red flags that Levy says to look for in a guy you may be seeing that usually mean he's the abusive type:

- He has an explosive temper, lashes out at others in a violent way (for example if he gets in fights or has hit an ex-girlfriend).
- He is very controlling, jealous, possessive, or tries to restrict your behavior (like he makes you feel guilty for spending time with family or friends, tells you what clothes to wear).
- You're afraid of him or what he might do.

A lot of young women have the idea that they'd never get involved in an abusive relationship. "Once he lays a hand on *me*," the thinking goes, "I'd be outta there." But the nature of abusive relationships is usually very intense, as in intensely good turning to intensely bad. Levy explains the cycle in four parts:

1. Honeymoon stage: Two people meet. They think the relationship is better than any they've ever had before. She thinks his jealousy is "cute" and loves the attention he gives her.

2. Tension stage: He's unhappy and moody. She tries to make him happy again, and he starts to expect her to make him feel better. No matter what she does, he gets more and more unhappy and tense.

3. Explosion stage: They have a huge fight where he is abusive towards her.

4. Return to honeymoon: He apologizes by being on good behavior, buys her gifts, and promises that it won't happen again. But it does.

Levy explains, "As the relationship goes on, the length of time from the honeymoon stage to the explosive stage gets shorter and shorter. She keeps trying to make him happy, hoping he'll change, but things only get worse."

Why Does He Abuse?

Try to picture an abuser and the image that comes to mind is an overheated, big, beefy jerk. Some of them are, but most are just Regular Joes, at least on the outside. "Abusers test normal in all areas of their personalities except in their aggression towards women," says Levy. "Even if they don't believe in abusing women, they justify their own abusive behavior."

Kaiser explains that men who abuse are also control freaks. "They abuse to gain power and control," Kaiser says, "and they feel they're entitled to that power over someone else." What separates abusers from other people is that they need to dominate women in order to feel good about themselves. But, as everyone knows, stepping on someone else or putting them down doesn't boost self-esteem.

Rather than getting a life of their own, abusers spend most of the relationship trying to rule others. Because they need a victim, Levy says, "Abusive men are very dependent people and are afraid of being left. He thinks that she has control over him and turns it around by constantly trying to control her." Oddly enough, most abusers actually see themselves as the victims! This view conveniently keeps them from taking responsibility for their actions.

As hard as it is to believe, many abusers don't believe it's right to hit women, but they tolerate violence towards women from others or themselves. For example, they may hang out with guys who think it's OK to slap a girl or give her a beeper to keep track of her. They believe that they own their girlfriends (you've heard the phrase "my woman") and can treat them as they wish.

Overall most men abuse because they can. "We all probably know an abuser," says Kaiser, "and we may even think he's terrific. But because he doesn't see women as his equals, he feels he has the right to harm them." It only stops when he isn't allowed to abuse anymore.

Why Don't Women Just Leave?

Saying good-bye to a mean, abusive guy seems like it would be a snap. Easy to say from the outside looking in, but those who have been abused by lovers or boyfriends know firsthand that leaving can be really tough.

In an abusive relationship the abuser constantly guilt-trips his partner into making her feel responsible for his moods and feelings. Levy explains that as a victim a woman is made to feel that she's not trying hard enough to help or change him and that's why he keeps exploding and hurting her. Her whole goal is to win back the wonderful guy she fell in love with at the beginning, and she can spend months or years trying to find that one thing to make him happy.

When the abuse gets really bad, things change. Levy calls this traumatic bonding. "If the victim is terrified of the person who shows her tenderness, she blocks out the terror and tries to meet the abuser's needs so she can be safe." She bonds so closely to the person who hurts her that she stops thinking of what she wants or needs and only thinks of the abuser.

As the good times disappear, it becomes clear that things aren't getting any better. Women who have survived abusive relationships look up at this point to find that their lives have been spent sacrificing for the abuser, and they haven't gained anything. These young women may have lost friends, dropped out of school, or become distant from their families. Then it hits that it's time to make a serious change.

Getting Out

If you're in an abusive relationship or if you know someone who's in an abusive relationship, here are some steps to getting out:

1. Come up with a good escape plan. You need to think about your safety first. According to Kaiser, the most threatening time in an abusive relationship is when the survivor decides to end it. For up to two to five years afterwards, women may have to be careful of their exes, but the vast majority of women leave without many problems. So have a plan that enables you to get on with your life while staying away from him.

2. Be prepared for the breakup blues. Levy says that for a few weeks after breaking up you'll probably feel lonely and will miss him. "If he calls," says Levy, "you'll probably feel guilty for having left him and making him unhappy." Remember that as time passes, it'll get better.

3. Get support. If possible, go away with your family or friends to get a new perspective. Or start building your social life again. You'll need to feel like you have control over your life again, and can get back on track where you left off.

4. Help yourself by getting help. Abusive relationships are damaging and extremely stressful. You'll need professional help to sort out your feelings of mistrust, confused sexuality, fear, loneliness, and having missed out on your life—not to mention nightmares and flashbacks that happen afterwards. Don't fool yourself into thinking you can "just get over it." Call an abuse hotline, battered women's shelter, or get a referral to a professional who deals with abuse.

Special note to friends of survivors: The best way to help your friend start rebuilding her life again is to be supportive and nonjudgmental. Ask her:

- What she needs. Don't assume or tell her what she needs.
- Why she's in the relationship, so you can begin to understand her perspective.
- If she wants any help or information and then help her get it. "Don't push it on her," says Kaiser, "or you'll be just like her abuser."
- Don't associate with her abuser.

"There's a lot of pressure on what the survivor has to do," Kaiser believes, "but we need to put as much pressure on men who abuse as we do on drunk drivers." So, no matter how cute or popular he may be, any guy who abuses women is no friend.

No More Sitting Ducks: Self-Defense Strategies

Nobody asks to be sexually violated. But according to Donna Chaiet, an expert in self-defense and author of the *Get Prepared Library: Violence Prevention for Young Women*, some of us are more vulnerable to attacks than others. "Teen girls don't have a sense of their personal boundaries," says

Chaiet. "Through advertisements that show women's body parts or parents not respecting their privacy, they learn that their bodies belong to someone else." Without understanding firmly where to draw personal boundaries, young women are sometimes left open for others to do harm.

But you can prevent violence and abuse. Start by enforcing your boundaries by taking charge in small ways. Chaiet says that by saying "no" to both adults and peers when you feel you're going against your gut feelings, you can learn how to avoid more serious problems later. For example, the next time a friend tries to mooch some cash that you suspect you'll never see again, tell her no. Letting people tread on you in the little ways, opens the doors for others to stomp on you in big ways.

You probably also need to view the world a little differently. Sadly, women must be on the lookout for danger. Chaiet believes predators look for three kinds of women to victimize. Those who are:

- unaware;
- lost or disoriented;
- overly compliant (go along with something that makes them uncomfortable).

So if you stay on your toes and are prepared to take action, you can avoid many dangerous confrontations.

Chaiet suggests three very important steps to take:

KEEP YOUR EYES AND EARS PEELED! Be aware of your surroundings by scoping the scene. If you get an "uh-oh" feeling, LISTEN TO IT. Your instincts are the best indicators of trouble. Don't compromise yourself by denying danger ("there's no problem"), minimizing it ("it's not that bad"), or confronting it ("I'll show him I'm not scared"). Whether it's a boss, bully at school, boy on a date, or a group of men who look threatening, avoid them by getting to safety.

SAY IT LOUD! If you can't avoid a dangerous encounter, you can at least take action. In clear and direct language, yell "Stop! Go away! Leave me alone!" Be sure your body language matches what you're trying to get across. "Most communication is nonverbal," says Chaiet, "so use your tone of voice and facial expression to let him know you're not a victim and you're not going to be quiet." This is hard for most young women, who've been told to be "ladylike" or not to cause a scene. But situations like this don't call for politeness. Ninety percent of women are successful at scaring away an attacker if they draw attention to themselves at this stage rather than hoping he'll go away.

FIGHT FOR YOUR LIFE! If the first two steps don't work, let your "fighting spirit" kick in. This is your inner strength that says "My life is worth fighting for." In emergencies like these, you must use whatever you have available to get him where he's vulnerable.

What you can use: voice, arms, legs, brain, a weapon like a key or pencil.

Where he's vulnerable: eyes, nose, throat, temple, groin, chin, instep of his foot.

What to do: ram your knee, pencil, or whatever's available into his weak spot with full force, ruthlessly and aggressively, while making as much of a racket as possible. Remember, this is your LIFE!

Other tips for specific situations:

AVOIDING SEXUAL HARASSMENT: If a boss at work, a boy at school, or a bully in the neighborhood harasses you verbally or physically, take action at the first incident. For example, if a boss brushes up against you, touches you, or speaks abusively, say "Stop touching my body" or "I'm going to speak to the manager." (Remember, these kinds of guys prey on women who keep quiet.)

AVOIDING DATE RAPE: If a guy tells you to change your outfit, cuts you off in midsentence all night, or puts his hands where they aren't welcome, these are all boundary violations that need to be nipped in the bud, quick. Always be prepared to end the date and have a way back home when you sense something's not right. "It's easier to say 'no' with your clothes on," says Chaiet. She also warns that most date rape begins in a public setting, involves drugs or alcohol and ends with the victim being isolated more and more away from female friends and a public setting.

AVOIDING STRANGER ASSAULT: Here are some basic rules that should be part of your life:

- Don't go out late alone, always take an escort.
- Wait where someone can see you at a subway stop.
- Stand under a light while waiting for a bus.
- Walk wide around corners.
- Be aware of your surroundings by looking 360 degrees.
- Trim the shrubs in front of your house or apartment.
- Make sure the entrance way to your house is well lit.
- Before going inside, look around to see that no one has followed you.

Though these life-saving tips are effective, Chaiet believes nothing can replace a good self-defense class. She suggests finding one that specializes in teaching girls or women, that has a simple technique that you can use under pressure (not a martial-arts type class with fancy moves that you'll never remember in an extreme situation), and that uses realistic role playing. It's best to visit a class or speak to an instructor before signing up.

STRANGER DANGER: QUICK TIPS TO AVOID ABDUCTION

When most of us think about missing children, we picture the young kids on the backs of milk cartons. But according to the National Center for Missing and Exploited Children, "Children aged twelve and older are actually the most likely victims of nonfamily abduction, 74 percent of whom are girls."

Don't be misled: an abductor is not going to be some stranger with some candy. A report released by the Center states that, "People who victimize teenagers seek easy access to them in order not to draw unnecessary attention to themselves." More shocking is that they may be adults whom victims already know, work with, or live near.

To avoid dangerous situations, the National Center for Missing and Exploited Children offers these tips for teens:

- Buddy up. Walk to and from school, the bus stop, mall, wherever with a friend.
- No shortcuts. Don't go on any isolated path alone.
- Tell your parents where you're going and when you'll be back. It doesn't make you any less independent, and it could save your life.
- Be aware of bogus offers or questions, such as:

    Directions: adults don't generally ask kids for directions, so tell them to ask someone else or ignore them.

    Modeling or acting: this is the oldest trick in the book! Never go with anyone who wants to take you back to his studio or office to be photographed or filmed.

- Never ever hitchhike. You're leaving yourself open to absolutely anything by getting into a stranger's car.
- Don't leave school with someone unless you've checked with the folks first. A typical ploy is someone saying they came to pick you up because of a family emergency. Remember that 19 percent of abductors are acquaintances.
- If someone approaches you, MAKE SOME NOISE AND GET AWAY. This is the fastest way to ditch a would-be perpetrator, because

you're drawing attention and saving yourself—something he doesn't expect or want.

- If you can't get away, fake it. If he has a weapon, or it's impossible to go anywhere, fake illness or fainting to throw him off. This will also give you a chance to get away.
- Always tell someone. If anyone has attempted to harm you in any way, tell an adult you trust ASAP.

For more information contact the National Center for Missing and Exploited Children, 2101 Wilson Blvd., Suite 550, Arlington, VA 22201-3052; (703) 235-3900.

Where To Turn

Recommended Reading

Deadly Consequences: How Violence Is Destroying Our Teenage Population and a Plan to Begin Solving the Problem, Deborah Prothrow-Stith, Harper-Collins, 1991.

Free to Fight Back: A Self-Defense Handbook for Women, Marilyn Scribner, Harold Shaw Publishers, 1988.

Get Smart! What You Should Know (But Won't Learn in Class) about Sexual Harassment and Sex Discrimination, Montana Katz and Veronica Vieland, Feminist Press, 1988.

I Never Called It Rape: The Ms. *Report on Recognizing, Fighting and Surviving Date and Acquaintance Rape*, Robin Warshaw, Harper & Row, 1988.

In Love and in Danger: A Teen's Guide to Breaking Free of Abusive Relationships, Barrie Levy, Seal Press, 1992.

Self-Respect and Sexual Assault, Jeanette Mauro-Cochrane, Tab Books, 1993.

Sexual Assault: How to Defend Yourself, Dan Lena and Marie Howard, Fell Publishers, 1990.

Sexual Harassment: High School Girls Speak Out, June Larkins, Second Story Press, 1994.

Staying Safe on Dates, Donna Chaiet, Rosen Publishing Group, 1995.

Staying Safe at School, Donna Chaiet, Rosen Publishing Group, 1995.

Stopping Rape: Successful Survival Strategies, Pauline B. Bart and Patricia H. O'Brien, Pergamon Press, 1985.

Support Groups and Organizations

The American Women's Self-Defense Association, 713 N. Wellwood Avenue, Lindenhurst, NY 11757; (516) 225-6262. An organization of women and men involved in female self-defense training, dedicated to furthering women's awareness of self-defense and rape prevention. Call for training facilities, rape crisis centers, victim assistance in your area.

Impact, Self-Defense, 6219 N. Sheridan Road, Chicago, IL 60660; (312) 338-4545. Includes a 24-hour self-defense course that teaches a variety of impact self-defense skills in a safe supportive environment. Women have opportunities to practice using their skills, judgments, and feelings in simulated attack scenarios.

Infolink, National Victim Center, 309 West Seventh Street, Suite 705, Fort Worth, TX 76102; (800) FYI-CALL.

Provides a comprehensive, toll-free source of information and referrals to victim service agencies throughout country and to national crisis hotlines that cover a specific area of victimization.

Model Mugging, Resources for Personal Empowerment, Box 20316, New York, NY 10028-0052; (800) 443-KICK. Teaches simple, effective, full contact fighting skills to vital areas like the head and groin.

National Coalition Against Sexual Assault (NCASA), 912 N. 2nd Street, Harrisburg, PA 17102-3319; (717) 232-7460. A national network of rape crisis centers and battered women's programs; call for local referral.

National Organization for Victim Assistance, 1757 Park Road NW, Washington, DC 20010; (800) TRY-NOVA or (202) 232-6682. Makes nationwide referrals to community programs for rvictims of violent crimes.

Native American Women's Health Education Resource Center, P.O. Box 572, Lake Andes, SD 57356; (605) 487-7072. Offers a guide to date rape which contains a list of all the domestic abuse and sexual assault services in South Dakota.

PACT (Policy, Action, Collaboration, Training), Contra Costa County Health Services Department, 75 Santa Barbara Road, Pleasant Hill, CA 94523; (510) 646-3797. A violence prevention initiative whose cornerstone is violence prevention leadership training for African American, Laotian, and Latino youth.

Positive Adolescents Choices Training (PACT), Ellis Institute, 9 N. Edwin Moses Blvd., Dayton, OH 45407; (513) 873-3490. Program helps African American youth develop skills to reduce their risk for becoming victims or perpetrators of violence.

PrePARE (Protection, Awareness, Response, Empowerment), 147 W. 25th Street, 8th Floor, New York, NY 10001; (212) 255-0505 or (800) 442-7273. Contact: Karen Chasen. Have a program called "Get Prepared Teens," which deals with everything from verbal harassment to rape and abduction.

Straight Talk About Risks (STARS): A Pre-K–12 Curriculum for Preventing Gun Violence, Education Dept., Center to Prevent Handgun Violence, 1225 Eye Street NW, Suite 1100, Washington, DC 20005; (202) 289-7319. This curriculum was developed to meet the need for educational materials about the dangers of carrying guns. Also encourages positive teamwork and emphasizes understanding emotions, particularly anger, and building conflict resolution skills.

Victim Services, 2 Lafayette Street, New York, NY 10007; (212) 577-7700. National referral service, 24-hour crisis-counseling hotline. Free services for crime victims and their families, such as individual counseling and peer-support groups for victims and their significant others, and assistance during police questioning, court appearances, and hospital exams. Also has a program called SMART that works with students to use mediation to settle disputes.

YWCA of the U.S.A., 726 Broadway, New York, NY 10003; (800) YWCA-US1. Sponsors a campaign called "A Week Without Violence." Call or write for a participation packet.

Hotlines

Check your local phone listings under "Rape Crisis Hotline" or "Rape Crisis Center."

National Organization for Victim Assistance (NOVA): (800) TRY-NOVA; (202) 232-6682 (in Washington, D.C.). Crisis counseling and referrals for crime victims.

CHAPTER 13

WHEN LIVING AT HOME HURTS

Home is supposed to be a safe place. Unfortunately, many young women (and men) live in violent homes where they are being abused or witness family members being abused. In a recent report, the National Committee to Prevent Child Abuse (NCPCA) estimated that nearly 3 million children were being abused and/or neglected in the United States. For those who are living in abusive situations, it's important to realize that it's not like that in all homes and there is hope.

Families and Abuse

Even for teens who aren't the ones being abused, seeing a loved one hit or degraded still makes a strong impression. Witnessing a mother being slapped down or another family member being beaten, may lead to anger, intimidation, and fear, because it seems there's no way to stop it.

Physical Abuse

Domestic violence or spousal abuse is not a new syndrome, but like other forms of abuse, it's not reported enough. The term "battered spouse syndrome" is often used when talking about the violence inflicted upon a woman by her partner. According to the National Coalition Against Domestic Violence, battering is "a pattern of behavior with the effect of establishing power and control over another person through fear and intimidation, often including the threat or use of violence."

Characteristics of domestic violence include:

- emotional and verbal abuse: name calling, playing mind tricks;
- threats of violence to the person or self (suicide);
- violence in the presence of victim: punching a hole in a wall, or throwing objects at the person;

- physical and emotional isolation: doesn't want the person to social-ize with family or friends;
- economic abuse: attempts to keep the person from getting or keep-ing a job.

Dr. Andrew Sappington, a domestic abuse expert and associate professor of psychology at the University of Alabama at Birmingham, says, "Many times a child will not tell anyone because it's difficult for them to see their parents as doing any wrong. In addition, from the very beginning of the abuse the child is taught that what goes on behind closed doors is family business and it should remain behind closed doors."

Is Your Parent Being Abused?

As with child abuse, there are specific signs to look for if you suspect a fam-ily member is being abused. Judy Johnson, M.Ed., a psychotherapist in South Carolina who counsels abused women and men, lists the following warning signs you should be aware of:

- Does your mom lie about what's going on or cover up for her part-ner's behavior? ("Oh, Daddy's not in a good mood today.")
- Is your mom afraid of her partner?
- Does your mom try to calm her partner if he comes home upset?
- Does the abuser isolate your mom from her friends and family?
- Does he keep very close tabs on her whereabouts?
- Is your mom angry or sad most of the time?
- Does she experience sudden mood changes? You notice she's in a cheerful mood until Dad gets home.
- Does your mom wear inappropriate clothing for the weather? Per-haps her long sleeves and turtlenecks in warm weather are hiding bruises.
- Are you able to see unexplainable scars or bruises?

These signs could indicate that your parent is being abused and needs help. If you have the wherewithal, you may want to suggest she contact a support group in your hometown.

The Ripple Effect of Abuse

When someone lives in an abusive household, it can have very damaging effects. Some teens display emotional and behavioral problems such as with-drawal, low self-esteem, nightmares, and self-blame. Says Johnson, "When a young person witnesses abuse it's as if they are also being abused."

Young women may grow up thinking it's okay for boyfriends and husbands to hit them or scar them emotionally. According to Dr. Sappington, "Young teen women that have been exposed to violence in the home are sometimes slower to spot danger. Although they may leave abusive relationships quicker than those that have not witnessed abuse, they tend not to see the red flags going up in the beginning."

For men, seeing abuse may teach them to control others through physical force, which continues the cycle of abuse. "With abuse, the behavior and responses are learned. If your dad is abusing your mom he more than likely came from an abusive home, and so on and so on," says Johnson. "But realize that once the belief system is instilled, even if you believe abusing someone is wrong, you can still end up being a victim or an abuser. This is why getting help is so important." (See "Enough Is Enough," later in this chapter.)

Here's a list of the effects of witnessing domestic violence, taken from *Who Will Speak for Me,* an information pamphlet put out by the Minnesota Coalition for Battered Women.

Emotionally:
• feel responsible for the violence;
• shame: you feel like you're the only one going through this;
• fear: of expressing feelings (especially anger), fear your parents will divorce, fear of the unknown;
• confusion: you may feel bad for wanting to tell because you don't want to get your parent in trouble;
• depression, helplessness, powerlessness;
• burdened: you may be acting as parent substitute.

Behaviorally:
• overachieve or underachieve;
• act out or withdraw;
• refuse to go to school;
• bedwetting, nightmares;
• taking care of others much more than yourself;
• aggressive or passive behavior.

Physically:
• head, stomach and other aches;
• sickly: have colds often;
• no reaction to physical pain;
• nervous;
• short attention span;
• personal hygiene neglected.

Socially:
- difficulty trusting others;
- poor conflict resolution skills;
- overly social as a means of staying out of the house;
- distant in relationships;
- inability to keep friends for a long period of time.

• •

- One woman is battered every fifteen seconds (National Victim Center).
- Up to 50 percent of all homeless women and children are fleeing domestic violence (National Coalition Against Domestic Violence).
- In a national survey of over 6,000 American families, 50 percent of men who frequently assaulted their wives also frequently abused their children (Family Violence Prevention Fund [FVPF]).
- Child abuse is fifteen times more likely to occur in families where domestic violence is present (FVPF).

• •

"One time my brother was beating my mother, and I had to lay on top of her to stop him from hitting her. He was hitting me too."

NAME WITHHELD, 18, WASHINGTON, D.C.

My mother was abused by my father and brother ever since I was nine years old. It started as verbal and then it turned into hitting. Right now I live in a shelter, because I couldn't deal with it anymore.

I remember the first time I saw my father hit my mother. I don't remember exactly what they were arguing about, but I know I was sitting down and the phone rang. My mother went to answer it, and my father just started beating on her and yelling. This was the worst time I can recall because he beat on her the whole night. I was upset at first but since no one was doing anything about it I forced myself to ignore it; that was how I coped.

And one time my brother was beating my mother, and I had to lay on top of her to stop him from hitting her. He was hitting me too. I'm not sure why my brother beat my mother, but I know he was on drugs at the time, and that had a lot to do with it. My brother, I noticed, would never fight guys in the street he had a problem with; he would come home and take his anger out on us. If he felt someone had disrespected him in the street, we would pay. And he would mainly start hitting my mom if she tried to stick up for me when he was beating me up.

Eventually, my mother started acting like she didn't care about anything, including me and my twin sister. My father would hit me too sometimes, usually with his hand or a belt buckle. My aunt and the next door neighbor knew what was going on. Basically everyone in my apartment building knows about it, but they never tried to do anything. Every time my brother beat me up, I would call the police but nothing would really happen.

This shelter is OK for now. My mother put me out of the house because of my brother. The day before yesterday he was beating on me and he started stomping on my head. I called the police. I pressed charges and the police arrested him. Then my mother told them if they were gonna take him then they better tell me to get out of her house.

The only advice I have for someone living in this situation is to get out, it will only get worse; it did for me. Right now, I'm worried about what's going to happen in the future. I can stay here until I'm situated, and then I'll move to transitional housing for people my age, up to twenty-one. From there I'll be placed with another program that will help me find a job. Then I can go into independent living and they will help me find an affordable place to live. I hope it all works out; I know I can't go back home and deal with all that.

Family and Substance Abuse

When parents abuse drugs and/or alcohol teens are left feeling alone and neglected and may even blame themselves for the problem. Alcoholics and drug users suffer from a disease, like diabetes. "Recognizing that these addictions are diseases is very helpful in helping people avoid the self-blaming and shame that goes along with equating substance abuse as a moral failure," says K. Dale Henfarling, executive director of the Center for Families in Shreveport, Louisiana. "The abuser really has no control over the addiction."

It's also important for teens to understand that they have no control over their parents' addiction. However, depending upon the relationship, parents may be open to suggestions from family members to seek help.

Before dropping hints about Alcoholics Anonymous or Nar-Anon, first assess the situation. According to Marianne Bozzi, L.C.S.W., C.A.C., a counselor at the St. Barnabas Medical Center outpatient program for addiction services, these signs may indicate a drug or alcohol problem:

• change in behavior: violent or erratic;
• smell alcohol on breath frequently;
• emotions out of control, lose temper over minor things;
• suicide threats, hallucinations;

- blackouts: you tell Mom something one day and the next day she has no memory of the conversation;
- family members and friends avoid parent;
- argumentative: you can't seem to do anything right, unreasonable resentments, hold grudges;
- nodding out;
- excessive weight loss (cocaine) or gain (drinking);
- not fulfilling parental responsibilities;
- the abuse causes problems: DWIs, job in jeopardy, lack of concentration;
- never goes through the day without a drink or using drugs;
- depression.

How It Affects Teens

According to Henfarling, teens who live with a parent who abuses drugs or alcohol tend to blame themselves. "Often with drug abuse, children will take on the blame, because they feel out of control," says Henfarling. "In their minds they feel that if they're the cause of the problem, maybe they can do something to make things better. A child would rather believe they're the one at fault than believe that there is no hope."

Living with an addicted parent can also throw the family balance into jeopardy. During a parent's drug- or alcohol-induced bout, children may be subject to abuse such as neglect, malnutrition as a result of the neglect, physical abuse, and often poverty. Many times teens are too embarrassed to talk about their parent's problem. But it's critical to get help. Seeking counseling or joining a support group such as Nar-Anon or Alateen (children and relatives of alcoholics) can be an important form of healing.

Some parents are so secretive that it's hard to determine if there is a problem. If you know your parent or parents drink or drug, but aren't sure how bad it is, ask yourself the following questions:

- Do you have a parent, close friend, or relative whose drinking or drug use upsets you?
- Do you tell lies to cover up for someone else's drinking or drug problem?
- Do you think their behavior is caused by you, other members of your family, friends, or rotten breaks in life?
- Do you feel that if your Mom or Dad loved you they'd give up the drugs and alcohol?

- Do you think your problems would be solved if the drinking stopped?
- Do you ever threaten or actually hurt yourself to scare your parents into saying "I'm sorry," or "I love you"?
- Do you stay out of the house as much as possible because you hate it there?

If you answered "yes" to some of these questions, it is time for you to share some of your feelings with other people who are facing the same problem. Look in your telephone directory for a group near you.

Being Abused

When you hear about someone being abused, you probably picture physical abuse—black and blue marks, bruises, and broken bones. However, there are other forms of abuse that leave no visible marks on the victim, but are just as damaging: emotional, verbal, and sexual abuse. These forms of abuse leave long-lasting scars on the inside and often take a long time to heal.

Dr. Gloria Griffith, child abuse expert and assistant professor in the School of Psychology at Tennessee Technological University, outlines the types of abuse as follows:

Emotional/Verbal Abuse
- Being yelled at for not doing well or showing enough interest in activities;
- Being cursed at;
- Constantly being put down: "You'll never amount to anything";
- Being compared to a sibling or another teenager: "You should be more like your brother. He always gets good grades";
- Being given too much responsibility or being treated like a spouse;
- Being ignored, for example, by a depressed parent.

Physical Abuse
- shoving and pushing;
- slapping;
- choking;
- tripping;
- twisting arms;
- pinching;
- biting;
- pulling hair;

* being shaken by the shoulders;
* burning (cigarettes or scalding water);
* kicking;
* punching;
* threats of any of the above.

Sexual Abuse
* penetration of the vagina with penis or other object;
* being forced to perform or receive oral sex;
* being fondled or forced to fondle the abuser;
* being touched in a seductive way;
* having sexual comments or suggestions made;
* being forced to watch or listen to adults having sex;
* being forced to watch pornographic movies.

Why Abuse Hurts So Much

Abuse is hardest to deal with when it's happening at home. "Abuse is especially harmful because of the long-term effects it can have on a teenager," says JoAnn Fuchs, clinical instructor in the School of Social Work at the University of Missouri-Columbia. "Older teens may be safer because they are able to run away from the abuser more so than a younger child."

According to Fuchs, if the abuse is not stopped, it can eventually lead to all sorts of problems. "In the young person's later years, they can experience relationship problems, on all levels. You can also become terribly passive and wind up a walking victim or do the opposite and end up overly defensive and hostile." Here are more effects of abuse according to ChildHelp USA:

Short term:
* medical problems;
* severe emotional problems;
* problems in school;
* low self-esteem;
* behavior/learning disabilities.

Long term:
* depression;
* hostility;
* anxiety;
* fear;
* criminal behavior;
* lack of coping skills;

- inability to enter into intimate relationships;
- inability to keep jobs;
- acting out, engaging in risky behavior (sex, drugs, etc.).

Coping can be hard for the abused teen who feels like there's no one else going through the same problem. Coping is a way of dealing with the abuse, surviving. It may mean trying to live a double life and acting like everything is okay around friends and other family members. Self-blame is another way that some teens deal with abuse. (See "It's Not Our Fault," later in this chapter.)

Some have other ways of coping. According to Ellen Bass and Laura Davis, authors of *The Courage to Heal: A Guide for Women Survivors of Child Sexual Abuse*, victims may:

MINIMIZE THE ABUSE. Pretending that the abuse wasn't really that bad, as in "Mom only hits me when she's had a bad day at work."

RATIONALIZE THE ABUSE. Saying things like, "Dad didn't really mean to put his hands on my breasts. He and Mom are having problems so he needed someone to turn to."

DENY IT. This coping mechanism is typical of children of alcoholics and those who have been sexually abused. By ignoring the problem it may feel as though it will mysteriously disappear. Remember, the abuse will continue until the *abuser* is ready to stop.

FORGET ABOUT IT. This is the most common way of coping; just put it in the back of the mind.

ESCAPE IT. Some teens run away from home, while others throw themselves into other activities (sports, watching TV, sleeping) to block out the pain.

BECOME ADDICTED AND/OR ISOLATED. Drugs, food, or sex can numb the feelings triggered by the abuse. However, these are very self-destructive methods of coping, because with them comes a whole new set of problems.

Although many survivors of abuse cope in these ways, these methods aren't very helpful as far as confronting the issue and moving on. Abuse is serious and in most cases requires a support system; the healing process cannot and should not be something that is done alone.

If you're being abused in any way, find an adult you trust—a family member, teacher, guidance counselor, or school nurse—who you feel comfortable talking to. Or you can look into joining a support group for people going through the same turmoil at home. These support systems may help you identify options you never knew existed (see "Enough is Enough"). "Survivors' groups can be really beneficial, because they can help a person through their pain; they've been there," says Fuchs. "In order to heal, you must grieve. It's much like dealing with the loss of a loved one. Once the grieving is over then you can move forward."

REASONS THOSE BEING ABUSED ARE AFRAID TO TELL

- fear of being accused of lying;
- fear of being taken away from their families, put in a foster home;
- thinking they are to blame;
- being afraid that the abuser will harm other family members (most abusers scare their victims into silence by threatening to hurt other family members);
- not sure of the reaction from whoever the abused person chooses to tell (passive, insensitive, isolated).

REASONS TO TELL

Just as there are a thousand reasons not to tell, there are at least as many reasons to tell. Once the survivor shares her pain with people who care or have been through a similar experience, it's like a weight has been lifted off her shoulders. She doesn't have to lie or feel alone because she now understands that there are others just like her. Bass and Davis give more reasons that telling is an important step towards healing:

- Moving through the shame and secrecy that breeds isolation and loneliness.
- Getting rid of denial and beginning to accept the truth of the abuse.
- Feeling more in touch with feelings.
- Making it possible to get understanding and help.
- Ending the abuse by breaking the silence in which it thrives.
- Becoming a model for other survivors.
- Eventually feeling proud and strong.

Abuse can alter the dynamic of a family. For example, a young woman who is being abused by one parent, may wonder why the other parent doesn't come to her defense. According to Dr. Griffith, "Many times the other parent knows the child is being abused but is afraid to say something because they don't want their lifestyle to change. If the mother is a house-wife, for instance, she may not want to go to the authorities because if they remove her husband from the household, there goes the steady income."

Also, in many cases, the mother whose daughter is being abused may be a survivor of childhood abuse herself. Facing up to the reality of her daughter's situation, may be too difficult—it would force her to deal with her own memories and pain.

Letting Go of Blame

The person who's being abused tends to feel that what's happening to her is her own fault. Why else would parents or other trusted adults do things this mean? Abuse is an act of control and power, just like rape is an act of violence. In order for any healing to begin everyone must understand that those who are being abused are not responsible for what's happened to them. And it's most important for the survivor to believe that it's not her fault.

That can be hard, because the abuser—who probably feels guilty or scared that the secret may come out—is saying things like "I'm only doing this to you because you're bad," or "I can't help myself, you're so sexy." And the abused young person may believe it. That's why it's critical to place blame where blame should lie: with the person doing the abuse. That person is wrong and needs help.

Shifting blame can also be a painful process because it means that the abused person must face the fact that her parents acted irresponsibly. All young adults have been taught the notion that parents and other adults are always right and always have their children's best interests at heart. But the reality is this: no matter how old a child is, it is the responsibility of her parents to not be sexual with her or abuse her in other ways. According to The American Human Association and ChildHelp USA, here are a few reasons parents abuse children (either physically or sexually):

• poor parenting skills, hitting instead of talking;
• history of abuse in their childhood, the only way they know how to discipline;
• unrealistic expectations of child;
• unemployment;
• low self-esteem;
• frustration over marital problems;
• involved in an abusive relationship;
• abuse drugs and/or alcohol;
• unable to handle stresses of parenthood, job.

In the vast majority of cases of sexual abuse, the abuser is a male—father, stepfather, uncle, brother, cousin, neighbor, grandfather, teacher. As far as physical abuse, such as beating and emotional and verbal battering, women—mothers, stepmothers, aunts, sisters, cousins, grandmothers—are also likely to abuse children, especially because they are likely to be the caretakers of the kids. And according to ChildHelp USA, about 95 percent of child abuse victims knew the perpetrator.

- Approximately six children are reported abused and neglected in America every minute.
- Every thirteen seconds a child is abused.
- As many as 38 percent of all women have been sexually abused by the time they finish adolescence.
- Sexual trauma has been found to occur frequently in families who are also dealing with alcohol abuse and violence.
- There are an estimated 60 million childhood sexual abuse survivors in America today.

"This lady was crying and praying for her daughter who had been raped by her uncle. I prayed for her daughter, and then I started crying, and I said, 'The reason I know how she feels is because it happened to me.'"

CAROLYN, 16, GOLDEN, COLORADO

I first started sundancing when I was twelve. Here on the reservation, we do it once a year. We're in a circle and we dance. As we dance we hear songs, and as we hear songs we pray. We believe sundancing brings about good health and wealth and all that good stuff.

When I first started I was dealing with being a survivor from rape. I was coming out of it. I was kind of blaming myself—that it was me, that's why it happened, that it was all me. I was only five when I was molested. And then when I turned eleven I was raped. The person that did this to me went on for three years, until I was thirteen. He threatened me, my family, my little sister—he threatened to kill them if I told. He threatened to kill me if I told what was happening.

I started going to these ceremonies and when they would pray, they would sing, I would sing with them, and I would cry because I couldn't say anything. So many people knew that something was happening because I would talk all the time about many other things—they couldn't make me shut up because I was very happy and I wanted to share with them how I felt. But when they asked me what was going on I wouldn't tell them anything; all I said was "nothing." And every time he'd pass by I'd shiver. I'd just sit there and put my head down. I just wanted to cry.

In my third year of sundancing, when I was fourteen, it finally started to hit me that this was wrong, and it wasn't my fault that this was happening. We were in a sweat and we were all praying and singing songs. This lady was crying and praying for her daughter who had been raped by her uncle. I listened to her pray for her daughter for five days during purification and when it came around to my turn, I couldn't help it. It was like I wanted to say something. And then when it came my turn to pray, I prayed for her daughter and then I started crying and I said, "The reason I know how she feels is because it happened to me."

And all these women started crying with me and it was very relaxing. That it wasn't only me that this happened to. After the sweat I still had tears running down my face, and I was still crying and all these women came up to me and said, "You're not alone." It finally started to hit me that it wasn't only me and that I could talk. It was the first time in so many years I'd been able to talk.

About two months later, I went and told the principal that I wanted to put on an assembly for the high school about rape. He said, "Rape? That's kind of a precious little thing to touch." And I said, "No it isn't, not when it happens to you." And he just looked at me and said, "OK, we'll set it up."

So they set it up and they turned off the lights. I didn't want anybody to know it was me right away, so I wore a costume and I walked out there and told them what happened to me. After the assembly, they said, "We want to know who you are." So they turned off the lights again, and I took my costume off. And everybody gasped, "Not her." It was scary because I was standing up there by myself and I was just coming out of it. But it was also refreshing to know that this was all off my chest.

After the assembly, about seventy-three girls from the high school came up to me to say it happened to them. They asked if they could talk to me, so I gave them my number and they started calling. I got so many calls that I started writing them down, and I still have a thick notebook of girls telling me what happened to them. And because of me, it brought them out. It brought out their stories.

It makes me feel happy that someone could open up to me. I began to feel more confident, hearing all those stories from the other girls. Knowing that I'm not alone, knowing that if anyone tried to do this again to me, I wasn't going to let it happen.

Enough Is Enough

Everyone eventually reaches a boiling point when something stresses them out. Being beaten, molested, or put down constantly is certainly grounds for reaching a boiling point. When confronted with these feelings, the choice is generally to either run away, or to confront the issue head on and hopefully put a stop to the abuse.

Connie Clark, teen counselor at the Youth Services Center in Provo, Utah, gives some reasons that people who are being abused reach the boiling point and decide to fight back or flee:

- The abuse is too much to handle.
- Constant turmoil in the family between everyone.
- Significant change in life—pregnancy, divorce, breakup with friend or boyfriend.
- Communication between teen and parent has broken down.
- Abuser starts abusing siblings.
- Responsibility of being oldest child is too much.
- Parents set down very strict rules and child rebels by running away.

Before Running Away

No one should be expected to stay in a home that is dangerous. However, running away isn't usually a great bet either, because of all the dangers out on the streets—even if it's just for a short period of time. Plus, running away is illegal in most states! Runaways stand the chance of being arrested or ending up a ward of the court. According to the National Runaway Switchboard, there are over 1.3 million runaway and homeless youth in the United States; 12,000 in Chicago alone. A part of growing up and becoming a responsible adult is learning to face difficult situations, not run away from them.

"When kids run away it's like a cry for help. By them creating chaos in the family, it's sometimes a good thing because we can then step in and help the family get things back on track," says Clark.

Whatever the reason may be, running away is not the answer. After three days on the street, most runaway and homeless youth are forced to become prostitutes (survival sex), sell drugs for food and shelter, steal and beg for money. In addition, many runaways are exposed to violence, sickness, and some feel guilty and lose their self-esteem because they have to engage in illegal or demeaning activities to survive. According to Clark, most runaways don't graduate from high school, they lose their family identity, and the opportunity to create a productive life for themselves.

Every effort should be made to work things out before packing up and hitting the road, because life on the streets is not easy. Gina Rogerson, direct service supervisor at the Denny Place Youth Shelter in Seattle, gives a few alternatives to those considering running away:

- Get your family involved in counseling before problems get out of hand; this can be done through a social worker. It's much easier to deal with issues when you're still at home rather than trying to set up meetings to get together after the fact.

- Make arrangements with a close friend or relative for alternatives when things get bad. For example, you could have a deal where you can spend the weekend with them when things are out of control at home.

- Call your local teen crisis hotline before making any rash decisions. These hotlines are answered by staffers who help you identify the problem and focus on key issues. They can also refer you to services available in your community.

- Consider joining job corps. Similar to a boarding, job corps is free to teens and it's a good opportunity to learn a skill they can use later in life. It's also possible to get two and a half years of college education for free.

Adds Clark: "In any case where the child is ready to leave the home, I would highly recommend them going to live with another family member. It's so important to maintain the family identity during these years because once it's gone, the teen loses a sense of who they are; they need to feel connected to family in some way."

The Foster Care Option

Another alternative to running away is placement in the foster care system. As a temporary situation, foster care is a last resort, because it requires you to live away from your family. But if the family is highly abusive, foster care may be a safer choice.

According to the Child Welfare League of America (CWLA), 540,000 children are expected to live in foster care in 1995. Most of these kids live in foster homes with other families. Others live in group homes, emergency shelters, or residential centers. And a lot of young people, especially in the African American community, have arranged to live with extended family.

Placement into foster care usually goes like this:

1. A social worker evaluates the home situation and determines whether it would be better for the young person to leave home or to stay and try to work things out.

2. Once it's determined that she should leave, she must appear before a judge who decides which type of foster care placement is best.

3. The foster family receives money from the state based on the child's age and any special care that's required, about $300 to $400 a month for foster families.

"The goal of foster care is to give support to the child and the family while the matter is being resolved," states Kathy Barbell, Director of Foster Care for CWLA. "Usually kids go back home after some time, but some kids are adopted." A good foster care situation can help provide a safe, stabilizing situation with reliable adults to count on. Most people going into foster care are still dealing with the trauma of leaving their original families, however chaotic or painful the situation might have been, and find it difficult to just "start fresh."

This can be made worse if the new living arrangements are just as unsafe as the old ones (if there's abuse or abandonment, for example). Then the young person may end up feeling like there's no place to go. For a foster child who ends up in a situation that's as bad or worse than her biological family, Barbell recommends contacting the following people/groups for help:

- police;
- the state's 800 Child Abuse Hotline number;
- someone at school (a teacher, counselor);
- a social worker;
- an advocate or attorney.

• **WHAT ARE YOU GONNA DO ABOUT IT?**

FOSTER CARE YOUTH UNITED

Living in the foster care system can be extremely difficult for a young person to adjust to. Although many people living in foster care turn out just fine, for others the experience is scary and even dangerous. Thus, the idea for *Foster Care Youth United (FCYU)*, a magazine geared toward those living in the system, was born.

The bimonthly, based in New York City, is mainly written by foster care youth and has a circulation of 10,000. It serves as an outlet for the built-up frustration often found in teens living in the system and aims to provide a voice to young people in foster care. Also, staffers hope that by writing about issues within the system they can break down the stigma and silence surrounding foster care so that young people won't feel alone or blame themselves for problems that adults caused them.

Wunika Hicks, eighteen, and Kenyetta Ivy, nineteen, both foster kids, regularly contribute to *FCYU*. Wunika first read about the magazine in another publication and immediately became involved. Kenyetta became aware of the magazine in 1993 through a woman she worked with on poetry readings. They both agree that writing for the magazine helped them turn negative energy into positive energy.

According to Wunika, who has been in the system for ten years, "The writing has helped me grow mentally and it has allowed me to get in touch with my feelings. It's good to be able to put things down on paper when I have a hard time talking it out, rather than keeping it all inside." Ivy, who resides in an independent living group home, says, "The whole system is designed to bring you down. There's a whole lot of physical, mental, and emotional abuse that goes on, and it gets to a point where you want to run away or commit suicide. My writing helped me overcome all of that and it kept me out of trouble."

For more information contact FCYU, 144 W. 27th Street, 8th Floor, New York, NY 10001; (212) 242-3270, ext. 106.

Where to Turn

Recommended Reading

The Courage to Heal: A Guide for Women Survivors of Child Sexual Abuse, Ellen Bass and Laura Davis, HarperCollins, 1993.

Living with a Parent Who Drinks Too Much, Judith S. Seixas, Beech Tree Books, 1991.

Living with a Parent Who Takes Drugs, Judith S. Seixas, Beech Tree Books, 1991.

Secret Survivors: Uncovering Incest and Its Aftereffects in Women, E. Sue Blume, Ballantine, 1991.

Shining Through: Pulling It Together After Sexual Abuse, Mindy Loiselle and Leslie Bailey Wright, Safer Society Press, 1994.

Straight Talk About Child Abuse, Susan Mufson, C.S.W., and Rachel Kranz, Dell, 1993.

Support Groups and Organizations

Al-Anon/Alateen, Family Group Headquarters, Inc., P.O. Box 862, Midtown Station, New York, NY 10018-0862; (212) 302-7240 or 800-344-2666.

Alateen is a fellowship of teenage relatives and friends of alcoholics who meet to help each other cope with the troubles brought about by another person's drinking.

Asian Task Force Against Domestic Violence, P.O. Box 120108, Boston, MA 02112; (617) 338-2350 or (617) 338-2355 (24 hours). The task force has opened the first shelter and transitional housing program in New England to serve Asian people. The shelter provides outreach and crisis intervention, counseling, English classes, legal assistance, and survival-skills training for Asian women and their children and distributes educational literature.

Childhelp U.S.A., Independent Order of Foresters National Child Abuse Hotline, P.O. Box 630, Hollywood, CA 90028; (800) 4-A-CHILD. Provides crisis counseling information and referrals to children and adults in crisis.

Child Welfare League of America, 440 First Street NW, Suite 310, Washington, DC 20001; (202) 638-2952. Deals with children's rights, including foster care.

Covenant House, 460 West 41st Street, New York, NY 10036; (212) 613-0300. Covenant House is a national organization with offices in many cities. It provides free AIDS education, referrals, peer counseling, addiction counseling, and street outreach programs. Several offices also offer residential programs for homeless and runaway youth as well as HIV positive young people. To find the Covenant House in your area, call (800) 999-9999.

Incest Survivors Anonymous, World Service Office, P.O. Box 17245, Long Beach, CA 90807-7245. Write to above address and include a self-addressed stamped #10 envelope to find a support group in your area.

Incest Survivors Resource Network International, P.O. Box 7375, Las Cruces, NM 88006-7375; (505) 521-4260. The Network provides information packets on incest and makes referrals to organizations and self-help groups.

Infolink, National Victim Center, 555 Madison Avenue, New York, NY 10022; (800) FYI-CALL. Provides a comprehensive, toll-free source of information and referral for victims of crimes and concerned citizens.

Kempe Center for the Prevention and Treatment of Child Abuse and Neglect, 1205 Oneida St., Denver, CO 80220; (303) 321-3963. Offers literature and educational materials and referrals to organizations.

National Association of Former Foster Children, Inc., P.O. Box 874, Wall Street Station, New York, NY 10268-0874; (212) 332-0078. A nonprofit organization concerned with the needs of all children formerly or currently in foster care.

National Clearinghouse on Child Abuse and Neglect Information, P.O. Box 1182, Washington, DC 20013-1182; (800)394-3366 or (703) 385-7565.

A national resource for information on the prevention, identification, and treatment of child abuse and neglect. Free publications catalog available upon request.

National Coalition Against Domestic Violence, P.O. Box 18749, Denver, CO 80218-0749; (303) 839-1852. Call for literature or a referral to a local support group in your area.

National Committee to Prevent Child Abuse, 332 S. Michigan Avenue, Suite 1600, Chicago, IL 60604-4357; (312) 663-3520. This organization runs a home visitation program, called "Healthy Families America," for new parents focusing on parenting skills, child development, child health, and other aspects of family functioning. Also publishes materials on child abuse, child abuse prevention, and parenting.

National Council on Child Abuse and Family Violence, 1155 Connecticut Ave., NW, Suite 400, Washington DC 20036; (202) 429-6695.

National Network of Runaway and Youth Services, 1400 I Street, Suite 330, Washington, DC 20005; (800) 878-2437. The Network publishes a series of fact sheets containing information on runaway and homeless youth, alcohol and other drug use, and HIV/AIDS prevention.

National Organization for Victim Assistance, 1757 Park Rd. NW, Washington, DC 20010; (800) TRY-NOVA.

National Resource Center on Child Abuse and Neglect, 63 Inverness Drive East, Englewood, CO 80112; (800) 227-5242 or (303) 792-9900. Provides general information and statistics about child abuse.

National Runaway Switchboard, 3080 North Lincoln, Chicago, IL 60657; (312) 880-9860. Offers free crisis intervention and counseling for runaway and homeless young people. Toll-free 24-hour national hotline (800) 621-4000.

One Voice, P.O. Box 27958, Washington, DC 20038-7958; (202) 371-6056. A resource center that provides legal referrals and information on childhood victimization to survivors as well as education and outreach programs.

Parents United International, Inc., 615 15th Street, Modesto, CA 95354; (209) 572-3446. With sixty chapters throughout the United States, Mexico, and Canada, Parents United International offers community-based programs. Daughters and Sons United organizes support groups for sexually molested children and their siblings.

YWCA. Check yellow pages; many local chapters house women's centers and offer access to shelters, or provide basic services such as referral to appropriate programs in your area.

Hotlines

Childhelp USA: (800) 4-A-CHILD (24 hour national hotline for crisis intervention and referrals).

Covenant House Nineline: (800) 999-9999. Crisis line for youth, teens, and families. Locally based referrals throughout the United States. Help for drugs, abuse, homelessness, runaway children.

Incest Helpline: (212) 227-3000. Strictly confidential gives referrals to victims and survivors of child sexual abuse.

National Center for Missing and Exploited Children: (800) THE-LOST. Crisis intervention and referrals.

National Domestic Violence Hotline: (800) 333-SAFE.

National Family Violence Helpline: (800) 222-2000. For referrals and intervention.

National Resource Center on Child Abuse and Neglect: (800) 227-5282. Offers information, resources, and referrals.

National Runaway Switchboard: (800) 621-4000 (24 hours). Provides crisis intervention and traveler's assistance to runaways. Gives referrals to shelters nationwide. Also relays messages to, or sets up conference calls with, parents at the request of the child.

Youth Crisis Hotline: (800) 448-4663 (24 hours). Provides counseling and referrals to local shelters. Responds to runaways and youth dealing with child abuse.

THE MEANING
OF LIFE

After reading this book, you should now know the meaning of life. Well, at least you should begin to see that the meaning of life is different for everyone, which means you must decide for yourself what the meaning of your life is.

Knowing the meaning of your life is more than just knowing yourself. It's about seeing how you fit into "the scheme of things" or what your special place is in the universe. A lot of people call this line of thinking spirituality. Whether you believe in God, Goddess, Buddha, Allah, Krishna, a Higher Power, or not, having some sort of spiritual base is extremely important.

Jacob Moody, M.Div., director of the Balboa Teen Health Center in San Francisco, defines spirituality as feeling in connection with everyone and everything. "This relationship," says Moody, "has meaning and gives us a sense of purpose as to why we are here." Though you can express your spirituality through organized religion, not everyone does. "Organized religion gives us a structure for helping us experience spirituality," explains Moody. However, some people find their own structure, like waking up every morning and meditating or praying. Without even realizing it, most people have spiritual experiences every day when they sing, dance, read, take a quiet walk, spend time with family or friends, sit quietly, write, or take a relaxing bath.

The importance of spirituality, Moody believes, is that it helps you know you're not alone. "In our society, which stresses being an individual, we constantly struggle to maintain a sense of community." But by being in a community, you learn how to be spiritual from your connection with others in a loving relationship. The lessons you learn through spirituality help the best parts of yourself come out, like being loving, patient, kind, compassionate, and giving.

Karen Baker-Fletcher, assistant professor of Theology and Culture at Claremont College in California, believes that spirituality is vital for all women. "When we view ourselves as sacred, we begin to value ourselves and see ourselves as having worth," she says. Feeling worthy gives you high self-esteem and the belief that you can accomplish your dreams in life. Media messages tell you to be sexy and make lots of money but say nothing about being a good person nor give you any direction as to how you can "make it." By contrast, spirituality makes you turn within to help you discover that you have your own internal resources to draw on. It gives you hope that you can do what it takes to make your life successful.

Most important, spirituality allows you to enjoy the present. The African American poet Gwendolyn Brooks has a line in her poem "Speech to the Young" that goes: "Live not for the end of the song/Live in the along." If you think about your favorite song, you don't want to rush through it. You want to savor every note and connect with the feeling the song is conveying. That's what Brooks means by living in the along: taking life in as it's happening. Her point is that life is as good as you make it *right now*.

So, even if you feel like your life sucks today, try to see the big picture. You're in a stage of tremendous growth that will lead to a stronger, wiser you with each new experience. As long as you're willing to "live in the along" and know you have a unique place in the world, you will come to understand what the meaning of your life truly is.

P.S. Write to us and let us know what you think of *Finding Our Way* or anything else. Allison and Linda, c/o HarperCollins, 10 E. 53rd Street, New York, NY 10036; aabner@aol.com, linvil@aol.com

INDEX

abduction, how to avoid, 282–283
abortion: 151–155; aftercare, 153; frequency of, 155; limits on, 154–155; reasons for, 151; resources on, 164, 165, 167; types of, 152–153; your right to have an, 154
abstinence from sex: 113, 114; as contraception, 115; personal story about, 116–117
abuse:
  in family: as act of control, 296; and addiction, 294; coping with, 294–295; denial of, 294; effects of on teenagers, 293–294; emotional/verbal, 292; escaping the, 294; and family dynamics, 295; forgetting, 294; frequency of, 286, 297; lack of family support and, 296; minimizing, 294; personal story about, 297–298; physical, 292–293; poor ways to cope with, 294; rationalizing, 294; reasons for, 296; recovery from, 295; and relationship problems, 293; resources on, 302–306; sexual, 293; support groups for, 295; talking about, 294–295; types of, 292–293
  in relationships: emotional/verbal, 276; and guilt, 277; how friends can support survivors, 279; how to avoid, 280–281; motivation for, 277; and need to control, 277–278; physical, 276; sexual, 276; types of, 276
  spousal. *See* violence, domestic
abusive personality, described, 276–277
abusive relationship: 276–279; how to leave an, 278–279; stages of an, 277

acne: causes of, 25; cleanliness and, 26; personal story about, 26–27; preventing, 26; treatment of, 25–26
acquired immunodeficiency syndrome (AIDS). *See* HIV/AIDS
adolescence, tough times in, ix
adoption: 156–159; personal story about, 157–158; resources on, 159; types of, 156
Afrocentric appreciation movement, 182–183
Afrocentricity, 35
AIDS. *See* HIV/AIDS
Aid to Children of Imprisoned Mothers, 215
Alan Guttmacher Institute, 160, 240–241, 243
Alateen, 291
alcohol: availability of, 60; binge drinking, 60; consequences of use of, 60, 62; and driving, 61–62, 238, 291; effects of, 62; parental abuse of, 290, 296; rape and, 273, 274; sex and, 115
Alcoholics Anonymous, 57, 60, 290
allergies and eczema, 28
All That She Can Be, 169
alphahydroxy acids (AHAs) in bleaching cream, 26, 28
A magazine, 20, 183
amenorrhea. *See* menstruation, lack of
American Academy of Cosmetic Surgery, 19
American Academy of Dermatology, 28
American Academy of Plastic and Reconstructive Surgery, 19
American Association of University Women (AAUW), 172, 188, 268, 269

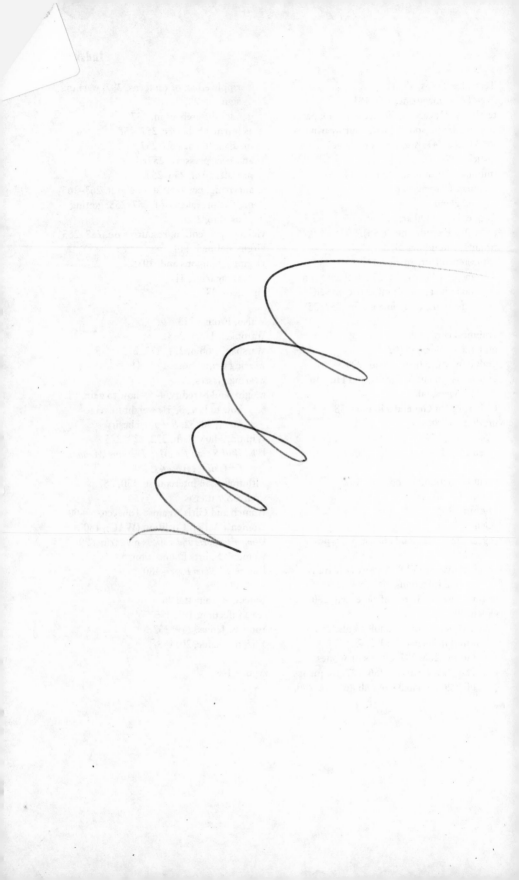